Citizens of Asian America

NATION OF NEWCOMERS
Immigrant History as American History

Matthew Jacobson and Werner Sollors
GENERAL EDITORS

Beyond the Shadow of Camptown: Korean Military Brides in America
Ji-Yeon Yuh

Feeling Italian: The Art of Ethnicity in America
Thomas J. Ferraro

Constructing Black Selves: Caribbean American Narratives and the Second Generation
Lisa D. McGill

Transnational Adoption: A Cultural Economy of Race, Gender, and Kinship
Sara K. Dorow

Immigration and American Popular Culture: An Introduction
Jeffrey Melnick and Rachel Rubin

From Arrival to Incorporation: Migrants to the U.S. in a Global Era
Edited by Elliott R. Barkan, Hasia Diner, and Alan M. Kraut

Migrant Imaginaries: Latino Cultural Politics in the U.S.-Mexico Borderlands
Alicia Schmidt Camacho

The Force of Domesticity: Filipina Migrants and Globalization
Rhacel Salazar Parreñas

Immigrant Rights in the Shadows of Citizenship
Edited by Rachel Ida Buff

Rough Writing: Ethnic Authorship in Theodore Roosevelt's America
Aviva F. Taubenfeld

The Third Asiatic Invasion: Empire and Migration in Filipino America, 1898–1946
Rick Baldoz

Race for Citizenship: Black Orientalism and Asian Uplift from Pre-Emancipation to Neoliberal America
Helen Heran Jun

Entitled to Nothing: The Struggle for Immigrant Health Care in the Age of Welfare Reform
Lisa Sun-Hee Park

The Slums of Aspen: The War against Immigrants in America's Eden
Lisa Sun-Hee Park and David Naguib Pellow

Social Death: Racialized Rightlessness and the Criminalization of the Unprotected
Lisa Marie Cacho

Love and Empire: Cybermarriage and Citizenship across the Americas
Felicity Schaeffer-Grabiel

Citizens of Asian America: Democracy and Race during the Cold War
Cindy I-Fen Cheng

CINDY I-FEN CHENG

Citizens of Asian America

Democracy and Race during the Cold War

NEW YORK UNIVERSITY PRESS
New York and London

NEW YORK UNIVERSITY PRESS
New York and London
www.nyupress.org

© 2013 by New York University
All rights reserved

References to Internet Websites (URLs) were accurate at the time of writing. Neither the author nor New York University Press is responsible for URLs that may have expired or changed since the manuscript was prepared.

Library of Congress Cataloging-in-Publication Data
Cheng, Cindy I-Fen.
Citizens of Asian America : democracy and race during the Cold War / Cindy I-Fen Cheng.
pages cm — (Nation of newcomers : immigrant history as American history)
Includes bibliographical references and index.
ISBN 978-0-8147-5935-6 (cl : alk. paper)
1.Asian Americans—History—20th century. 2. Asian Americans—Ethnic identity. 3. Asian Americans—Cultural assimilation. 4. Asian Americans—Civil rights. 5. Cold War—Social aspects—United States. 6. United States—Social conditions—1945- 7. United States—Race relations—History—20th century. I. Title.
E184.A75C486 2013
305.895'07309045—dc23   2012049433

New York University Press books are printed on acid-free paper, and their binding materials are chosen for strength and durability. We strive to use environmentally responsible suppliers and materials to the greatest extent possible in publishing our books.
Manufactured in the United States of America
10 9 8 7 6 5 4 3 2 1

CONTENTS

List of Illustrations	vii
Acknowledgments	ix
Introduction: Asian American Racial Formation and the Image of American Democracy	1
1. Legislating Nonwhite Crossings into White Suburbia	21
2. Living in the Suburbs, Becoming Americans	57
3. Asian American Firsts and the Progress toward Racial Integration	85
4. McCarran Act Persecutions and the Fight for Alien Rights	117
5. Advancing Racial Equality and Internationalism through Immigration Reform	149
Conclusion: Cold War America and the Appeal to See Past Race	191
Notes	209
Bibliography	247
Index	261
About the Author	273

ILLUSTRATIONS

1.1. Map of common neighborhood names in the southeast Los Angeles area	36
1.2. Map of Los Angeles–area neighborhoods near the homes of Amer and Kim	37
1.3. Map of Tommy Amer's home	38
1.4. Map of Yin Kim's home	39
2.1. Sing Sheng with family, 1952	79
3.1. Sammy Lee with gold medal at the 1952 Olympics	107
3.2. Jade Snow Wong at a reception in Rangoon, Burma, 1953	107
3.3. Municipal Judge Delbert Wong with family, 1959	108
4.1. Terminal Island, 1950	135
4.2. Diamond Kimm before House Committee on Un-American Activities, 1955	135
4.3. David Hyun with family, 1953	136
4.4. Diamond Kimm with wife, Fania Goorwitch, 1965	136

ACKNOWLEDGMENTS

The research and writing of this book were completed with the generous fellowship support of the Office of the Provost of the University of Wisconsin–Madison, the University of Wisconsin Institute on Race and Ethnicity, the University of Wisconsin Institute for Research in the Humanities, and the University of Wisconsin–Madison Graduate School. At an earlier stage, the research and writing of this project were supported by the Andrew W. Mellon Postdoctoral Fellowship in the Humanities at the University of Southern California Program in American Studies and Ethnicity and the University of California Regents. I am indebted to the generosity of Mark Stuart Ong and Marshall Wong for giving me photos to use in this book and to my dear friend Joseph P. Adriano for drawing maps to fit my narrative on postwar Los Angeles.

Citizens of Asian America grew out of the support of family, friends, and colleagues who saw me through the long journey of completing my first book. Their love and feedback are imprinted on its pages. I especially want to recognize the support of four individuals. I owe my deepest gratitude to Leslie Bow, whose mentorship and friendship guided me through the challenging task of writing this book. I benefitted immensely from her insightful readings of my work and her unabated belief in the importance of my project. I would also like to thank Leslie, Russ, Julian, and Maya for welcoming me into their home and the many happy meals that we shared together. During my first quarter as a graduate student at the University of California-Irvine, I had the good fortune of taking Jon Wiener's course on U.S. Cold War culture. Jon not only inspired my interest in this field but also oversaw my research on race and U.S. Cold War politics. Jon has provided invaluable feedback on this project and I am humbled by his continual support and friendship. Nan Enstad has been a tireless advocate for me at the University of Wisconsin–Madison. Her caring mentorship has helped me navigate the demands of teaching and research, and I am grateful for our many conversations over hot tea. Finally, I want to thank Laura Hyun Yi Kang for her unflagging concern for my well-being. From Laura, I learned that change happens when people are not afraid to see that others have an easier time in the academy than what they experienced. I am a product of that ethos and I owe my tenure in the academy to her generous and revolutionary spirit. I also want to thank Laura for always having me over, Paul Yi for cooking the most delicious meals, and their two boys, Junsu and Minsu, for being endless sources of fun and playfulness.

At the University of Wisconsin–Madison, I am surrounded by a wonderful group of colleagues and friends. I am grateful for their camaraderie and their belief in my teaching and scholarship. From the Department of History, I would like to acknowledge Leslie Abadie, Thomas J. Archdeacon, Florence Bernault, Ned Blackhawk, Laird Boswell, the late Jeanne Boydston, the late Paul Boyer, Maggie Brandenburg, Scott Burkhardt, Mike Burmeister, Steve Cantley, Charles L. Cohen, William Cronon, Avi Cummings, Ashley Cundiff, Suzanne Desan, Colleen Dunlavy, A. Finn Enke, Nan Enstad, Brenna Greer, Kori Graves, Camille Guérin-Gonzales, Nicole Hauge, Mark Hessman, Francine Hirsh, Jennifer Hull, Doria Johnson, Susan Johnson, William Jones, Stephen Kantrowitz, Charles Kim, Marc Kleijwegt, Neil Kodesh, Christine Lamberson, Faron Levesque, Alfred W. McCoy, David M. McDonald, Tony Michels, John Persike, Brenda Gayle Plummer, Haley M. Pollack, Jennifer Ratner-Rosenhagen, Mary Louise Roberts, Francisco Scarano, Jim Schlender Jr., Amy Schultz, Brett Sheehan, Karl B. Shoemaker, James Sweet, Sarah Thal, Teri Tobias, Carrie Tobin, Zoe Van Orsdol, Lee Palmer Wandel, Stephanie Westcott, Jane Williams, Thongchai Winichakul, André Wink, and Louise Young. I especially want to acknowledge the support of Florencia Mallon and Steve Stern. I would also like to thank Chong Moua and MaiGer Moua for being a source of support and inspiration. I hold the deepest respect and admiration for Chong and her commitment to Hmong/American history. I look forward to working many more years with her.

I want to recognize the Program in Asian American Studies for being my intellectual home at UW–Madison. It is a privilege to work with Leslie Bow, Peggy Choy, Joan Fujimura, Leena Her, Victor Jew, Stacey Lee, Bao Lo, Yer Lor, Ella Mae Matsumura, Jan Miyasaki, Mytoan Nguyen Akbar, Linda Park, Hemant Shah, Atsushi Tajima, Betty Thao, Michael Thornton, Lillian Tong, Lynet Uttal, Paj Ntaub Vang, Morris Young, and Timothy Yu as we collectively aspire to foster interdisciplinarity, transnationality, and critical race studies in our research, teaching, and program activities.

I have made some dear friends at Madison. The caring friendships of Ikuko Asaka, Mary Beltran, Karma Chávez, Marc A. Hertzman, Sara

ACKNOWLEDGMENTS

McKinnon, and Leah Mirakhor have filled my time here with fun, laughter, stimulating conversations, and a sense of humor about who we are and what we do. I would like to extend a special thanks to all those with whom I have worked in my graduate and undergraduate courses at UW–Madison. I have learned so much from my interactions with you, and the pedagogical relationships that we forged have been the most rewarding aspect of my time at Madison thus far.

I was also fortunate to build some lasting relationships while in graduate school at the University of California–Irvine. I am particularly indebted to the continual support of Wilson Chen, Lan Duong, Inderpal Grewal, Jane Hseu, the late Wiebke Ipsen, Laura Hyun Yi Kang, Mike Masatsugu, Randy Ontiveros, Jennifer Terry, and Jon Wiener. I also want to recognize the museum director and curator of El Pueblo Historical Monument, Suellen Cheng, along with Glenn Omatsu and Meg Thornton, with whom I had the pleasure of working during my undergraduate study at the University of California–Los Angeles, for their unwavering commitment to social justice and the field of Asian American studies. Their activisms have made an enduring impact on my intellectual and political pursuits.

The Southern California Library for Social Studies and Research had a profound impact on the research and writing of my book, for it was there that I came across the files for David Hyun and Diamond Kimm and learned of the activities of radical Asian Americans who dared to go against the government's persecution of people for their political beliefs. I met some amazing people during my time at SCL, and I want to thank Raquel Chavez, Diana Flores, Krystin Hence, Huong Hoang, Susan Jones, Olivia Kardos, the late Annette McKinley, Gabriel Milton Nimatuj, Yusef Omowale, Rukshana Singh, and Michele Welsing for their help with my research and for making research less alienating of an endeavor. At the Huntington Library, I want to thank Meredith Berbée, Juan C. Gomez, Kadin Henningsen, and Catherine Wehrey for their friendly assistance in retrieving records for my research.

My study of Asian Americans and the Cold War began with a series of interviews that I conducted while in graduate school with Chinese Americans in the Los Angeles area. I remain forever indebted to Tommy Amer, Abe Chin, Clara Chin, Bill Chun-Hoon, Carol Chung, Dr. James Chung Jr., Dr. Robert Eng, Dr. Rose Eng, Gim Fong, Jim Fong, Don Hall, Teddy Hall, Nell Hong, James Hong, Jerry Jann, David Lee, Margie Lew, Albert Lew,

Herbert Leong, Louise Leong, Steve Leong, Ella Leong, Mei Ong, Ella Quan, Peter Soo Hoo Jr., Edith Tom, Herb Tom, Judge Delbert Wong, Dolores Wong, Estelle Wong, Patrick Wong, Tom Woo, Nancy Yee, and Clarence Yip for their willingness to share their life stories with me.

I want to thank Eric Zinner and Ciara McLaughlin of New York University Press for their help in getting this book published. I also want to acknowledge Brandy Liên Worrall-Soriano for her work in copyediting early drafts of this manuscript.

My close family and friends are my primary source of sustenance and happiness. I am lucky to have them in my life. I met Margaret Chao when we were both eight years old, and we became the best of friends and sisters ever since. I want to thank Marge, Ray, Dylan, Tiffany, Tristan, and Luke for filling my life with love and joy. My friendship with Joseph P. Adriano has also extended past two decades. I am immensely grateful for the love and support that Joe and Grace Mandac have given me over the years. I owe so much to Tina Tran and Michael Kidder. They have fed me, sheltered me, and spent long hours listening to all of my musings about life. Ava is a blessing and I am so happy that she came into their lives. My deepest love and gratitude go to my mom, Li Lin Proud, my brothers, Michael Yu-Hao Cheng and Howard Yu-Hsiang Cheng, and my pup, Xiao Bao, for believing in me and sticking by me.

I dedicate this book to the memory of my beloved dad, James Chien-Hua Cheng.

Introduction

Asian American Racial
Formation and the Image
of American Democracy

Shortly after World War II ended, the President's Committee on Civil Rights released its 1947 report entitled *To Secure These Rights*, which dedicated a section to discussing the injustice of Japanese internment. It noted that not since the days of slavery had the nation witnessed such a wholesale displacement and incarceration of a group of people. The committee worried about the implications of Japanese internment for the future of American civil rights and advised the federal government to explore other means to ensure national security that did not entail mass accusations based on national heritage.[1] Besides detailing the injustice of Japanese internment, the committee called attention to discrimination against the Japanese, who were denied the right to citizenship by naturalization. It deplored the way this inequality had impinged on their economic opportunities, particularly through California's 1913 Alien Land Law, which made it illegal for aliens ineligible for citizenship to purchase agricultural land or lease it for more than a period of three years. While the committee believed that a democracy could establish reasonable tests to determine an individual alien's eligibility for citizenship, it nevertheless considered the racial qualification to naturalized citizenship an unjust rule, given that a standard based solely on race had "nothing to do with a person's fitness to become a citizen."[2] To correct this inequity, the committee recommended that the federal government go beyond adding Japanese to the list of exceptions to the whites-only rule that already included Chinese, Filipinos, South Asians, and persons of African descent. It urged the government to remove all racial barriers to naturalized citizenship.

The President's Committee on Civil Rights sought to explain why it was so essential to ensure civil rights for all in the postwar period.[3] To that end, it pointed to the rise of a new world conflict, particularly the ideological battle being waged against the United States by the Soviet Union. In this emerging struggle, the Soviet Union disseminated stories on the rampant racism in U.S. society that proved U.S. democracy "an empty fraud" and in so doing, replaced the World War II propaganda of Germany and Japan that sought to accomplish the same. The committee beseeched the federal government to take seriously the way U.S. racism was becoming an issue in world politics. It echoed the concern of the undersecretary of state Dean Acheson that broadcasting the mistreatment of Asians and blacks in the United States was hampering the nation's ability to build trust and cooperation with non-Western countries. The committee asserted that in this highly interdependent world, American racism compromised the security of not only the United States but also the world.[4]

Arguing that racism was undercutting the ability of the United States to be the leader of the "free world," the committee looked to establish the importance of civil rights reforms to advancing the nation's Cold War policy of internationalism and communist containment.[5] It maintained that racialized minority integration was critical to reclaiming the legitimacy of American democracy and that this restoration could help contain the influence of communist ideologies and foster trust and cooperation between the United States and non-Western countries. In charting a new civil rights frontier, the committee did not merely map out what the federal government had yet to do to secure the rights of all. It also delineated a place where democracy and national security interacted and became mutually constitutive.

The interplay between democracy and national security, between Cold War internationalism and communist containment, did not, however, simply hinge on racial integration, it also appeared to necessitate the suppression of those suspected of espousing communist beliefs. This explained why President Truman not only enacted measures to desegregate the armed forces and the federal workforce, but also passed the Federal Employees Loyalty Program to oust suspected communists from the federal government. In this expanded framework, the inclusion of racialized minorities and the exclusion of political dissenters both functioned to promote the credibility of U.S. democracy. In this view, the federal government was influenced by the need to show the international community the nation's commitment to democratic principles when it backed civil rights reforms. It further acted to safeguard the legitimacy of American democracy by supporting measures that limited the rights of those who promoted communism or called into question the superiority of the American political system.

This book examines how both securing and infringing upon the rights of Asian Americans worked to promote the superiority of U.S. democracy over communism during the early Cold War years from 1946 to 1965. It analyzes the ways Asian American racial formation gave rise to this dual effect, specifically how popular perceptions of Asian Americans as the foreigners-within cast them at once as "loyal citizens" to be integrated into dominant society and as "alien subversives" to be deported. The racialization of Asian Americans as the foreigners-within positioned their inclusion as well as their exclusion from dominant society as responses to the demands of Cold War internationalism and communist containment.[6] My analysis of this effect goes beyond detailing how changes in U.S. foreign relations with countries in Asia impacted the social standing of Asian Americans; I aim to develop an understanding of how these changes shaped the kinds of stories that the state told about race and U.S. democracy. These state-generated stories were important not only for promoting the nation's Cold War agenda but also for influencing the efforts by Asian Americans to secure their social and political legitimacy in Cold War America and the stories they told about race in the United States.

The communist revolution in China in 1949 along with the outbreak of the Korean War a year later provide the context in which to see the federal government's desegregation measures and liberalization of immigration laws as actions geared toward advancing the credibility of U.S. democracy abroad. Following the escalation of the Cold War into open conflict with the outbreak of the Korean War, the federal government drew on the successful incorporation of Asian Americans within the nation's suburbs and workplaces to promote the benefits of the American way of life and to show the nation's goodwill toward "free countries" in Asia. However, it also implemented policies that monitored the activities and scrutinized the loyalties of Chinese and Korean Americans. Through these measures, the federal government sought to promote the superiority of the American political system by suppressing any dissenting views. Still, the Cold War formation of "two Chinas" and "two Koreas" helped to avert a wholesale association of Chinese and Korean Americans with communism.[7] The rise of the U.S.-backed Republic of China in Taiwan in 1949 and the Republic of Korea in the southern Korean peninsula in 1948 generated different means to assess the loyalties of Chinese and Korean Americans, illuminating the ways racial discourses worked to promote the benefits of the American way of life.

The belief that Asian Americans were direct extensions of people in Asia, regardless of place of birth or length of stay in the United States, allowed the political shifts that occurred between the United States and Asia to generate conflicting articulations over their place in Cold War America. The communist revolution in China along with the outbreak of the Korean War advanced beliefs about the likelihood that Asian Americans, particularly Chinese and Korean Americans, were communist agents who needed to be ousted from the nation. The nation's endeavor to contain communism in Asia, however, also promoted Asian American integration as a means of demonstrating the legitimacy of American democracy and the goodwill of the United States toward all "free countries" in Asia. In light of these conflicting imperatives, mainstream periodicals and government reports alternated between depicting Asian Americans as fully assimilated Americans whose cultural ties were an asset to the nation's Cold War effort and as unassimilated aliens whose ties to their country of origin needed to be monitored and regulated. As these shifts demonstrated, the construct of assimilation functioned to reveal the goals and aspirations of the state: state-generated narratives drew on the successful adjustment of Asian Americans in U.S. society to establish the superiority of the American political system.

Many Asian Americans thereby drew on their designation as assimilated Americans and as representatives of Asia to show that they deserved acceptance in mainstream society and were willing to advance the credibility of U.S. democracy in Asia. Such displays of Americanness and loyalty not only helped to deter the systematic harassment of Chinese and

Korean Americans following the communist revolution in China and the outbreak of the Korean War, they also enabled Asian Americans to press for greater civil liberties. These gains explained why so many were complicit with the state when it depicted at times the perceived cultural and national differences of Asian Americans as traits to be contained and erased, and at other times preserved and valorized. These gains did not, however, secure the consent of all to the dictates of U.S. foreign policy in Asia. Some Asian Americans promoted instead communist ideologies in their campaign to establish a "free Asia" and to create a society that was free of racist practices. This book intends to explore these varied responses and show Asian American culture as a site that generated competing stories about race and U.S. democracy.

Race and Cold War Democracy

One of the central concerns of this study is to explicate the different ways race worked to demonstrate the preeminence of the American way of life during the Cold War. To that end, this book utilizes Asian American racial formation as its primary mode of analysis to explore the effects of U.S. foreign affairs on domestic civil rights. Asian Americans, as the main subjects of this historical inquiry, also define and shape its methodological approach. This approach draws on the insights of Asian American studies scholars who examined how Japan's bombing of Pearl Harbor and the forging of an alliance between the United States and China to combat Japanese aggression resulted in a split in the views and treatment of Chinese and Japanese Americans.[8] As the cultural critic Elena Tajima Creef has shown, the shifts in U.S. foreign relations with Asia during World War II generated a need to discern what was previously seen as "inscrutable."[9] While these changes pushed the federal government to distinguish the Chinese as friends from its enemies, the Japanese, they did little to unsettle the perception of Chinese and Japanese Americans as extensions of people in China and Japan, regardless of whether or not they were American-born. The policies that the federal government enacted to mitigate wartime concerns over national security, which resulted in the internment of Japanese residents on the West Coast in 1942 and the repeal of the Chinese exclusion acts in 1943, revealed the ties that were thought to bind Asian Americans to their countries of ancestry—ties that continued to differentially affect the social standing of Asian Americans in Cold War America.

For the historian Ronald Takaki, the perception that Japanese Americans were "strangers from a different shore," more than any other reason, led the government to adopt the policy of evacuation and internment of Japanese residents on the West Coast, in contrast to the policies that addressed concerns over the loyalties of German and Italian immigrants during World War II.[10] Similarly, the historian Mae Ngai drew on the wartime phrase "A Jap is a Jap" to show how the belief that all Japanese were "racially inclined to disloyalty," regardless of place of birth, resulted in the suspension of the civil liberties of 120,000 internees, two-thirds of whom were citizens, given that the government never formally nullified the citizenship of Japanese Americans.[11] The 1943 Magnuson Act, which repealed the Chinese exclusion acts, set up an annual Chinese quota of 105, and granted naturalization rights to the Chinese, was passed to increase the status of Chinese in the United States; nevertheless, the act demonstrated how the racial formation of Asian Americans as the foreigners-within continued to make the social standing of Chinese Americans contingent on U.S. foreign relations with Asia, albeit in a contrary fashion than what Executive Order 9066 had exacted on the Japanese.

According to the legal scholar Neil Gotanda, President Franklin Delano Roosevelt urged Congress to revoke the Chinese exclusion acts in order to counter Japanese propaganda that blasted the nation's racist immigration laws for banning the entry of Chinese to the United States and for denying to them the right to naturalization.[12] The Magnuson Act was thereby enacted to thwart the efforts of the Japanese government to unite Asia under its leadership with the formation of the Greater East Asia Co-Prosperity Sphere. Its passage, moreover, showed how the credibility of U.S. democracy and the nation's treatment of its Chinese residents became consequential factors in winning the Pacific War and securing an alliance with China.[13] The political scientist Fred Riggs corroborated this view as he detailed how special interest groups had lobbied for the repeal of the Chinese exclusion acts because they believed that the extension of civil rights to Chinese Americans would help the nation's war effort in the Pacific.[14] The passage of the Magnuson Act enabled the state to generate a story about race and U.S. democracy that delineated the superiority of the United States over Japan and the totalitarian regime of Nazi Germany with its espousal of Aryan supremacy.[15] In a similar fashion, the policy of "military necessity" that the federal government adopted to legalize Japanese internment safeguarded the credibility of American democracy by designating the incarceration of Japanese Americans a matter of national security and not a case of racism.[16]

Despite the many works that focus on the split in the views and treatment of Japanese and Chinese Americans during World War II, African American history has taken center stage in studies of the impact of U.S. foreign affairs on domestic civil rights. For instance, the historian Brenda Gayle Plummer is noted for opening up the field of race and U.S. foreign affairs with her 1996 study *Rising Wind: Black Americans and U.S. Foreign Affairs, 1935–1960*.[17] Unlike most scholars of U.S. diplomatic history, Plummer showed that black Americans maintained a sustained engagement with U.S. foreign affairs; far from being apathetic about such matters, they actively opposed the spread of fascism and the rise of the Japanese empire. African American organizations, she revealed, made use of the United Nations during the postwar era to gain political leverage in the United States. Most notably, Plummer examined the implications of the 1954 landmark U.S. Supreme Court case *Brown v. Board of Education* on U.S. foreign policy by detailing how the movement for racial equality was pivotal to advancing the nation's efforts to contain the spread of communism abroad during the early Cold War years.

Plummer's pathbreaking study has influenced the works of many scholars, including the legal historian Mary Dudziak. In her 2000 book *Cold War Civil Rights*, Dudziak analyzed how race relations in the United States influenced the nation's foreign affairs during the early Cold War years.[18] According to Dudziak, the federal government was engaged in a sustained effort to tell a particular story about race and U.S. democracy as it sought to counter Soviet propaganda, which was calling attention to racist practices in the United States in order to undermine the benefits of the American way of life. The lesson of this story was always that "American democracy was a form of government that made the achievement of social justice possible, and that democratic change, however slow and gradual, was superior to dictatorial imposition."[19] With this in mind, Dudziak detailed how the fight against racism became linked to the fight against communism, establishing that civil rights reforms were vital to advancing the nation's Cold War agenda.

This book does not merely extend Plummer's and Dudziak's concerns to include a discussion of Asian Americans. It depicts the ways civil rights reforms worked together with laws that limited the rights of racialized political dissenters to maintain the credibility of American democracy. It further seeks to complicate Dudziak's conception of how race operated to promote the superiority of U.S. democracy over communism. The inquiry into how Asian American racial formation shaped the discourses surrounding U.S. democracy unsettles the practice of using African Americans as the only signifiers of race in the historiography on Cold War civil rights. It shows how the federal government drew on the relative positioning of Asian Americans vis-à-vis blacks and whites and on the racialization of Asian Americans as the foreigners-within to establish the superiority of the American way of life.

Dudziak, whose work has been formative to developing this field of study, adopted a black/white paradigm to explore the impact of U.S. foreign affairs on domestic civil rights reforms because policy makers and foreign observers of the early Cold War years saw race as "quintessentially about 'the Negro problem.'" Her use of the black/white paradigm, which she regarded as a "narrowed conception of American race relations," was in this respect "not an attempt to assert that race is a black/white issue." Rather, it was an effort to "capture the way race politics were understood at a time when 'the Negro problem' was at the center of the discourse on race in America."[20] But in this endeavor to recuperate the mindset of policy makers and foreign observers of the Cold War era, Dudziak left unexamined the possibility that policy makers and foreign observers used the category of blacks to represent the circumstances of all racialized minorities. She did not consider that their understanding of the "Negro problem" might have extended beyond the disparities and conflicts between blacks and whites. As a result, Dudziak importantly overlooked how race functioned as a relational construct even during the early Cold War years.

The 1947 report *To Secure These Rights*, by the President's Committee on Civil Rights, provides a clear example of how government reports of the time conceived blacks to stand in for the interests of all racialized groups in the United States. A striking aspect of the 1947 report was the amount of attention it paid to all minoritized groups in the United States with respect to racial, ethnic, national, cultural, and religious differences. The report's analysis recognized that Asian American racialization was unlike that of European immigrants, leading it to conclude that the marginalization of Chinese and Japanese immigrants was "intensified by physical characteristics which no amount of acceptance of western ways could change."[21] As mentioned earlier, the 1947 report also spoke out against the internment of Japanese Americans and decried the way Japanese immigrants were unfairly denied the right to citizenship by naturalization.[22] But what made this study even more noteworthy than its attempt to provide a comprehensive overview of racism's effects on all racialized groups in the United States was the way it accounted for its particularities. The 1947 study made known that while it aimed to show civil rights violations in all sections of the country, it honed in on the southern states because "the most sensational and serious violations of civil rights have taken place in the South." It subsequently focused on the problems facing "Negroes" because they were the "most visible minority group" in the South.[23] The report's placement of blacks at the center of discussions on civil rights violations was, in this view, an attempt to rally behind the most serious of abuses rather than a display of its inattentiveness to the problems confronting other racialized groups, as Dudziak has suggested. While working to construct southern blacks as the *primary* signifiers of race, this placement did not conceive blacks as the *only* signifiers of race. What this centering did was to link the concerns of northern blacks, Asians, and Mexicans in a chain of equivalences in order to show the overarching problem of civil rights violations. The conflation of these concerns enabled "the Negro" to signify the needs of all racialized groups while allowing the state to fix the problem of racism by addressing only the issues of southern blacks.

Unlike the 1947 report, other state-sponsored studies sought to downplay the impact of structural racism. Accounts such as the 1958 *Where Shall We Live?* called attention to the rising number of Asian Americans in the nation's suburbs in order to attribute the disparities between blacks and whites in U.S. society to the cultural failings of blacks rather than to the whites-only restrictions in housing.[24] In this context, blacks did not work to represent the interest of all racialized groups in the United States. Rather, the report exemplified what the political scientist Claire Jean Kim has described as the "relative valorization" of Asian Americans vis-à-vis blacks and whites.[25] The cultural critic Leslie Bow has, moreover, developed the notion of "racial interstitiality" to detail how the black/white binary situated Asian Americans "within the space between normative structures of power."[26] As I reveal, Asian Americans were likewise figured in state narratives to be at times "like whites" and at other times "like blacks." This relative positioning of Asian Americans, I argue, importantly shaped popular images of American democracy during the early Cold War years.

Notably, state narratives of the early Cold War years also defined Asian Americans in relation to Asians in Asia. Numerous scholars of Asian American studies have noted the caricature of Asian Americans as the perpetual foreigners-within to be the quintessential racial formation of Asian Americans. This racialization encapsulated the idea that Asian Americans regardless of place of birth or length of stay in the United States remained unmediated extensions of people in Asia. Its historical roots lay in the exclusionist movements of the late nineteenth and early twentieth centuries, which drew on beliefs in the incompatibility of the East and the West and the unassimilability of Asian immigrants to justify barring Asian immigrants from the United States and to block businesses from relying on Asian immigrants as their main source of cheap labor. The state codified this understanding by making Asian immigrants ineligible for citizenship by naturalization and in so doing, bolstered popular perceptions of Asian Americans as the perpetual foreigners-within.[27] These historical events critically reveal how the movement toward the systematic disenfranchisement of Asian immigrants established Asian Americans as knowable subjects. Racialization reduced the complexities of an entire population from East, Southeast, and South Asia to a few simple traits and habits and made Asian Americans indistinguishable from people in Asia.

The racial formation of Asian Americans as the perpetual foreigners-within thus allowed the government to draw on the successes of a very select group of Chinese, Korean, Japanese, and South Asian Americans to represent the rising status of all Asian Americans in U.S. society. The government used this generalization to demonstrate not only the validity of U.S. democracy but also the nation's goodwill toward noncommunist countries such as Japan, the Philippines, India, Burma, and Malaysia. But the effect of Asian American racial formation to elide group differences was not without qualification, even as Soviet propaganda was working to turn the social status of all racialized groups into a measure of the validity of American democracy. This was because the escalation of the Cold War in Asia that resulted in the formation of "two Chinas" and "two Koreas" prompted the federal government to hone in on the activities of Chinese and Korean Americans for political scrutiny. During World War II, the shifts in U.S. foreign relations with Asia had incited the federal government to distinguish Chinese Americans as its "friends"—distinct from its "enemies," the Japanese Americans; similarly, in the geopolitical situation of the Cold War, the inclusion and exclusion of Chinese and Korean Americans from dominant society took on greater political significance than the inclusion and exclusion of Japanese, Filipino, and South Asian Americans. After Japan's bombing of Pearl Harbor, the federal government had systematically designated Japanese Americans as "enemy aliens"; in the new Cold War context, the communist revolution in China along with the outbreak of the Korean War pushed the federal government to see Chinese and Korean Americans as likely communist spies. In examining these developments, this study extends the cultural critic Christina Klein's observation that Cold War internationalism enhanced the value of Asian Americans as Americans; the nation's campaign against communism, I will argue, intensified the tendency to view Chinese and Korean Americans as subversives.[28] This book focuses on the activities of Chinese and Korean Americans in order to call attention to the way U.S. foreign affairs differentially impacted the social standings of Asian Americans in Cold War America.

Citizens of Asian America brings to the fore these varied and conflicting understandings of Asian Americans in order to show how these ideas informed the stories that the state told about race and U.S. democracy during the early Cold War years. Despite this focus, this study does not analyze race as just an ideological construct shaping human and institutional actions. It also examines race as a discursive sign that is formative to constructing the image of national progress. Once again, the 1947 report *To Secure These Rights*, by the President's Committee on Civil Rights, serves as a solid example of how government reports of the early Cold War years developed race in relation to state agendas. Specifically, the report revealed the importance of positing the American heritage of freedom and equality as the unquestioned basis for the American way of life. This epistemological grounding was useful, for it allowed the report to talk about racism as a phenomenon that showed American democracy to be an ideal that "still awaits complete realization," rather than as a flaw that undermined the superiority of the American political system.²⁹ The 1947 study was therefore able to recognize that a gulf existed between American ideals and practice while maintaining that these discrepancies did not shake the committee's belief that civil rights would soon be extended to all.³⁰ By framing racial equality to be foremost a matter of time, the report obscured even its own discussion of how the Cold War had turned racial equality into a national priority. American democracy was in this way credible because the nation remained always already on the path toward social progress.

My book seeks to explore how the rising status of Asian Americans affirmed the belief in the inevitability of national progress and effectively distinguished the superiority of the American way of life over communism. It departs in this way from the project of the historian Brenda Gayle Plummer, as it goes beyond casting racialized minorities as active agents of history and unsettles the facticity of master narratives by uncovering their constructedness. As this study looks to denaturalize the belief that racial equality is the anticipated outgrowth of American democracy, it examines how racial constructions are connected to state agendas.

In my reluctance to limit this study to a foregrounding of Asian American responses to U.S. foreign policy, I take a page out of the feminist historian Joan Wallach Scott's work on gender as a useful category of historical analysis.³¹ Under this framework, the term "race" is not a synonym for Asian Americans, just as "gender" is not a synonym for women. Race, like gender, is an ideological construct that helps to make sense of human actions and a discursive sign that unfolds the making of metanarratives. Asian American racial formation uncovers these processes, revealing assimilation to be an ideological construct that the state drew upon to construct Asian Americans as deserving of integration and as a discursive sign that operated in conjunction with Cold War civil rights to develop a narrative of progress. This approach also importantly explores how the coherence of metanarratives is forged through the elision of differences and contradictions.

Finally, I hope to offer a view of Asian American activism that takes into account the impact of ideological and institutional structures on human actions. My study thereby analyzes how state-generated narratives on the benefits of the American way of life provided Asian Americans a discourse through which to articulate their own self-conception. These tales

INTRODUCTION

not only gave Asian Americans a way to make sense of their racialization in U.S. society, they also prompted some to generate different accounts on race and U.S. democracy. In taking on this approach to understanding the activities of Asian Americans during the early Cold War years, I draw from the work of the cultural critic Lisa Lowe, who examined in her 1996 book *Immigrant Acts* the effect of state narratives on the development of an Asian American culture. For Lowe, Asian American culture can work to reimagine popular understandings of American democracy and social progress.

As Lowe has argued, the racial formation of Asian Americans as the foreigners-within revealed the narrative strategies that the state deployed, especially the immigration and naturalization laws that it enacted to conceive a national identity that was homogenous in its whiteness but still inclusive of racially and culturally marked groups. While the racialization of Asian Americans as perpetual foreigners kept intact this image of the nation, Lowe argued that it generated a clash in the social standing of Asian Americans, evidenced by the way immigration and naturalization laws designated the Asian immigrant to be a desired commodity within the nation's workplaces but "linguistically, culturally, and racially" outside of and foreign to the national polity. The tension between being economically central and culturally marginal, between being "within" and "foreign," formed the basis of what Lowe described as the contradictions of Asian immigration.[32] In state-generated accounts, Asian Americans figured as both "persons and populations to be integrated" and as "contradictory, confusing, unintelligible elements to be marginalized and returned to their alien origins." These contradictions also turned Asian American culture into an alternative site "where the palimpsest of lost memories is reinvented, histories are fractured and retraced, and the unlike varieties of silence emerge into articulacy."[33] The very ideas that kept Asian Americans at odds with the state worked, in this view, to generate competing visions of the nation, visions that showed how the United States was not homogeneous in its whiteness or inclusive of racialized groups.

My analysis of the writings and oral histories of Asian Americans during the early Cold War years employs this view of Asian American culture as an alternative site where Asian Americans generated competing stories about race and U.S. democracy. It shows how some contested the discriminatory practices in the United States by contending that communism and not American democracy worked to ensure freedom and equality for all. For the few who managed to cross the racial divide and achieve a high level of professional success, this distinction did not always incite them to tout the benefits of the American way of life. Rather, many drew on the singularity of their experiences to point out that Cold War America remained a deeply segregated society. As for the many who professed support for the U.S. Cold War effort in Asia, their professions of support were often accompanied by statements that called upon the United States to relax its immigration policies toward Asia. This link importantly showed that many Asian Americans declared support for the U.S. Cold War effort in Asia as a means to increase their civil rights in the United States rather than as blind expressions of their belief that spreading American democracy in Asia would in fact lead to the betterment of Asian societies. State-generated stories on race and U.S. democracy are thereby important not only for promoting the nation's Cold War imperatives, but also for shaping the ways Asian Americans went about fighting for civil rights and against the belief in the inevitability of national progress.

Asian Americans and the Historiography on Cold War Civil Rights

As this study examines Asian American racial formation in order to make sense of the conflicting depictions and treatment of Asian Americans during the early Cold War years, it draws on this approach to redefine and broaden the scope of Cold War civil rights historiography. Specifically, it brings together works on civil rights reforms and works on government persecution of people for their political beliefs for the purpose of reframing the conceptual compass of both fields of study. Of the scholarship on the anticommunist crusade of the early Cold War years, the legal historian Michal Belknap has written one of the most definitive studies. In his 1977 book *Cold War Political Justice*, Belknap examined the Smith Act prosecution of Communist Party leaders as a prime example of American political justice.[34] For Belknap, the Smith Act trials demonstrated how the judicial system was intricately bound to partisan politics and did not exist apart from that. Other scholars have similarly remarked on this contingency of

American democracy in their analysis of postwar anticommunist hysteria. Victor Navasky, for instance, explored the domestic attack on political dissenters with the creation of the Hollywood blacklist in his 1980 study *Naming Names*, while Ellen Shrecker provided a comprehensive overview of the ways the government limited the rights of a nation during the McCarthy era in her 1998 study *Many Are the Crimes*.[35] Like Belknap, these scholars highlighted the government persecution of political dissenters in order to track the development of the American political justice system and its compromise of constitutional protections.

Despite revealing U.S. democracy as a mediated ideal that was shaped by the political agendas of the state, these scholars did not seek to explain why the government's blatant disregard of constitutional protections failed to undermine the legitimacy of the American political system in the minds of the American public. In other words, why has the notion of political justice been ineffective in unsettling fully the image that the United States is always already on the path toward the full realization of democratic principles? This study addresses this dilemma and analyzes the government harassment of Chinese and Korean Americans for their political beliefs as a mechanism to maintain the credibility of U.S. democracy during the early Cold War years. In so doing, this study looks to extend the analytical weight of American political justice and details how the suppression of dissent, although compromising the freedoms guaranteed by the Bill of Rights, critically upheld the belief that American democracy was valid, credible, and superior to all other forms of government. The study of Cold War civil rights is for this reason not complete without an analysis of how the government enacted laws that placed limits on the freedom of expression and due process. My book develops the need to explore how civil rights reforms worked together with the legal suppression of political dissent to establish the validity of the American political system.

As this book foregrounds the political ventures of Asian Americans, it further brings to the fore how the liberalization of immigration laws, particularly the 1965 Immigration and Nationality Act, was an important Cold War civil rights measure. Given that Asian Americans were racialized not only through color but also through national differences, this racialization enabled the federal government to employ both immigration laws and segregation policies to limit the rights of Asian Americans. The campaign among Asian Americans for greater civil rights had for this reason included immigration reform. Like desegregation measures of the early Cold War years, the 1965 Immigration and Nationality Act demonstrated that granting civil rights to racialized minorities was crucial for promoting the nation's foreign policies. The federal government promoted Cold War internationalism by placing Asian Americans on equal footing with European Americans and Asia on par with Europe. Scholars such as the immigration historian Daniel Tichenor and the legal scholar Gabriel Chin have noted this as a distinguishing feature of the 1965 act.[36] This study develops the insights of these scholars, and argues that the study of Asian Americans necessitates an inquiry into how immigration reform worked alongside desegregation measures to advance the nation's Cold War agenda.

In light of the reforms that were passed during the early Cold War years, scholars of Asian American history have largely seen the postwar era as a time when society opened up and when second-generation Asian Americans successfully assimilated into mainstream society. Many of these scholars have not taken into account the fact that racial restrictions were lifted as a result of collective struggle and the nation's foreign policy endeavors; instead, they have portrayed social progress as a natural outcome of the passage of time. The historian Charlotte Brooks's 2009 study *Alien Neighbors, Foreign Friends* offers a refreshing account of race relations in postwar California that, for the most part, avoids the reductive reading of racial integration as a testament to the nation's progress toward the full realization of its democratic principles.[37] In her endeavor to chart California's shifting race relations through the residential patterns of Asian Americans, Brooks examines the move from racial segregation to racial integration as an indication of how U.S. foreign affairs shaped domestic civil rights reform. Nevertheless, she overlooks the importance of interracial activism in bringing about social change in California; in so doing, she makes light of the historian Scott Kurashige's analysis of interracial organizations' pivotal role in ridding postwar Los Angeles of its racist practices.[38]

While my study similarly examines how U.S. foreign affairs connected the fight against housing segregation to the fight against communism during the early Cold War years, it also takes note of the ways U.S. Cold War politics influenced employment practices, limited the political activities of a nation, and shaped immigration reform. I therefore do not share Brooks's contention that housing is the best way to understand California's postwar racial dynamics.[39] My study takes seriously the role of interracial activism in effecting social change in California. Moreover, it analyzes how the communist revolution in China and the outbreak of the Korean War prompted the federal government to focus on the activities of Chinese and Korean Americans over other Asian groups. My book does not for this reason foreground the experiences of Chinese and Japanese Americans the way Brooks's project had. Rather, it highlights the activities of Chinese and Korean Americans in order to explain why their activities were of greater political significance for U.S. foreign affairs than those of other Asian American groups during the early Cold War years. It hopes to reveal through this analysis the structural forces that treated all Asian American groups as the same as well as those forces that distinguished between groups.

The book explores in five chapters how the processes of securing and infringing upon the rights of Asian Americans worked to establish and uphold the legitimacy of the American political system during the early Cold War years. It begins in chapter 1 with an examination of how the fight to end race-based restrictions in housing emerged at the forefront of the federal government's attempts to show before an international audience the validity of American democracy. The legal campaign to outlaw residential segregation culminated with the U.S. Supreme Court ruling unconstitutional the practice of race-based restrictions in housing. Notably, in its ruling against housing segregation, the Supreme Court designated blacks to represent the interest of all racialized groups. Despite having accepted for review two cases involving Asian Americans due to uncertainty as to whether a ruling on blacks would apply to other nonwhite groups, the Court nevertheless moved to hear only the cases on black Americans. This decision cemented the way blacks functioned in future landmark civil rights cases to signify the capacity of American democracy to secure the rights of all. The examination of Asian American participation in the national legal campaign to invalidate the whites-only rule in housing reveals the creation of this racial understanding. State-generated stories on race and U.S. democracy were thus able to narrate the progress of American democracy by focusing only on the experiences of black Americans.

Chapter 2 suggests that the path to residential freedom entailed not just the outlawing of race-based restrictions in housing but also nonwhite assimilation to the values and lifestyle of white middle-class suburbanites. In state-sponsored studies focused on the increased number of Asian Americans in the nation's suburbs, assimilation was seen as an effective means to rectify the housing disparities between whites and nonwhites. The reports downplayed the effects of structural racism, attributing the low number of blacks in the nation's suburbs to their failure to adjust to the white middle-class lifestyle. Assimilation emerged in these state-sponsored studies as an important ideological construct that prevented racism from undermining the credibility of U.S. democracy. Against the claims of these studies, the case of Sing Sheng showed how a fully assimilated Chinese American was barred from residing in an all-white suburb of South San Francisco because of his race. But while the Sheng case revealed how the outbreak of the Korean War turned the social standing of Asian Americans into a measure of the credibility of U.S. democracy, it also revealed how U.S. Cold War politics was working to enhance the desirability of racial integration. In this context, the caricature of Sheng as a fully assimilated American helped move the nation past its racial preferences and toward racial integration.

I examine in chapter 3 how mainstream periodicals supported the government's efforts to promote the credibility of U.S. democracy by regularly running stories that recognized the first of a particular ethnic and racial group to obtain a high level of social and professional distinction in mainstream society. Features on the firsts drew on the successes of racialized minorities to show how the nation was progressing toward a racially inclusive society. Following the outbreak of the Korean War, the U.S. State Department commissioned notable Asian American firsts such as the Olympic gold medalist Sammy Lee and the author Jade Snow Wong to embark on tours throughout East, Southeast, and South Asia for the purpose of being the living examples of the benefits of the American way of life. The federal government sought to make use of the racial heritage of Lee and Wong to authenticate the superiority of U.S. democracy over communism and to show the nation's goodwill toward "free countries" in Asia. But as Wong recollected, her Chinese heritage did not provide an inroad into the hearts and minds of the people in Asia. She became convinced after her tour of Asia that there did not exist a shared Asian sensibility. Her recollections were in this respect an attempt to contest the racial formation of Asian Americans as the foreigners-within. In this chapter, I also examine the writings and recollections of other notable "firsts," including the oral history of Judge Delbert Wong, who sought to call attention to his status as the *only* Chinese American judge. Judge Wong drew on this distinction to highlight the way Cold War America remained a deeply segregated society. His story was in this way notable as it looked to unsettle state narratives' use of the firsts to demonstrate the progress of American democracy.

Chapter 4 details the federal government's endeavors to protect the integrity of the American political system by suppressing the political activities of Korean radicals in the United States. The outbreak of the Korean War saw the federal government impose sanctions that limited the rights of a nation while heightening its scrutiny of the political activities of Korean Americans. A study of the arrests of David Hyun and Diamond Kimm for subversive activities charts this increased scrutiny, and reveals the rise of progressive organizations that defended the right of Hyun and Kimm to espouse communist ideologies. The government persecution of Hyun and Kimm further brought to the fore how the U.S. government had adopted a very narrow understanding of communist activities and had construed all such activities as supporting the expansion of a Soviet empire. This misconception caused the federal government to overlook how Hyun and Kimm were working to establish a sovereign Korea that was free not only from the vestiges of Japanese colonial rule but also from the dominance of wealthy landowning elites. It also led the government to dismiss the way racist practices in the United States pushed Hyun and Kimm to activism. As the federal government refused to recognize the liberatory potential of communist ideologies, it upheld the American way to be the only way toward creating a socially just society.

Finally, I explore in chapter 5 how the communist revolution in China and the outbreak of the Korean War prompted the federal government to launch two campaigns to monitor systematically the political activities and loyalty of Chinese Americans. In its campaign against the extortion racket, the U.S. government sought to keep money sent by Chinese Americans to their relatives in China from falling into the hands of the communist government in China. In its campaign against the slot racket, the U.S. government implemented tighter sanctions against Chinese immigration in order to prevent the infiltration of Chinese communist spies to the United States through illegal channels. Notably, these two campaigns did not merely document how the government sought to maintain the integrity of the American political system by infringing on the rights of Chinese Americans. They also importantly detailed the efforts of Chinese Americans to fight for greater civil rights through immigration reform. To that end, many professed their support for the U.S.-backed Republic of China not only to prove their loyalty to the United States but also to remind the government of a viable overseas Chinese population that could help advance the nation's Cold War efforts in Asia. They therefore appealed to the nation's desire to create better relations with "free countries" in Asia in their call for greater civil rights through immigration reform. These efforts effectively showed how Chinese Americans made use of U.S. Cold War politics for their own gain, as I argue, contributing to the enactment of the 1965 Immigration and Nationality Act. Civil rights reforms of the early Cold War years thus centered not only on desegregation measures but also on the liberalization of immigration policies.

Citizens of Asian America reveals how the shift in U.S. Cold War policies toward Asia greatly enhanced the ways Asian American racial formation shaped discourses on civil rights during the early Cold War years. This study, at its core, seeks to explicate the mechanisms that worked to construct and maintain the superiority of the American political system. Specifically, it highlights how the legal suppression of dissent is vital to maintaining the belief that the American heritage is indeed rooted in the principles of freedom and equality. During the early Cold War years, the outlawing of political opposition worked together with civil rights reforms to bolster the perception that American democracy remained steadfast on the path toward social equality. Asian American representation was central to this narration. My attention to this matter aims to anchor stories on race and U.S. democracy to the goals and aspirations of the state, and thus to unsettle the practice of using historical progress to mask state agendas. Given the recent emergence of postraciality and how it is working to denote the next step toward social advancement, I consider it an important task to call into question racial equality as the anticipated outcome of American democracy. My study of race and Cold War civil rights thereby puts forward the need to examine how racial constructions are conceived in relation to state agendas and how this conception has, in turn, transformed race into a category of analysis that can work to reveal the goals of the state.

CHAPTER 1

Legislating Nonwhite Crossings into White Suburbia

Just two days after Tommy Amer moved into his newly purchased home in South Los Angeles, his neighbors stopped by to inform him that they had filed an injunction against him. The petition before the Los Angeles Superior Court demanded that Amer be removed from the premises of his home. As Amer recounted many years later, his neighbors emphasized that the filing of the injunction was nothing personal; they merely acted to protect their property values from diminishing with the residence of an Asian American in their suburban tract. While Amer was aware that the home he purchased in 1946 was in a covenanted area—that homeowners had come together since 1941 to sign an agreement limiting the residency of the Firth Main Street Boulevard Tract to persons of white or Caucasian race—he claimed not to have understood how this racial restrictive covenant could actually ban him from living in the house that he lawfully purchased. Amer noted that he was only twenty-four at the time and had just returned home from fighting in World War II. He believed in earnest that his rights were protected by the Constitution and was not aware that the U.S. Supreme Court had ruled in 1926 that racial restrictive covenants were the actions of private individuals and not of the state and were thereby not in violation of the Fourteenth Amendment.[1]

There were other reasons that led Amer to believe that his living on 127 West 56th Street was not going to incite the ire of his neighbors. From what Amer could tell, the area where he purchased his home looked as if it were on the verge of being integrated. His neighbors across the street, the Hickersons, were black. Amer learned only after he was served with the injunction that the Hickersons were also embroiled in a legal battle to retain the ownership and occupancy of their home. Amer remembered how the previous homeowner had hinted to him that his white neighbors would not go after him since they were mainly concerned with ridding the neighborhood of the two black families that had moved in. But as he learned, the whites-only restriction that worked to prohibit his black neighbors from living in the Firth Main Street Boulevard Tract had applied to him, a Chinese American, as well. Following the receipt of court papers, Amer embarked on a two-year legal battle to reside in his home in South Los Angeles. Later he recalled in an interview that his campaign against residential segregation was born not out of a desire to fight for equal rights but out of an imposed necessity to do so, as he was unable to find housing elsewhere and was unsure if he could recover financially from the loss of his home. What Amer did not foresee was that his case would be among the seven lawsuits admitted for review by the U.S. Supreme Court that resulted in the 1948 landmark ruling against the state enforcement of racial restrictive covenants.[2]

This chapter examines the Amer case, along with a companion suit that involved a Korean American, Yin Kim, to explicate the various forces that called into question the practice of race-based restrictions in housing during the early Cold War years. While the housing shortage of the postwar period triggered a rise in the number of lawsuits that contested the legality of racial restrictive covenants, the advent of the Cold War incited the federal government to come out in support of the legal struggle against housing segregation. Much of the federal government's efforts to invalidate the whites-only rule grew out of the need to counter Soviet propaganda that highlighted racist practices in the United States to undermine the credibility of American democracy. The campaign against race-based restrictions in housing had thereby enabled the state to tell a different story about U.S. democracy, one that emphasized the nation's commitment to creating a socially just world. This chapter details how the Amer and Kim cases importantly shaped this story about race and U.S. democracy in the national legal campaign against the state enforcement of racial restrictive covenants.

Before these two lawsuits gained national prominence, they were embroiled in California's legal campaign to end housing segregation. The Amer and Kim cases thus provided a window into the contestations that were taking place on a local level, particularly in Los Angeles, to invalidate the whites-only housing restrictions. These local struggles were notable because it was during these campaigns that civil rights activists and liberal supporters began to organize across racial lines to challenge the whites-only rule. The interracial activism importantly put Los Angeles on the map for legal battles against housing segregation while drawing national attention to the problem of unequal property rights between whites and nonwhites. The efforts further supplied the national campaign with a rationale for securing the equal rights of all. Drawing on sociological studies on urban and suburban America, advocates of housing integration argued that residential freedom was key to mitigating urban and suburban decay, as residential segregation gave rise to the formation of black ghettos across the United States. This line of thinking put forward in concrete terms how the granting of equal access to housing benefited the whole of society and moved the nation toward social progress. In so doing, it helped to turn racial desegregation into a desirable endeavor in Cold War America.

The Amer and Kim cases also played an essential role in the national legal campaign against housing segregation. They revealed how the construct of Asian Americans shaped legal understandings of race in the landmark civil rights cases before the U.S. Supreme Court. The Amer and Kim cases achieved national significance after the U.S. Supreme Court admitted these lawsuits for review as it prepared to reconsider the constitutionality of racial restrictive covenants. The Court agreed to review the two cases because it wanted to see whether the experiences of other racialized groups were relatable to those of blacks in regard to housing segregation. It further recognized that significant proportions of Asians in the United States were American citizens and thus entitled to equal protection under the law. As the Court ultimately decided to hear only the cases that involved blacks, it determined to use blacks as the representative racial category that would speak to the interests of all racialized groups. This maneuver critically established that rulings to secure blacks' rights functioned to safeguard the rights of all.

But the move in favor of legal expediency, where a ruling on blacks applied to all racialized citizens, generated some adverse effects. Not only did it bolster the perception that race was a black/white issue, it also relied on this simplified view of race relations to simplify the problem of racism and turn it into a containable matter. By sidelining the Amer and Kim cases, the U.S. Supreme Court allowed people to forget that the fight against residential segregation was an interracial effort. The desire to make coherent the problem of racism further ignored the way interracial tensions had worked to shape the unequal access to housing. What these effects promoted with this limited understanding of race and property rights was the advancement of a story about the nation's unwavering commitment to democratic principles and how this adherence had prompted the Court to strike down the whites-only rule in housing. As this chapter traces how the category of blacks came to represent the interests of all racialized groups in the landmark ruling on property rights, it explores how Asian Americans were figured into discourses surrounding race and U.S. democracy.

Whiteness as Property

The early Cold War years witnessed a decided shift in the efficacy of the whites-only restriction in housing. In ruling unconstitutional the state enforcement of racial restrictive covenants, the U.S. Supreme Court upended a trail of legislative acts that previously worked to build and preserve the worth of whiteness as property. According to the legal studies scholar Cheryl Harris, the recognition that whiteness was both a characteristic to inhabit as well as a resource to be accessed came about with the systematic seizure and appropriation of lands from Native Americans, blacks, and other racialized groups by Anglo Americans.[3] The legislative history of land use segregation based on race demonstrated the repeated attempts of the state to preserve the value of whiteness and the property rights of whites in the face of challenges to that privilege. Moreover, it detailed the making of a nonwhite category that functioned to assess the worth of whiteness as property.

Prior to the rise of the nonwhite category in land use segregation laws, a set of disparate policies had been enacted during the late nineteenth century that worked together to uphold the value of whiteness as property even as individual legislations functioned to limit the property rights of a particular racialized group. While restrictions leveled against one group often served as the legal basis for restrictions against another, they also exposed ambiguities about the applicability of these prohibitions. As the cultural critic Leslie Bow has detailed in her 2010 book *Partly Colored*, the institution of Jim Crow laws to segregate blacks from whites in all public facilities had turned Asians in the South into an anomaly in the colored/not colored binary.[4] For Bow, the inability of these categories to neatly determine the place of Asian Americans showed not just the constructedness of racial classifications but also their instability. Outside the South, this instability was apparent as Asian Americans during the postwar period were on occasion granted access to restricted neighborhoods of the West Coast, as whites regarded Asians as less troublesome than blacks. The shakiness of this black/white schema is even more pronounced when the uncertainty over the place of Asian Americans in postwar America is juxtaposed to the situation of the late nineteenth century, when Asians were the principal targets of urban residential segregation.

During the height of anti-Chinese sentiments in the late nineteenth century, California amended its constitution to include Article XIX, simply entitled, "The Chinese," for the purpose of limiting Chinese residents access to state resources and services. Among the restrictions outlined in this 1876 measure was the confinement of the land use of the Chinese to certain portions of cities and towns.[5] In addition to this constitutional amendment, state officials passed a series of Alien Land Laws during the early decades of the twentieth century that importantly showed how the category of "aliens ineligible for citizenship" and not just ethnic and racial designations functioned to restrict the property rights of all Asians in California.[6] These laws documented how Asian Americans emerged as the principal targets of exclusionary measures on the West Coast during the late nineteenth and early twentieth centuries, during a time when Mexican Americans were legally classified as whites in the California census. This legal classification resulted in the uneven enforcement of laws to limit the land use of Mexican Americans.[7]

As the civil rights lawyer Loren Miller noted in his 1947 study on residential segregation laws, restrictions that were leveled against the Chinese during the late nineteenth century laid the groundwork for the development of urban residential segregationist measures to prohibit the land use of all racialized minorities. According to Miller, the first attempt to impose urban residential segregation occurred with the passage of the 1890 Bingham Ordinance in San Francisco. As this city zoning ordinance requested the removal of all Chinese who were residing or conducting business within a designated area, it carried out the provision of the 1876 California State Constitution that granted to incorporated cities and towns the authority to enact measures for the removal of the Chinese.[8] But almost as soon as the ordinance was enacted, the case of *re Lee Sing* rose to challenge its legality. Notably, the San Francisco judge who presided over this case ruled that the Bingham Ordinance was in violation not only of the Equal Protection Clause of the Fourteenth Amendment but also of the 1868 Burlingame Treaty, which granted to Chinese in the United States certain rights and privileges in accord with China's most-favored-nation status.[9]

In light of this ruling, the 1890 case of *re Lee Sing* took on an added significance. It revealed how the Equal Protection Clause of the Fourteenth Amendment necessitated the development of a different approach to preserving the worth of whiteness as property that did not explicitly rely on the state to enforce land use segregation based on race. When state-mandated zoning laws were outlawed, residential segregation policies arose in the form of private agreements between consenting parties that were incorporated into property deeds to limit the use and occupancy of specified lands to white Americans. The first court case that tested the legality of such agreements took place in 1892. In *Gandolfo v. Hartman*, a covenant in deed was signed by two consenting individuals to prohibit the use and occupancy of a designated tract of land in San Diego by Chinese residents. The San Diego district judge who deliberated on the case ruled against this practice and issued a telling statement on how the legality of racial restrictive covenants rested on one's interpretation of the Fourteenth Amendment, specifically the interpretation of what constituted state action.[10] This was because the use of racial restrictive covenants in the form of private agreements to protect the privilege of whites did not appear to be the direct result of state action. But as the judge noted,

> It would be a very narrow construction of the constitutional amendment in question and of the decisions based upon it, and a very restricted application of the broad principles upon which both the amendment and

the decisions proceed, to hold that, while state and municipal legislatures are forbidden to discriminate against the Chinese in their legislation, a citizen of the state may lawfully do so by contract, which the courts may enforce. Such a view is, I think, entirely inadmissible.[11]

Thus the San Diego judge determined that the court's upholding of such agreements constituted state action. He thereby ruled racial restrictive covenants in the form of private agreements unenforceable. Despite obtaining the backing of the U.S. Circuit Court of Appeals, which denied the request for an appeal, this decision was overturned by the California Supreme Court in 1919.

Two key developments prompted the widespread use of racial restrictive covenants to grant white Americans greater access to property rights than other racialized groups. Following the huge influx of blacks to urban areas from 1915 to 1929, known as the Great Migration, the noticeable increase of black residents in the nation's cities spurred the enactment of policies to limit the land use of blacks, not just of the Chinese.[12] The reliance on racial restrictive covenants to maintain white privilege further grew after the U.S. Supreme Court outlawed in 1917 all forms of state and city ordinances that restricted the use and occupancy of lands by racialized minorities.[13] The Court's 1917 *Buchanan v. Warley* decision, which upheld the 1890 *re Lee Sing* ruling, had thereby set constitutional limits on state action even though the Court believed that residential segregation helped to mitigate racial hostility.[14] This decision, together with the increase of black residents in urban areas and the barring of Asian immigration to the United States in 1924, importantly worked to turn blacks into the main targets of urban housing restrictions.[15] The shifts that took place in residential segregation policies after the passage of the Fourteenth Amendment further documented how restrictions leveled against the Chinese during the late nineteenth century became antecedents to the prohibitions directed against blacks during the first part of the twentieth century.

Following the *Buchanan v. Warley* ruling, racial restrictive covenants became the primary method of enforcing residential segregation, as state courts began to uphold the validity of such agreements. Louisiana became the first state to support the use of racial restrictive covenants, after its Supreme Court ruled in 1915 that private contracts made between consenting parties for the purpose of imposing whites-only restrictions in land use did not violate the Fourteenth Amendment as these agreements were not state-imposed legislations or ordinances. The Missouri Supreme Court concurred in 1918. A year later, the California Supreme Court reached the same conclusion, overturning the 1892 *Gandolfo v. Hartman* ruling, and in 1922 the Michigan Supreme Court also upheld the practice of racial restrictive covenants.[16] Finally, the U.S. Supreme Court legitimized the interpretation that private agreements made between consenting parties did not constitute state action in its 1926 ruling on a case that came from the District of Columbia. The Court declared in *Corrigan v. Buckley* that "the prohibitions of the Fourteenth Amendment have reference to state action exclusively, and not to any action of private individuals. Individual invasion of individual rights is not the subject matter of the Amendment."[17] It also ruled that the Fourteenth Amendment did not apply to the District of Columbia and that racial segregation was not against public policy in that territory. With this deliberation, the Court sanctioned the practice of racial restrictive covenants.

After the *Corrigan* decision, the use of racial restrictive covenants proliferated. These covenants generally consisted of one of three types of restrictions: (1) those restricting sale, lease, conveyance to, or ownership by members of a designated racial or religious group; (2) those restricting use or occupancy by that group; and (3) those restricting both ownership and use and occupancy by that group.[18] These contractual agreements also took on two distinct methods of barring the ownership or use of designated lands by nonwhites. The first had restrictions written into the title deeds of individual property listings. Individuals, land companies, or real estate firms typically signed this type of deed covenants. The second method, which was used mostly for the purpose of restricting a large tract of land, contained the signatures of a number of property owners within a particular district that not only bound themselves but also heirs, successors, and assigns to a contract even if they were not originally part of the property title or deed. This second type of agreement was generally initiated and regulated by neighborhood associations or a real estate board.[19] It was this type of contract that restricted Tommy Amer from living in his home in South Los Angeles. A sample of this contract reads as follows:

> It Is Hereby Mutually Covenanted and Agreed by and between parties hereto that each and every of the lots or parcels of land designated

and particularly described as opposite the respective signatures of the parties hereto shall be forever subject to the following restrictions and covenant which shall apply to and be binding upon the parties hereto, their and each of their heirs, devises, executors, administrators, successors and assigns, namely: That no portion or part of said lots or parcels of land ever shall be used or occupied by, or be permitted to be used or occupied by, any person not of the White or Caucasian race. That no person ever shall live upon said property at any time whose blood is not entirely that of the Caucasian race, but if persons not of the Caucasian race are kept thereon by such Caucasian occupant strictly in the capacity of servants or employees of such occupant, such circumstances shall not constitute a violation of this covenant.[20]

As racial restrictive covenants became the primary means of maintaining residential segregation from 1917 to 1948, it bears emphasis that these agreements were rarely contracted between individuals, as the designation "private agreements" might suggest. Rather, the practice of racial restrictive covenants was the standard policy of the housing industry and, as such, detailed a systematic approach to securing race-based restrictions in land use. This method of safeguarding white privilege was supported and regulated by real estate brokers, builders, financial institutions, and the government.[21] It was written into Article 35 of the Code of Ethics of the National Association of Real Estate Boards, which states, "A realtor should not be instrumental in introducing into a neighborhood a character of property or use which will clearly be detrimental to property values in a neighborhood."[22] While the language of this statute did not explicitly specify nonwhites as a detriment to property values, it was nevertheless the subtext of the code. Additionally, neighborhood associations assembled to maintain the worth of whiteness as property as they endeavored to mobilize property owners through meetings, the dissemination of propaganda, and house-to-house visits for signatures and funds to help enforce the whites-only rule in housing.[23]

What further deserves emphasis is how the advancement of racial restrictive covenants connected the development of suburbs to that of the city, given how suburban development carried forward practices that were already in place to advance white privilege.[24] This continued use of race to assess property values was apparent in the construction of postwar suburbs, exemplified by the building of Levittown in Long Island, New York. The formation of sameness in this suburban tract, widely heralded as the paragon of suburban postwar homogeneity, manifested not just in the similarity in architectural design of its 17,400 homes, but also in the creation of a whites-only district, resulting from long-standing policies of land use segregation based on race. While racial restrictive covenants had always covered the suburban tracts developed by the Levitt family since the 1930s, they became the stipulated criteria of the Federal Housing Authority that the Levitts had to abide by in order to receive federal aid in 1946 for the construction of Levittown in Long Island.[25] It was this employment of race-based restrictions in housing that importantly enabled and structured postwar residential patterns to appear as "white flight." In the case of Levittown, the whites-only restriction continued to be in effect for about twenty years after the U.S. Supreme Court banned the practice of racial restrictive covenants.[26] The growth of housing tracts led to the building of institutions such as schools, banks, and hospitals, which bolstered not just the worth of whiteness as property but also the need for the whites-only rule.[27] The translation of this worth into dollars, moreover, cultivated the belief that the enforcement of racial restrictive covenants was nothing personal—that racial preferences were in fact secondary to concerns over housing values rather than the measure of that value. This logic helped to justify the enforcement of racial restrictive covenants by deflecting its racist premises.

Notably, the growth of residential segregation during the postwar years also brought the designation "nonwhite" increasingly into use. Racial restrictive covenants began to impose the whites-only rule so that the covenants worked to limit the ownership and occupancy of lands of all racialized groups without having to name each group. Racialized minorities were in this way restricted from living in whites-only suburbs on the basis of being nonwhite. The conflation of various racialized groups under one designation to maintain the value of whiteness was, however, an unstable construction. As Amer's experience with residential segregation showed, the category of nonwhite was ambiguous because of the disparate ways racial differences worked to determine the value of whiteness. The previous homeowner had suggested to Amer that his living in the restricted suburban tract of South Los Angeles would not incite the ire of his neighbors as they rallied mostly to rid the neighborhood of its black residents.

The nonwhite classification thus revealed a level of uncertainty over the place of Asians in the suburbs during a time when blacks emerged as the main targets of residential segregation. This uncertainty made it acceptable at times for Asian Americans to be incorporated in whites-only suburbs, even though the majority of cases during the immediate postwar years detailed circumstances that kept them out. These inconsistencies showed the battle over property rights as a process of creating and re-creating racial boundaries.

The struggle over property rights during the early Cold War years further revealed a striking scenario. The U.S. Supreme Court ruled unconstitutional the practice of racial restrictive covenants during the height of its use, and the federal government put its full weight behind the campaign to outlaw the practice, even though the FHA was instrumental in implementing race-based restrictions in both the building and the selling of federally funded housing. What prompted this change was the Cold War. In this war, the whites-only rule became a liability to the growth of the nation, as racist practices in the United States compromised the nation's image abroad and called into question the superiority of American democracy over communism. By lending its support to the legal campaign against residential segregation, the Truman administration sought to prove to the international community that U.S. democracy worked to secure the rights of all.[28] To that end, the government built on the efforts of racialized minorities and liberal supporters who prior to the advent of the Cold War had rallied against the legality of race-based restrictions in housing. Many of these contestations took place in Los Angeles.

The Battle in Los Angeles

When Gus and Frances Kroeger, together with B. H. and Harriet Randall, filed an injunction with the Superior Court of the State of California requesting the removal of Amer from the premises of the Firth Main Street Boulevard Tract on March 25, 1946, the city of Los Angeles saw an upsurge in both discriminatory activities against racialized minorities and legal actions to protest such acts.[29] The situation in Los Angeles exposed the tensions that pervaded the practice of race-based restrictions in housing, tensions that had been brewing for the past decade. While the influx of nonwhites to Los Angeles to work in the growing defense industry prompted the enforcement of policies to limit their land use, the housing shortage of the postwar years led to an increase in the number of lawsuits that challenged the legality of the whites-only rule. This legal fight witnessed a burgeoning interracial effort to challenge race-based restrictions in housing and turned Los Angeles into one of the key urban centers of the battle over property rights. For many who called for an end to housing discrimination, the atrocity of the mass extermination of Jews throughout Europe during World War II weighed heavy on their minds as they contended that racism had no place in the United States. Opponents of housing segregation also drew on sociological studies to condemn residential segregation for inciting the spread of ghettos across the nation. The efforts of those who organized to challenge the whites-only restriction in housing were critical in drawing national attention to the problem of unequal access to housing.

Between 1940 and 1950, the booming defense industry in Los Angeles prompted a surge in the number of nonwhites moving to the city. The number of blacks increased by 107,435 and, more so than in previous decades, made up a significant portion of all migrants coming to Los Angeles.[30] While the influx of blacks to the city had steadily increased since the 1920s, by 1950 the number had skyrocketed as blacks made up 10.7 percent of the total inhabitants of Los Angeles. In the decade previous, blacks comprised 6.5 percent of the total population. Another notable trend was that 78 percent of all blacks in Los Angeles County resided in the city of Los Angeles.[31] The Chinese population in the city of Los Angeles increased from 4,736 in 1940 to 8,067 in 1950. In Los Angeles County the number also grew, from 5,381 to 9,187. The availability of jobs in the defense industry proved to be a notable draw, given how, except in the case of Los Angeles, the population of Chinese in cities across the United States was significantly lower than the 1890 peak, due to the passage of the Chinese exclusion acts.[32] Mexicans in Los Angeles County in 1950 were also reported to have greatly increased from the estimated count of 212,000 in 1940.[33] The Japanese population in Los Angeles County, however, decreased from 38,350 in 1940 to 36,761 in 1950.[34] The city of Los Angeles also saw a slight drop in the number of Japanese residents, from 25,502 in 1940 to 23,321 in 1950.[35] Despite the decline of its Japanese residents, the city of Los Angeles witnessed the overall growth of its nonwhite population. This growth was consistent with the national trend: the number of nonwhites living in the 168 Standard Metropolitan Statistical Areas (SMSA) increased from 5.72 million to 8.25 million between 1940 and 1950. The proportion of nonwhite movement was twice that of white movement to SMSA—44 percent compared to 20 percent. By 1950, 52 percent of the nation's nonwhite population was living in the 168 metropolitan areas, compared to 42 percent in 1940 and 39 percent in 1930.[36]

The vast majority of blacks who migrated to the greater Los Angeles area between 1940 and 1950 settled in already established black communities such as Pasadena, Long Beach, Santa Monica, Compton, and Monrovia.[37] In the city of Los Angeles, blacks tended to reside south and southwest of the downtown area. World War II, however, brought blacks to the Little Tokyo or Bronzeville district, which was just east of downtown, following the wartime evacuation and internment of Japanese Americans.[38] While the residence of blacks in Little Tokyo was foremost triggered by the city's massive housing shortage, it nevertheless importantly demonstrated how blacks expanded into the areas where Chinese and Japanese had resided. The settlement patterns of blacks detailed in this respect how racial restrictive covenants severely impinged on the areas where blacks could live freely, just as these restrictions had limited the land use of Asian Americans since the late nineteenth century. By the end of World War II, racial restrictive covenants hemmed blacks into four segregated regions: the Central Avenue district, the Watts district, the West Adams district, and the Little Tokyo district.[39] Notably, these were also the areas where the burgeoning numbers of Korean immigrants to Los Angeles had settled. In the postwar era, the Vermont and Jefferson area of the West Adams district was home to a visible community of Korean residents.[40]

Japanese postwar resettlement patterns also paralleled in part the residence patterns of blacks, as many were forced to live in districts south and southwest of downtown Los Angeles. A sizable group of evacuees, however, settled in areas east of the city's downtown district.[41] As many returned to Boyle Heights following internment, they joined an expanding Mexican American population and overtook an area that was previously dominated by Jewish and other ethnic white residents. Since the 1920s, Mexican Americans began to migrate out of the dilapidated old Plaza district of downtown Los Angeles and move to the east side. Their residence stretched from the Belvedere district, also known as Maravilla Park, to Boyle Heights.[42] The Chinese, for the most part, lived in the Ninth Street and South San Pedro area as well as in the area around East Adams Boulevard, which were both just south of downtown Los Angeles. They began residing in the Ninth and San Pedro area during the 1920s, following the rise of the City Market district in 1909, which brought together the produce businesses in Los Angeles. Chinese residence in this area grew after the 1931 razing of Old Chinatown and the building of a main railway terminal, Union Station, in its place. The two Chinatowns, China City and New Chinatown, that were subsequently constructed around the downtown area following the demolition of Old Chinatown served as tourist attractions rather than as residential hubs. After the influx of Japanese residents to the Ninth and San Pedro districts during the 1930s and 1940s, the Chinese began to spread out to the area around East Adams Boulevard.[43]

During the housing crisis of the immediate postwar years, many of these segregated areas experienced extreme overcrowding and slum-like conditions. The residential occupancy rate of these locales was approximately 40 percent higher than the city's average, which was already over 100 percent.[44] For instance, Little Tokyo, which prior to the Japanese evacuation housed about 7,500 Japanese, contained in the immediate postwar years approximately 30,000 blacks.[45] Some middle-class minorities were able to find better living conditions by purchasing older homes in whites-only areas that were on average 10 to 15 percent above market price. While a few managed to secure the approval of white neighbors before purchasing homes, others found houses where the terms of restriction had expired or were not yet covenanted. What emerged as a notable trend was that the movement of a nonwhite into a restricted area would spark a process of succession that triggered other nonwhites to move into the same locale.[46] A study of residential patterns in Los Angeles using the 1940 census showed that 13 percent of the city's Mexican population and 14 percent of its Asian population lived in the twenty-nine census tracts where black concentration was the greatest.[47] The majority of nonwhites were, however, unable to purchase homes outside segregated districts due to the enforcement of racial restrictive covenants.[48] By 1946, no new subdivision was created in Los Angeles without covenants written into the original subdivider's deed.[49] In the following year, the city employed the help of commercial enterprises to implement racial restrictive covenants that imposed restrictions over multiple tracts of land at one time. A public relations firm was started in October 1947 to conduct the business of promoting land use segregation, particularly the technique of blanketing large areas of land with a single expandable contract. The practice of residential segregation thus became a public or semipublic endeavor.[50]

Unlike the few racialized minorities who found houses in restricted areas that were not yet covenanted, the majority of those who broke into the suburbs had purchased covenanted homes. Many were served with injunctions and, like Amer and his neighbors, the Hickersons, took up the fight to challenge the legality of race-based restrictions in housing. Some remained steadfast in their attempts to hold onto their places of residence even after acts of violence had been committed to forcibly coerce their relocation out of whites-only locales. For instance, two weeks before Amer received the petition requesting that he be removed from his home in South Los Angeles, the Hickersons awoke to find that a burning cross had been placed in their front yard. While H. G. Hickerson believed that the cross burning was intended to serve as a warning to those who dared to break the whites-only rule, he did not think that his neighbors were responsible for the crude act. Instead, he believed that the cross burning was the activity of the Ku Klux Klan, which had learned of his fight against racial restrictive covenants from newspaper accounts. Despite this threat of violence, Hickerson vowed to remain in his home until the U.S. Supreme Court issued a ruling on the legality of race-based restrictions in housing.[51]

The Council for Civic Unity in Los Angeles corroborated Hickerson's charge, as did the attorney general of California, Robert W. Kenny, that the assault on Hickerson's home was the activity of the KKK, particularly the Klan of Kalifornia. In fact, the cross burning on the front lawn of the Hickersons' home on May 13, 1946, triggered a wave of Klan attacks in Los Angeles. Between May 19 and May 23, four more flaming crosses appeared in different locations. One of the fiery crosses was placed on the front lawn of the home of a black family who lived in an area densely populated by black residents. Two more crosses were found on the area surrounding the University of Southern California campus and on the campus itself. One was placed on the parking lot of the Zeta Beta Tau Jewish Fraternity, where the front walls of the fraternity building had the letters KKK painted on them. The other was found on the USC campus with the KKK symbols daubed on the Trojan statue. KKK symbols were also found on seven different

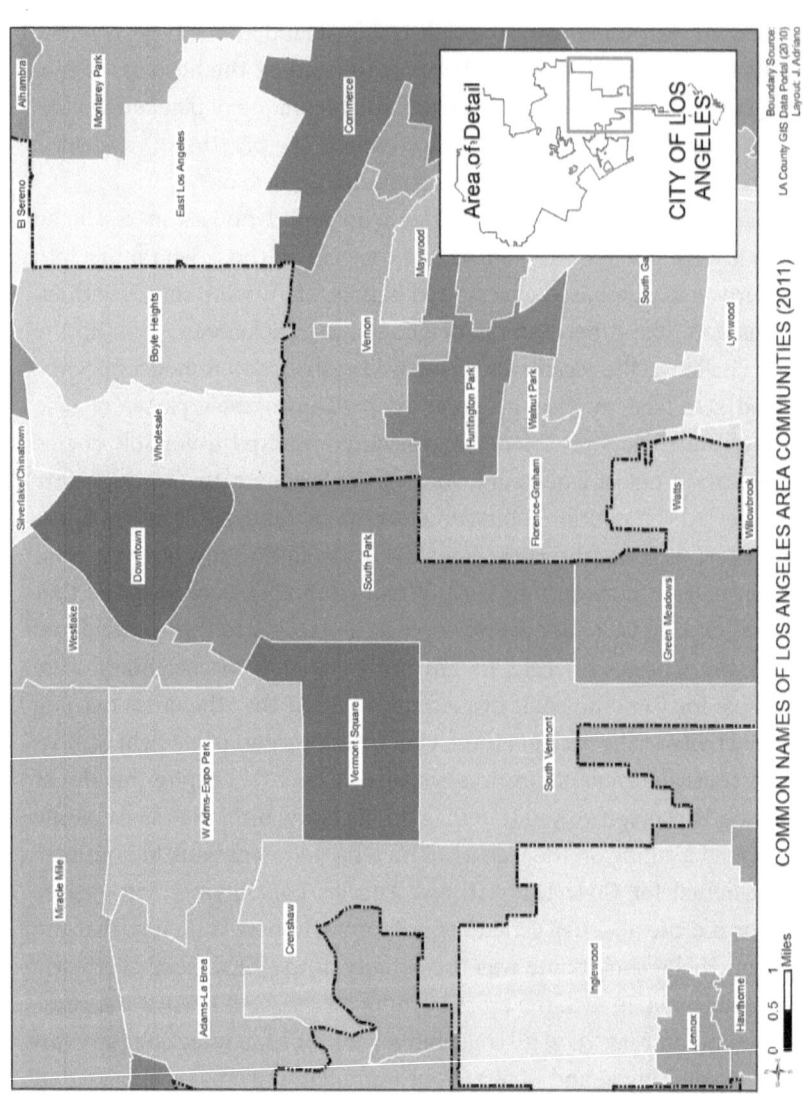

Fig. 1.1. Map of common neighborhood names in the southeast Los Angeles area

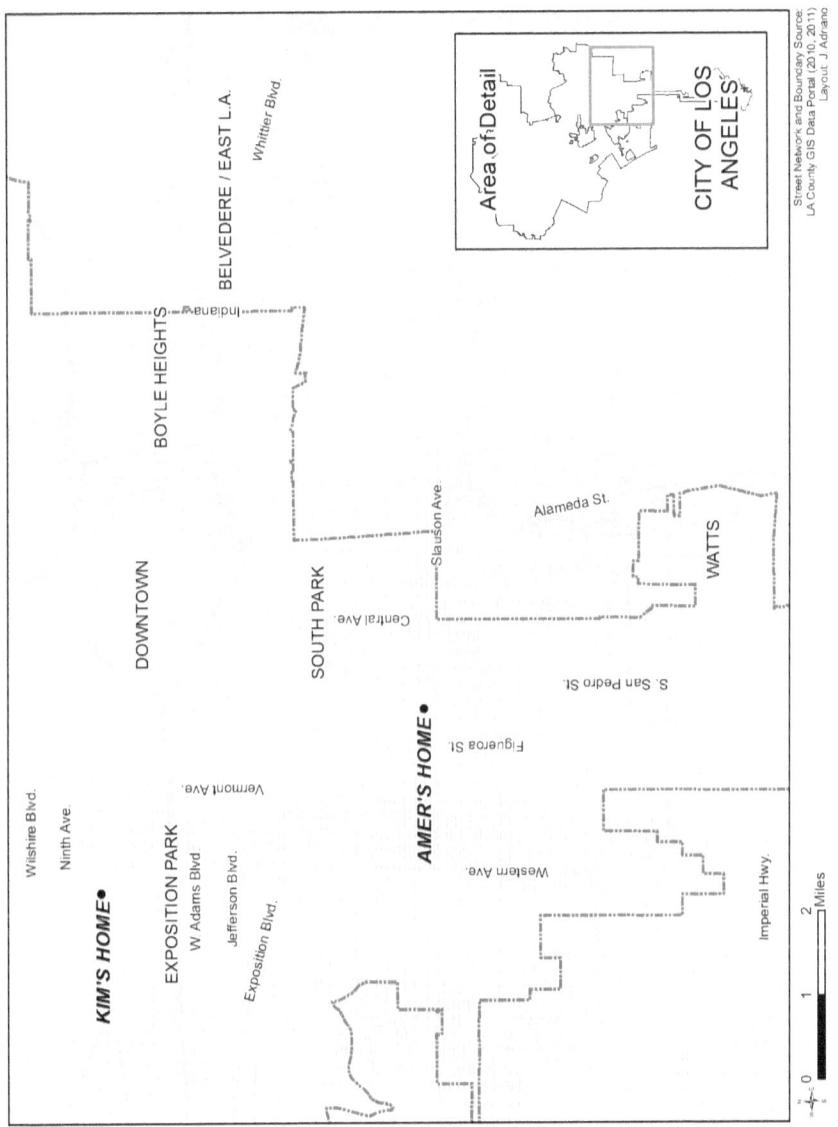

Fig 1.2. Map of Los Angeles–area neighborhoods near the homes of Amer and Kim

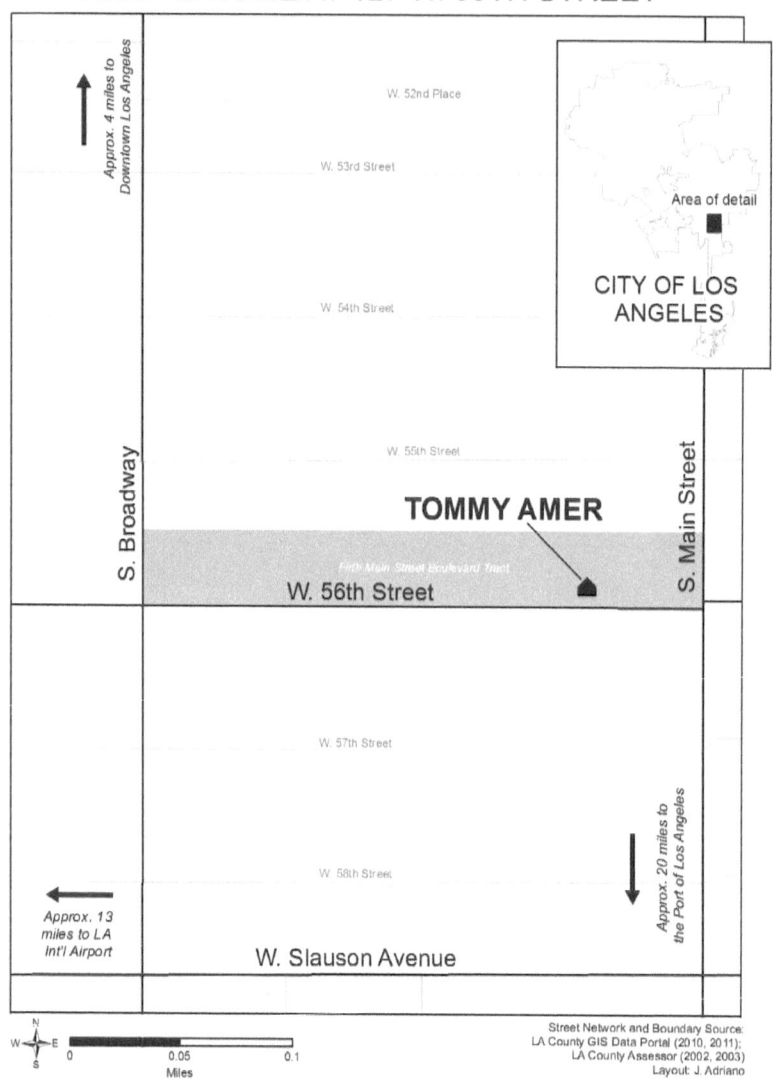

Fig. 1.3. Map of Tommy Amer's home

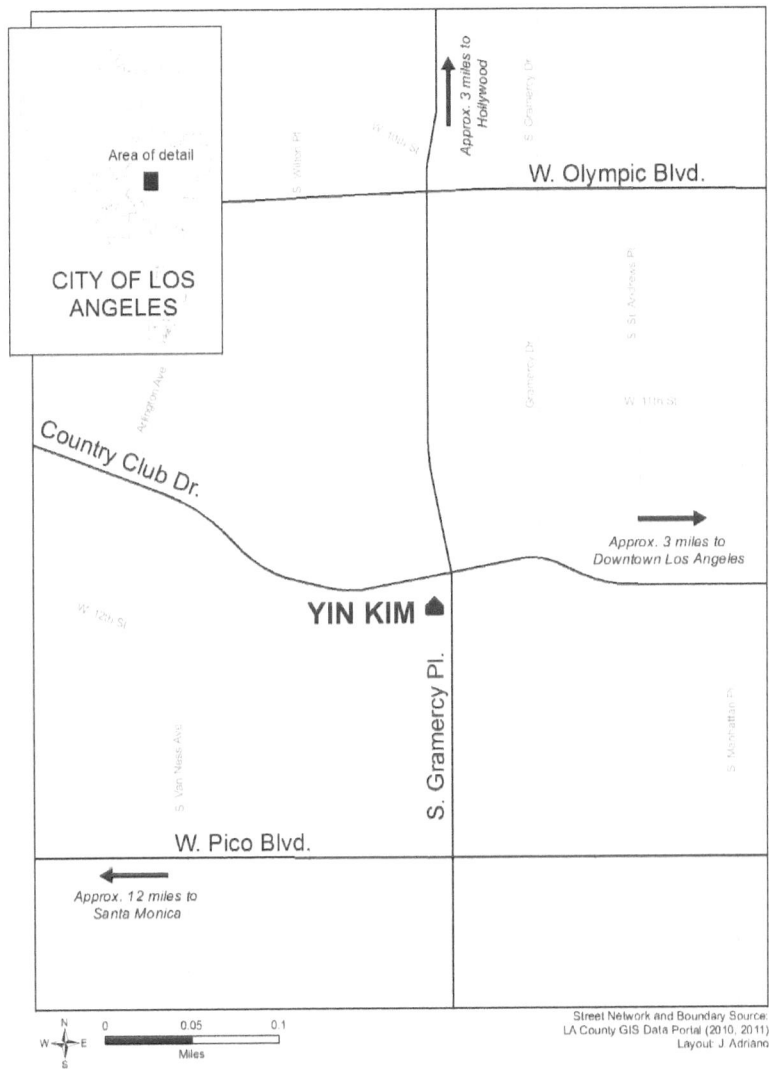

Fig. 1.4. Map of Yin Kim's home

places on the administration building. The fourth cross was set on fire in an open field in Eagle Rock, a neighborhood just northeast of downtown Los Angeles. In addition to the burning of the four crosses, vandals were reported to have desecrated the Temple Israel of Hollywood by ripping apart religious banners and destroying a rare religious scroll. A Nazi slogan and two swastikas were also scrawled on the walls of the temple.[52]

Immediately following the cross burnings and vandalism, Attorney General Kenny revoked the KKK's charter in California. He acted quickly, believing that the cross burnings and the synagogue's defacement represented a serious effort at reviving the KKK on a national scale. He considered these acts of violence a systematic campaign of provocation and intimidation.[53] Meanwhile, students at USC held a mass rally to denounce the racist assault on their campus and on the Jewish fraternity house. A host of community meetings composed mainly of civil rights leaders, members of the NAACP and the ACLU, celebrities such as Lena Horne and Earl Robinson, and religious leaders also took place at the Independent Church of Los Angeles and the First Congregational Church of Los Angeles to protest the practice of race-based restrictions in housing and the job market.[54] These gatherings importantly demonstrated the sustained efforts of community activists in Los Angeles to fight for racial equality since before the outbreak of World War II. As organizers endeavored to muster community support for those engaged in lawsuits against the practice of racial restrictive covenants, their efforts not only brought the petitioners together but also made known the rise of a widespread legal campaign waged to invalidate the whites-only restriction in housing.

While many took legal action to challenge the whites-only rule in housing, the more common tactic, as previously discussed, was for racialized minorities to participate in the process of succession. Dr. Yin Kim described this methodical approach to housing integration when he recounted how, following his occupancy in a restricted Arlington Heights neighborhood southwest of downtown Los Angeles, a wave of nonwhites began to move into the area. Kim recollected how he and his wife, Winifred L. Kim, had adopted a plan that many racialized minorities employed to secure their physical residence in the homes that they purchased. During escrow, unbeknownst to their neighbors, Kim and his wife began moving their belongings into 1201 South Gramercy Place. On the night before escrow closed, they quietly moved in. Even though they were spotted by a neighbor that evening, the Kims managed to evade the filing of an injunction before the move-in date, a filing that could have prevented their physical occupancy in their newly purchased home. The following morning, Kim was served with an injunction. But as he noted, as long as there was an ongoing lawsuit, he and his family could remain living in their home. In addition to fighting the pending lawsuit against him, Kim joined a community organization that helped another forty-six nonwhite families move into the Arlington Heights neighborhood. Many of these families were subsequently embroiled in lawsuits as they fought to hold onto their places of residence. When Kim was sharing his story with an interviewer just eighteen months after he and his wife purchased their home, he directed the interviewer's attention to the house across the street, where a black family was in the process of moving in at eight o'clock in the evening, in order to bypass the scrutiny of their white neighbors.[55]

As Kim recounted his involvement with community organizations that assisted the efforts of nonwhites to break into the restricted neighborhoods of Los Angeles, he described how progressive organizations in the city organized across racial lines to fight against residential segregation. These interracial organizations also helped Amer obtain legal representation for his lawsuit. Amer remembered how he went to the All People's Christian Church and Community Center, a progressive interracial church and social justice center in Los Angeles, to ask for help following the receipt of the injunction against him.[56] Amer had heard about the place from his brother, who attended services there. After a meeting with Reverend Dan B. Genung, Amer was put in contact with the ACLU and the American Youth for Democracy. The ACLU not only agreed to represent Amer and assigned A. L. Wirin, a prominent civil rights lawyer, to his case, but also assisted Amer by covering the bulk of the legal costs for his case.[57] As a result of his involvement with the ACLU, Amer met with and received the backing of the Los Angeles–based attorney Loren Miller of the NAACP, who later served as the principal lawyer for the cases from Missouri, Michigan, and the District of Columbia before the U.S. Supreme Court against the state enforcement of racial restrictive covenants.

The rise of this interethnic activism supports the analysis of the historian Scott Kurashige, who detailed in his 2008 study *The Shifting Grounds of Race* how black and Japanese Americans had come together to challenge the whites-only rule in postwar neighborhoods in Los Angeles such as Crenshaw. For Kurashige, the fight for housing integration on the west side of downtown Los Angeles importantly built the foundation for an interethnic alliance that helped to further the city's civil rights agendas during the 1960s, 1970s, and 1980s. This alliance helped Los Angeles become the nation's preeminent multicultural and multiethnic center.[58] In a similar fashion, in her 2011 study *Bridges of Reform*, the historian Shana Bernstein has shown how the early Cold War years saw the emergence of interracial activism in Los Angeles.[59] Like Kurashige, Bernstein abandoned the black/white approach to understanding the struggle for civil rights and highlighted how progressive organizations that cut across racial lines worked to bring about social change in the city. What she also sought to develop through this attention to interethnic cooperation was the importance of Los Angeles to deepening understandings of integrationist politics in the postwar years. Specifically, both of these authors presented studies of integration that extended beyond a focus on blacks who challenged the whites-only rule, and examined as well the forging of an interethnic solidarity that worked to secure the rights of a nation.

But as Amer's experience highlighted, this interracial cooperation did not erase the hostilities that existed among the various racialized groups in Los Angeles. Rather, these conflicts compromised the fight against housing discrimination during the immediate postwar years. As Amer recalled, despite his father's lifelong participation in the Chinese Consolidated Benevolent Association of Los Angeles and in the regional family association, these organizations did not come to his aid. Amer attributed the CCBA's lack of support in part to his father's passing and remarked that if his father were alive, the CCBA might have felt obligated to contribute funds to help with the cost of his case. However, Amer also believed that the reason no Chinese organization had come to his aid was that many of the Chinese were striving to reside in white neighborhoods that prohibited the residence of blacks.[60] As the sociologist Wen-Hui Chung Chen has noted in her 1952 study of the changing sociocultural patterns of Chinese in Los Angeles, Chinese Americans during the immediate postwar years often flocked to restricted neighborhoods that welcomed Asians but barred blacks. The prevalence of this interracial hostility limited, in Chen's view, the ability of racial succession to make obsolete the whites-only rule in housing and charted an uneven and spotty progression toward residential integration.[61] This pattern revealed the disparate ways

Asian Americans had situated themselves within the black/white schema. It also revealed how the positioning of Asian Americans near whites did not always indicate a move toward racial integration, but worked instead to affirm and uphold the worth of whiteness as property.

When Amer and Kim brought their cases before the Los Angeles Superior Court, they were unable to sway the court to rule against the injunctions. They also lost their appeal before the California Supreme Court. What prevented the enforcement of the injunctions against Amer and Kim as well as against those who were similarly embroiled in such legal actions was the U.S. Supreme Court's decision to reopen hearings on the constitutionality of racial restrictive covenants. As the Court prepared to rule on the legality of the whites-only rule, it accepted for review both the Amer and Kim cases along with five other cases during its 1947 October term. Following the Court's decision to reopen hearings on the legality of housing segregation, there were approximately 250 cases on hold nationally that awaited the Court's deliberation.[62] Twenty-two of these cases were from the state of California. Since 1943, more than seventy individual actions involving over 160 parcels of land were filed in Los Angeles County alone.[63]

The lawsuits from Los Angeles included the first postwar case involving a Japanese American, Sakuo Saito, who was served with an injunction a few months after Amer was issued his.[64] They also included the *Swift v. Rogers* suit, which detailed the struggle of an American Indian to reside in a restricted neighborhood.[65] The litigations further contained the high-profile Sugar Hill case, which involved the attempt to ban well-to-do blacks such as the actress Hattie McDaniel from residing in the affluent West Adams Heights district. Another notable lawsuit was the infamous Laws case, where Henry Laws, his wife, Anna, and their daughter, Pauletta, were fined and then imprisoned for failing to comply with the injunction before them.[66] Although the Amer and Kim cases lacked sensational appeal, they nevertheless captured an aspect of residential segregation that the Sugar Hill and Laws cases could not. The Amer and Kim cases made known how other nonwhite groups, besides blacks, were affected by the practice of racial restrictive covenants. During the late nineteenth century, the barring of Asian Americans from certain portions of cities and towns might have been the status quo, but in the postwar period, these restrictions revealed how exclusionary measures imposed against blacks had spilled over to infringe upon the rights of all racialized minorities. With this in mind, the legal counsels for Amer and Kim submitted these cases to the U.S. Supreme Court for review. In so doing, they sought to locate Asian Americans near blacks in their efforts to move the nation away from residential segregation.

Residential Freedom and the Discourse of Social Progress

The legal campaign against race-based restrictions in housing, involving numerous efforts by racialized minorities and community organizations to secure equal access to housing for all, historicized the circumstances and ideas that made residential freedom desirable in Cold War America. Sociological studies on urban America provided a way to connect the needs of racialized minorities to that of society at large. Even though many of these studies reinforced the image of urban ghettos as the locus of blight, they nevertheless offered a way of making sense of this social ill that also worked to unsettle certain racist assumptions. For instance, Robert Weaver's 1948 book *The Negro Ghetto* challenged the belief that racialized minorities possessed an innate proclivity toward crime and poverty; instead, he argued that residential segregation was the main cause of urban blight.[67] Unlike surveys such as Louis Wirth's 1928 work *The Ghetto*, which emphasized cultural differences to account for why racialized areas such as Chinatowns and Jewish tenements persisted in U.S. society, Weaver's study of black ghettos described how institutionalized racism built a divided world that kept the racialized underclass away from white America.[68] In this view, the biggest impediment to an integrated society was racist laws, not the unwillingness of ethnic minorities to assimilate. Moreover, the solution of residential freedom strove not only to move the nation away from the deterioration of neighborhoods and toward urban renewal, but also to move it away from racist practices and toward social progress.

Notably, for both Weaver and Wirth, World War II had increased the stakes in the struggle for residential freedom. As Weaver developed in his hugely popular 1945 circular *Hemmed In: ABC's of Race Restrictive Housing Covenants*, the racial strife caused by residential segregation ultimately hurt the nation by generating "internal weakness and the loss of international prestige."⁶⁹ Wirth, who dedicated much of his research and writing during the immediate postwar years to arguing for equal access to housing for all, echoed this sentiment. In a 1946 piece entitled "The Unfinished Business of American Democracy," Wirth maintained that the very denial of civil rights by "enemies of democracy abroad" in World War II furnished the nation with an incentive for their reaffirmation and realization at home.⁷⁰ Both this rationale and the findings of postwar sociological studies on the rise of urban ghettos directly impacted the legal campaign against race-based restrictions in housing. As the historian Clement Vose indicated in his 1959 study *Caucasians Only*, the U.S. Supreme Court's 1948 landmark ruling against the practice of racial restrictive covenants demonstrated the influence as well as the development of the sociology of law.⁷¹

Prior to acting as the chief counsel for the petitioners contesting the legality of racial restrictive covenants before the U.S. Supreme Court, the Los Angeles–based attorney Loren Miller represented a number of cases that fought against this practice in the lower courts of California. In these proceedings, Miller began to hone his use of sociological studies to build a case against housing discrimination. He drew on these findings not only to outline the social problems caused by housing discrimination, but also to explain why racialized minorities could not be held liable for refusing to comply with injunctions, since they were compelled to refuse because of the lack of decent housing in segregated areas. Likewise, community groups in their endeavor to rally public support against the whites-only rule cited the results of sociological surveys to frame race-based restrictions in housing as a social ill that was hurting the advancement of society at large.⁷² The Los Angeles Superior Court judge Stanley Mosk echoed these sentiments when he dubbed housing discrimination "un-American" in his groundbreaking ruling against the practice of race-based restrictions in housing. His decision was only the second ruling issued in the United States since 1892 that declared racial restrictive covenants invalid on the grounds that they violated the Fourteenth Amendment. Both rulings came from Los Angeles, further suggesting the influence of progressive interracial activism in bringing about social change in the city. In his deliberation Mosk declared,

> This court feels that there is no more reprehensible un-American activity than to attempt to deprive persons of their own homes on a "master

race" theory. Our nation just fought against the Nazi race superiority doctrines.[73]

Taken together, these various examples detailed the emergence of a state discourse that employed racial desegregation as a marker of social progress and the superiority of U.S. democracy over totalitarian regimes. The rise of this ideology was critical to turning racial desegregation into a desirable ideal in Cold War America.

When the President's Committee on Civil Rights released its 1947 findings, it identified housing as one of five areas that required the federal government's intervention. The committee notably cited Judge Mosk's ruling against race-based restriction in housing to indicate the direction that the federal government should be moving the nation toward.[74] But instead of emphasizing that World War II had increased the stakes for civil rights reforms, the committee called attention to the burgeoning Cold War and how it turned the credibility of U.S. democracy into an issue in world affairs. Extending equal rights to all was for this reason essential, since it worked to curtail the spread of Soviet propaganda that broadcasted racist practices in the United States in order to undermine the benefits of the American way of life. With this in mind, the committee recommended that the federal government support measures to desegregate the suburbs. It believed that securing residential freedom for all could help establish the validity of U.S. democracy and show the world that the United States was superior to the Soviet Union.[75]

The recommendation of the President's Committee on Civil Rights thus served as a telling example of how the fight to end race-based restrictions in housing became enveloped in the federal government's efforts to shape the nation's image during the early Cold War years. It also detailed how the legal battle in Los Angeles was instrumental in calling the nation's attention to the problem of residential segregation and in petitioning the U.S. Supreme Court to reopen hearings on the constitutionality of racial restrictive covenants. The Court's choice of the Amer and Kim cases for review not only imbued these lawsuits with national significance, but also cemented the role they would play in shaping the meaning of race in landmark civil rights cases before the U.S. Supreme Court. This influence importantly illuminated the ways Asian Americans informed the stories that the state told about race and U.S. democracy.

Housing Desegregation and the Story of American Democracy

The historian Clement Vose, in his 1959 study of the national legal campaign led by the NAACP to ban the practice of racial restrictive covenants, disseminated ideas that prevented a serious inquiry into how Asian Americans shaped the meaning of race in landmark civil rights cases before the U.S. Supreme Court. One example is the way Vose accounted for why the Amer and Kim cases were not heard before the U.S. Supreme Court despite being accepted for review. According to Vose, the Court showed a readiness in 1945 to revisit questions about the legality of racial restrictive covenants after repeatedly refusing to accept for review cases on this matter since 1929.[76] Two years later, on June 23, 1947, the Court granted writs of certiorari to the Supreme Courts of Missouri and Michigan for the cases of *Shelley v. Kraemer* and *McGhee v. Sipes*. On October 20, 1947, the Court granted to the federal court of the District of Columbia writs of certiorari for both the *Hurd v. Hodge* and *Urciolo v. Hodge* lawsuits. In addition to these two state and two federal lawsuits, the U.S. Supreme Court accepted three more cases for review at the end of its 1947 October term. The Court granted writs of certiorari to the Ohio Supreme Court for the *Perkins v. Trustees of Monroe Avenue Church of Christ* suit and to the California Supreme Court for the *Tom D. Amer v. Superior Court of the State of California* and the *Yin Kim v. Superior Court of the State of California* cases.[77] Vose explained that out of the seven cases accepted for review, the Court chose to hear only the ones from Missouri, Michigan, and the District of Columbia because these lawsuits dealt centrally with constitutional questions raised by the judicial enforcement of racial restrictive covenants, whereas the Perkins, Amer, and Kim cases raised only "peripheral issues of church-state relations and the rights of aliens."[78]

Notably, the Perkins case did not deal with church-state relations, and the Amer and Kim cases did not address matters pertaining to alien rights, as Vose has contended. Moreover, the Court's admission of these lawsuits for review appeared to have adhered to the same logic that governed the acceptance of the other four cases for review, which was to assemble lawsuits that provided a comprehensive but not overlapping overview of the ways racial restrictive covenants were put into effect. What the seven cases had thereby collectively detailed was how the judicial enforcement of racial restrictive covenants occurred in both the state and federal courts and violated the civil rights of blacks, of mixed-race populations, and of other nonwhite groups. Whereas the four cases from Missouri, Michigan, and the District of Columbia showed how residential segregation denied to blacks protection under the Equal Protection Clause of the Fourteenth Amendment, the Perkins suit was an example of this infringement on a mixed-race individual.[79] Specifically, the Perkins suit detailed the refusal of the plaintiffs, Fred Perkins et al., to sell a single residence property to a racially diverse church that had wanted to use the house as a parsonage for Reverend Lloyd L. Dickerson because Dickerson was "part Negro."[80] Meanwhile, the distinction of the Amer and Kim cases was that they showed the effect of race-based restrictions in housing on nonwhite, nonblack groups.[81] With these points in mind, the Court in electing to hear just the cases from Missouri, Michigan, and the District of Columbia determined that the category of blacks was sufficient for illustrating how the judicial enforcement of racial restrictive covenants affected all nonwhite groups in both state and federal courts. The Court chose blacks to be the representative racial category because it sought to recognize that blacks were affected to a greater extent than other nonwhite groups by race-based restrictions in housing. This decision thus made the racial distinctions of Dickerson, Amer, and Kim redundant in the legal sense. It further established that a ruling on blacks would be applicable to all nonwhite groups in landmark civil rights cases before the U.S. Supreme Court.

While Vose's misguided speculations on why the Perkins, Amer, and Kim cases were sidelined may have pointed to his principal interest in the other four cases that were heard before the U.S. Supreme Court, they also exposed, as his statements about the Amer and Kim cases suggest, the espousal of a particular racial thinking that saw all Asians in the United States as aliens. It was this thinking that rendered peripheral the study of Asian American participation in the struggle for equal access to housing. As the idea of civil rights was popularly understood to denote rights accruing to citizens and not necessarily to aliens, the caricature of Asian Americans as the perpetual foreigners-within meant that their involvement in the fight for residential freedom was seen as distinct from the struggle for civil rights. The Court's selection of blacks as the archetype of race generated in this respect an unwitting result. It advanced a racial paradigm that sought to recognize that other nonwhite groups, like blacks, were not only affected by but were also challenging the whites-only restriction in housing; this recognition, however, was eventually forgotten because of the Court's singular focus on the experiences of blacks over other nonwhite groups in civil rights cases.

Interestingly, the petitions submitted to the U.S. Supreme Court requesting that the Court grant writs of certiorari to the California Supreme Court for the Amer and Kim cases had sought to prevent the reading of these cases as lawsuits on alien rights. The briefs for the two cases had for this reason repeatedly emphasized that Amer was a U.S. citizen of Chinese ancestry and that Kim was a U.S. citizen of Korean ancestry. Unlike the briefs for the four black cases, which utilized the racial category of "Negro," the briefs for Amer and Kim drew on their legal status as citizens in order to qualify their lawsuits as civil rights cases. In addition to employing this distinction, the Kim brief cast Kim as an exemplary citizen who graduated from the University of Southern California and was a practicing dentist in the Los Angeles area, in order to establish him as a desirable candidate for residence in the suburbs. It further noted that Kim was a highly decorated solider of the U.S. army who was honorably discharged with the rank of captain.[82]

The Amer brief similarly drew on Amer's service as a combat photographer in World War II in order to show him as a patriotic American who was fit for residence in the suburbs.[83] As Amer was also the recipient of numerous awards for his service in World War II, such as the Purple Heart and the Oak Leaf Cluster, his emergence as a local war hero in Los Angeles further worked to cast the whites-only restriction in housing as an unjust rule that did not befit one who had put himself in harm's way in order to obtain accurate photographs of battle conditions.[84] Local newspapers such as the *Los Angeles Times* ran headlines that read, "Neighbors Try to Oust Purple Heart Veteran" and "Chinese Hero of Burma War Fights Eviction," for the purpose of teasing out this irony.[85] The attempts to distinguish Amer and Kim as American citizens and as veterans worked in these ways to show the whites-only rule as an unjust stipulation.

But the appeal to recognize Amer and Kim as U.S. citizens served another purpose. Besides qualifying their cases as civil rights lawsuits, it served as a reminder that the failure to see Asian Americans as American citizens had resulted in the unjust internment of Japanese Americans during World War II. The Japanese American Citizens League sought to make this point in its amicus brief for the national campaign against racial restrictive covenants. The JACL thus pointed to the detrimental impact of the judicial enforcement of residential segregation on American citizens of Japanese descent, specifically the way this form of institutionalized racism had made Japanese Americans "alien." It argued that racial restrictive covenants caused Japanese Americans to appear to have a natural tendency to be "clannish" and "unassimilated." The JACL maintained that were the Japanese not forced to live in segregated areas, "the 'clannishness' that General DeWitt found so inimical to national safety [during World War II] would not have existed." Moreover, given the dire consequence of Japanese internment, the JACL found it deeply troubling that evacuees upon their return to Los Angeles were once again forced to "'Little Tokyoize' themselves" and reside in segregated areas of the city.[86] It thereby urged the U.S. Supreme Court to outlaw a practice that functioned to perpetuate the racialization of Asian Americans as unassimilable aliens.

Finally, the brief for the Amer and Kim cases, besides establishing these cases as civil rights lawsuits, showed how other nonwhite groups, besides blacks, were affected by the judicial enforcement of racial restrictive covenants. As stated in the Amer and Kim brief,

> The petitioners here are of different "non-Caucasian" races but are similarly affected by the restrictive covenant. The cases should all be considered together so that this court can examine into the extent to which restrictive covenants have spread themselves over the land and how they are affecting all the racial minority groups.[87]

Likewise, the amicus brief of the JACL for the Amer and Kim cases stressed that the U.S. Supreme Court should consider cases where the petitioners were not black. The brief of the JACL thus argued,

> The petitioners in the cases at bar are similarly affected as are petitioners in the four cases above mentioned. They are not, however, Negroes.... The cases illustrate how the enforcement of the covenant affects persons of other than Negro birth. They present to this Court the actual facts, not by way of judicial notice, of the operation of race restrictive covenant against persons of other races living in the United States.... The Court should have before it concrete cases involving persons of different ancestry.[88]

As the legal team for the Amer and Kim cases petitioned to have the U.S. Supreme Court review cases that involved other nonwhite groups, they sought to avoid any loopholes that might arise if the Court did not consider the impact of housing segregation on all racialized groups. The legal counsels for the Amer and Kim cases adopted this cautionary approach because they recognized that the granting of rights to one group did not work in all instances to secure the rights of another. For example, the federal government passed separate laws to grant the right to naturalization to specified groups. The designation of blacks as an exception to the whites-only rule in naturalization during the nineteenth century did not thereby apply to other racialized groups. Rather, from 1868 to 1952, when racial restrictions in naturalization were finally abandoned, the federal government employed a group-by-group approach to grant the right to naturalization.[89] With this in mind, the legal team for the Amer and Kim cases sought to present to the Court two cases that related the experiences of nonwhite, nonblack populations so as to prevent this step-by-step method of securing the residential freedom of all minoritized groups.

The petition to have the U.S. Supreme Court review the Amer and Kim cases historicized the contestation of a particular racial thinking that rendered Asian Americans peripheral in the fight for civil rights. Moreover, it documented the need for lawsuits that showed how housing segregation affected all racialized groups, not just blacks. But as the Court ultimately decided to base its ruling on the constitutionality of racial restrictive covenants on the four cases that involved blacks, it determined to recognize the struggle of Asian Americans for residential freedom through the experiences of blacks. This choice was important not only for establishing a level of legal expediency in civil rights cases, where the securing of rights to blacks worked to safeguard the rights of all; it was also significant for advancing the belief that race was a black/white issue. The understanding of race that was developed in the landmark U.S. Supreme Court case on property rights thereby demonstrated that the Court, in its endeavor to affirm the ability of blacks to speak on behalf of all racialized groups, sidelined the Asian American destabilization of the colored/not colored schema. As the campaign to invalidate race-based restrictions in housing was enveloped in the federal government's efforts to counter Soviet propaganda, this simplified view of race facilitated the government's endeavor to promote the superiority of U.S. democracy over communism.

The construct of Asian Americans helped to make coherent the problem of racism for U.S. democracy to fix.

In December 1947, the U.S. Justice Department submitted an amicus brief for the case against racial restrictive covenants.[90] The filing of this brief marked the first time that the federal government intervened in a case to which it was not a party and for the purpose of securing rights guaranteed by the Fourteenth Amendment.[91] By taking on the role of advisor to the court, the federal government sought to make good on its promise to secure the civil rights of all while recognizing the international implications of its domestic civil rights policies. As it identified the conduct of foreign affairs as a key reason for its support of residential freedom, the federal government reiterated the concern of the President's Committee on Civil Rights that racial discrimination had hampered U.S. foreign relations.[92] The government's attention to this matter further echoed the concerns of other amicus briefs, particularly the brief submitted by the American Association for the United Nations on how racist practices in the United States had compromised the nation's international prestige.[93] The federal government had in this way made use of the struggle against residential segregation to establish the credibility of U.S. democracy abroad. It sought to employ civil rights reforms to shape the image of U.S. democracy during the early Cold War years.

The federal government notably drew on sociological studies on urban and suburban America to cast race-based restrictions in housing as a social ill, responsible for a host of societal problems such as overcrowding and the slum-like conditions of many of the nation's urban areas. As it noted in its amicus brief, blacks were impacted the most by residential restrictions even though "Mexicans, Armenians, Chinese, Japanese, Jews, Persians, Syrians, Filipinos, American Indians, and other 'non-Caucasian' or 'colored' persons" were similarly affected.[94] The federal government's use of this narrative pattern to describe the problem of the whites-only rule in housing was noteworthy because it affected the way nonwhite groups figured in the national legal campaign against residential segregation. Not only did this description rely on other nonwhite groups to indicate the reach of race-based restrictions in housing, it also utilized its listing of various racialized groups to create a coherent argument that racism worked to divide society neatly along the lines of colored and not colored. The development of this one-dimensional understanding of racism effectively enabled the ready collapse of other nonwhite groups into the category of blacks, advancing the perception that all social ills related to housing segregation could be understood through the focus on black Americans.

The U.S. Supreme Court's choice to deliberate on just the four black cases further shaped the strategies that the legal team representing these lawsuits developed to argue against the state enforcement of racial restrictive covenants. In matters pertaining strictly to judicial concerns, the counsels for the petitioners drew solely on the experiences of black Americans to argue how the state by upholding the validity of racial restrictive covenants had failed to abide by the Equal Protection Clause of the Fourteenth Amendment. Specifically, they argued that concerns over the implementation of property use restrictions could not be reviewed apart from the effect that these stipulations had on different groups of people. In other words, the Court could not rule on just the method of restriction without regard to the way this practice granted to white Americans greater access to property rights than it did to blacks. According to these counsels, the clearest evidence that racial restrictive covenants had violated the Fourteenth Amendment was the fact that, without the intervention of both state and federal courts, all of the petitioners before the Court would be peaceably residing in the homes that they purchased.[95] The fact that blacks were subjected to legal duress to move thus demonstrated how the state failed to ensure equal access to property rights for all Americans.

But as the historian Clement Vose has contended, the tipping point for the case against the practice of racial restrictive covenants was the extralegal concerns that the legal team brought forward. While the counsels for the petitioners called attention to the international implications of this case, they relied mostly on sociological studies to make known the detrimental impact of residential segregation on urban development. The NAACP considered these sociological studies critical for supplying the moral argument, given the way these studies presented housing desegregation as a sign of national progress. It therefore assembled a committee to compile all relevant studies that argued against the practice of race-based restrictions in housing, which was headed by the sociologists Louis Wirth and Robert Weaver. In light of how the U.S. Supreme Court had selected blacks to represent the interests and experiences of all racialized groups, the bulk of the nonjudicial materials that were compiled and written for the national legal campaign concentrated on the effects of residential segregation on blacks.⁹⁶ Because of this focus, black ghettos, rather than Chinatowns, Little Tokyos, or the barrios, emerged as the preeminent symbol of residential segregation. The focus on blacks further obscured the interracial struggle that was waged for residential freedom. Moreover, considering how racial restrictive covenants had structured social inequality through race, this effect also deterred sociological studies from taking a serious look at the ways class affected one's access to decent housing. This oversight importantly left unexamined the way residential freedom could also trigger the expansion of racialized ghettos, not just their elimination.⁹⁷

On May 3, 1948, the U.S. Supreme Court ruled judicial enforcement of racial restrictive covenants unconstitutional for violating the Equal Protection Clause of the Fourteenth Amendment. Many progressive organizations criticized this ruling, as it stopped short of invalidating the right to make racial restrictive covenants and only determined that such covenants could not be enforced in state and federal courts.⁹⁸ Despite these misgivings, the ruling was widely heralded by elected officials and civil rights activists alike as an important step toward racial equality and a true testament to the credibility of U.S. democracy. As Loren Miller remarked, the Court's ruling was a victory not just for blacks but for all Americans. Miller's framing of the significance of the 1948 decision in this fashion was important for revealing the way the Court had relied on the experiences of blacks to make known the civil rights abuses of all in U.S. society and in so doing, made the securing of civil rights to blacks applicable to all racialized minorities.⁹⁹ Because the *Shelley v. Kraemer* decision became the first landmark civil rights ruling of the U.S. Supreme Court, the Court's use of blacks as the representative racial category set the terms by which blacks would continue to function as the archetypal racial category in future civil rights cases.

Notably, Charlotta Bass, editor of the *California Eagle*, a leading black newspaper in the Los Angeles area, chose to frame the importance of the legal struggle for equal access to housing differently. Rather than affirm the symbolic weight of blacks, Bass sought to promote the fight for civil rights as an interracial effort:

> The question of minorities might be treated two ways—as separate complete units in themselves, with each group to improve its own lot; or as a more comprehensive study of the struggle of all minority

groups—Orientals, Jews, Mexicans, Indians, Haitians or Negroes—in the wider field of race relations.[100]

The Amer and Kim cases importantly documented the rise of this interracial activism in Los Angeles. The two lawsuits, however, also charted the process that led to the marginalization of accounts of interracial cooperation in the national legal campaign against residential segregation. In this way the Amer and Kim cases helped to shape state narratives of the early Cold War years that emphasized the extension of civil rights to black Americans as a testament to American democracy's capacity to ensure freedom and equality to all. Specifically, these cases revealed how this image of American democracy was forged through a particular conception of Asian Americans that related their experiences to those of black Americans. Even though the state would draw on other conceptions of Asian Americans, some of which emphasized the differences between Asian and black Americans, to establish and promote the benefits of the American way of life during the early Cold War years, in matters pertaining to civil rights reforms, the experiences of Asian Americans were employed to uphold the perception that American democracy worked to secure not just the rights of blacks but the rights of all nonwhite groups.

CHAPTER 2

Living in the Suburbs, Becoming Americans

Postwar suburbanization is often portrayed as a process that spatially reified racial divisions in society, where the separations that manifested in the built environment expanded on the privilege of whites. As the historian Eric Avila has explained, postwar suburbanization, as a course of white flight, fortified racial segregation by building whites-only neighborhoods that kept at bay the racialized underclass.[1] The lines that were drawn importantly set the stage for what the historians Scott Kurashige and Shana Bernstein described as the rise of an interracial activism that strove to break down the color divide. But as Avila also took note of the capacity of postwar suburbs to reconstitute the terms of racial belonging, he demonstrated that there were other forces at work to blur the color line besides the legal campaign to outlaw race-based restrictions in housing. Avila analyzed how postwar suburban growth prompted middle-class ethnic whites to "discover [themselves] as white," and argued that suburbs were conduits of racial assimilation, not just racial separation, such that the suburbanization of Jewish, Italian, and Irish immigrants appeared to have made them like Anglo Americans.[2] Notably, the transformative potential of suburban living extended well beyond reconstituting the meaning of whiteness and worked during the early Cold War years to promote the nation as a place that was accepting of all people regardless of racial and ethnic differences.

This chapter examines suburbanization as a process of Americanization. It argues that what made this process noteworthy was the way racialized minorities, particularly Asian Americans, came to be regarded as assimilable during the early Cold War years. The shift that took place in the way Asian Americans were perceived by dominant society, from unassimilable to assimilable, importantly documented the changes that occurred in Cold War America to make racial equality a desirable ideal. As the cultural critic Caroline Chung Simpson has noted in *An Absent Presence*, her 2001 study of postwar Japanese American cultural representations, the entry of a Japanese war bride in the suburbs of Melrose Park, Illinois, marked a significant occasion, for it offered a new way for the nation to imagine itself. Unlike news features on the resettlement of Japanese Americans following their release from wartime internment, stories on Sachiko Pfeiffer and her successful adjustment to life in the United States showed the nation to be a place that embraced people of all backgrounds without having to confront its racist past.[3] This chapter expands Simpson's analysis and explores how U.S. Cold War politics cultivated this pluralist view of the nation. It analyzes the ways sociological studies along with popular newspaper and magazine accounts of the early Cold War years emphasized the inclusive and transformative capacity of postwar suburbs in order to establish the superiority of U.S. democracy over communism following the outbreak of the Korean War.

The study of Chinese residence in postwar suburbs seeks to bring to the fore in a more extensive way than the study of a Japanese war bride had how the assimilation of Asian Americans into dominant society provided a means to account for racial divisions in society without having to tackle the problem of structural racism. As state officials justified the passing of exclusionary measures against Asians since the mid-nineteenth century by pointing to their supposed unassimilability, the use of this rationale importantly shaped the rise of segregated ethnic neighborhoods like Chinatowns to appear foremost to be the result of cultural differences rather than racist practices. State-generated narratives that noted how the Chinese during the postwar period were moving out of Chinatowns and into the suburbs thus used this change of residence to speak to how succeeding generations of Asian Americans were starting to let go of old world ways and take up the social mores of mainstream society. What these accounts neglected to mention was how this movement may have also stemmed from a lack of decent housing in segregated neighborhoods and the lifting of race-based restrictions in housing. The failure to address such issues elevated the belief that racial equality was truly just a matter of time and that social divisions based on race did not necessarily mean that the U.S. justice system prior to World War II worked largely to protect the interests of white Americans.

The 1952 Sing Sheng case offered a counternarrative to this belief by laying bare the inability of assimilation to live up to its remedial benefits. The Sheng case was in this way significant, for it not only detailed how Sheng tapped into the government's need to build alliances with noncommunist countries in Asia following the outbreak of the Korean War to argue for the extension of civil rights to Asian Americans. It also showed how mainstream presses depicted Sheng and his family as fully assimilated Americans in order to establish them as suitable for residence in the suburbs. But given how these attempts were unable to sway residents of a South San Francisco neighborhood to accept a nonwhite family into their suburban tract, the banning of the Shengs importantly challenged the belief that racism could be readily remedied once racialized minorities displayed a willingness to take on the ways of Anglo Americans. Instead, it revealed assimilation to be a narrative device that worked to make racial integration desirable during a time when the nation's civil rights record was an issue in world politics. The values that made nonwhites acceptable for residence in the suburbs exposed the terms of Americanization during the early Cold War years.

Suburbanization as a process of Americanization highlighted the values that made some Americans more desirable than others. Specifically, what this process showed was that those who conformed to the archetype of middle-class heterosexual nuclear families were seen as more fit for residence in the suburbs than those who deviated from that norm. In the case of the Chinese, their transformation into an assimilable population required that dominant society recognize Chinese women as mothers and wives and not just as prostitutes, which was a popular stereotype that exclusionists developed during the late nineteenth century to justify the barring of Chinese women from the United States. The shift in the popular perception of Chinese women was in this way critical to generating portrayals of the Chinese as an assimilable population of heterosexual nuclear families and not as a deviant community of aged bachelors.[4] The presence of Chinese women as wives and mothers thus enhanced the cultural citizenship of Chinese Americans and made them seem like other white Americans. This chapter develops the significance of this effect as it seeks to call attention to the ways ideas about gender and sexuality bolstered the desirability of Asian Americans in Cold War America.

Race and Immigrant Assimilation

The first major civil rights case of the postwar era saw the Truman administration take unprecedented measures to back the NAACP-led legal battle to outlaw the practice of race-based restrictions in housing. The government's efforts highlighted the added meaning that civil rights reforms took on during the early Cold War years. Besides working to affirm the nation's commitment to ensure the rights of all, civil rights reforms functioned to show how the United States was superior to communist countries. The endeavor to secure decent housing for all detailed in this respect how the nation came to connect the fight against racism to the fight against communism.

The Commission on Race and Housing assembled in 1955 to study the housing problems confronting minorities. Its formation coupled civil rights reforms with communist containment both in ideological discourse and in the political economy that financed this discursive production. The Fund for the Republic, which underwrote the cost of this research, began pursuing its interest in civil liberties independent of the Ford Foundation after the latter made a sizable contribution to establish the fund in 1953.[5] Under the direction of the former chancellor of the University of Chicago, Robert Maynard Hutchins, the Fund for the Republic sought to tackle the contradiction of communist containment: the aspiration to create a "free world" by fostering a domestic climate of hysteria and infringing on personal freedoms. The Fund for the Republic endeavored therefore to develop a different approach to combating the internal communist threat and championed causes such as academic freedom and the protection of minority rights by supporting research to achieve that end.[6] With this goal in mind, it brought together a group of men of high repute that included the university presidents Charles S. Johnson of Fisk University and Clark

Kerr of the University of California, Berkeley; the publishing executives Elliot Bell of McGraw-Hill and *Business Week* and Henry R. Luce of *Time, Life, Fortune, House & Home, Architectural Forum,* and *Sports Illustrated;* and corporate and banking presidents to conduct a fact-finding study on race and housing.[7] Committee members, careful to maintain an image of impartiality, indicated that they had assembled based on their individual capacities and not as representatives of any businesses or organizations.[8] Of the publications that the commission released, the 1958 study *Where Shall We Live?* and the 1960 report *Residence and Race* offered a striking look at how these reports promoted cultural assimilation as the overriding remedy to the housing problems facing racialized minorities.

The 1958 study, which collected data primarily on blacks, Puerto Ricans, Mexican Americans, Chinese, and Japanese, found no significant improvement in the housing conditions for nonwhites between 1940 and 1950. Whites, in contrast, reported gains in housing space per capita despite the general postwar housing shortage in cities across the nation. Segregation barriers were also markedly tighter in 1950 than they had been ten years earlier. While the out-migration of whites from cities to outlying suburbs during this time did produce some housing opportunities both in quality and quantity for nonwhites in inner-city areas, the majority of nonwhites continued to inhabit substandard buildings that had deteriorated due to age and neglect.[9] The study pointed to poverty, racial discrimination, government policies, the housing industry, and financial institutions as the ongoing causes of residential segregation.

Despite citing a familiar list of reasons to account for the disparities in housing opportunities between whites and nonwhites, the 1958 study proposed a new solution. In a section aptly titled "An Old Problem in New Perspective," it declared that "the time-honored solution" to the housing problems facing minorities was "contained within the process of Americanization." Whereas the 1947 report released by the President's Committee on Civil Rights emphasized the need to change unjust laws, the 1958 study called upon immigrants and their children to learn the values and behaviors of white Americans, which would enable them to "move out of slums and find dwellings in middle-class 'American' neighborhoods."[10] It argued that when immigrants assimilated to the ways of dominant society and resided in nonethnic neighborhoods, they would cease "to be identified or to identify themselves as members of ethnic groups" and their compact ethnic communities would also "gradually disappear."[11] The report concluded that the shift in residence from slums to suburbs was "both a condition for and a symbol of upward mobility, with emancipation from minority status."[12]

The remedy of Americanization that was prescribed by the 1958 study was notably part of a broader national conversation about the benefits of suburban life that took place during the early Cold War years. Vice President Richard Nixon, for instance, famously used the suburban home to display the advantages of American democracy and capitalism at the 1959 American National Exhibition in Moscow.[13] What Nixon sought to show by means of the suburban home was that the American Dream of domestic and political stability coupled with social and economic mobility was available to all.[14] In much the same way, the social critic William Whyte touted the inclusive capacity of suburbia in his 1956 study of U.S. Cold War culture. For Whyte, the suburbs were distinctive for their ability to transform inhabitants into Americans. He thereby deemed suburbia a "melting pot" that encouraged immigrants from urban enclaves to shed previous cultural and ethnic ties and form a middle-class collective.[15] Suburbanization was in this view a conduit for Americanization rather than being Americanization's end goal. Moreover, cultural assimilation was believed to be an ideal that went hand in hand with social and economic mobility.

Notwithstanding its promotion of suburbanization, the 1958 study by the Commission on Race and Housing recognized that a major impediment was impinging on the social rewards of suburban life. It argued that the benefits of Americanization could not be fully realized by all since a "color barrier" had obstructed the pathway to residence in the suburbs. Accordingly, even though blacks had narrowed the gap with whites as they lived longer in cities, gained more education, and rose in economic status, they, unlike white persons of immigrant origins, were prohibited from moving into the suburbs.[16] The notion of suburbs, rather than operating as a color-blind term of residential location, was in fact deeply racialized as white. Moreover, the experience of moving into the suburbs was available unevenly to white persons of immigrant origins, native-born blacks, and nonwhite immigrants. But instead of exploring the ways racism contributed to the unequal access to housing opportunities, the 1958 report, along with the subsequent 1960 study, reconciled this comparatively restricted movement into the suburbs with an assimilationist ideology by racializing blacks as either "too black" or "almost Americans." These designations allowed the reports to alternately emphasize the differences (especially the nonnormative composition of black households) that kept blacks out of white neighborhoods, and to acknowledge the future potential of blacks for assimilation by comparing them to immigrant groups. The inquiry into how blacks could be remade into full-fledged Americans thus emerged as a key concern of the two studies, overshadowing the problem of race-based restrictions in housing.

The 1958 study maintained that blacks, as newcomers to the North and West, depended on segregated neighborhoods, in much the same way that immigrants did, for their social sustenance and adjustment. By positing a similarity between blacks and immigrants, the report sought to apply to blacks the same conceptual framework commonly used to explain how immigrants could change to improve their social standing. The report's attention to the similarities between the two groups looked in this way to boost its espousal of assimilation to overcome the color line. With this in mind, the 1958 study examined the double bind of racialized enclaves. It contended that even though black neighborhoods helped to meet the social needs of black newcomers to the North and West, the residence of blacks in these enclaves had, nevertheless, slowed down their assimilation into dominant society. Racial discrimination was thus cast as an impediment to social and cultural assimilation instead of being the chief reason that blacks deviated from the educational, occupational, and behavioral standards of dominant society during the early Cold War years. Specifically, the report pointed to the way racism had caused "the lower class of Negroes to carry forward certain patterns of family life [that were] at variance with white middle-class customs."[17] As the 1958 study portrayed this variance as a class issue, it sought to downplay racism's impact on the composition of all black families. A focus on gender, particularly the report's attention to the high incidence of black working wives, further worked to reveal what was aberrant about black families. As the 1960 report *Residence and Race* detailed,

> The Negro population has long been characterized by distinctive features of family and household organization significantly affecting its housing conditions. Compared to the white population, Negroes have a greater frequency of large families, a higher incidence of broken families,

and more frequent presence of multiple families and unrelated persons in the household. A high proportion of working wives has also been traditionally characteristic of Negroes.[18]

To back this observation, the 1960 report drew on statistical data to establish what was nonnormative about black households. The study noted that the average number of persons per household for nonwhites in 1950 was 3.90, notably higher than the white average of 3.29.[19] It also noted disapprovingly that female-headed households among nonwhites composed almost a third of nonwhite renter families in New York and New Orleans.[20]

The discourse that characterized black families as nonnormative was constructed through a biased framework that neglected to engage in any meaningful discussion of the structural inequities that gave whites greater access to society's institutions than racialized minorities, and hence allowed them to constitute the norm. Without a serious inquiry into how institutionalized racism constructed the deviance of blacks, the 1958 study's prescription of assimilation proved to be an ineffective remedy to the problems facing minorities in housing. The report suggested that nonwhites conform to the very standard that racist laws and social conventions had prevented them from obtaining in order to qualify for equal housing opportunities. The remedy of assimilation placed the burden of social change disproportionately on the shoulders of blacks. And instead of dulling the remedial potential of assimilation, racism explained how blacks, despite "centuries of residence in America," possessed "some of the characteristics of an incompletely assimilated immigrant group."[21] Like persons of immigrant origins, blacks were not quite, not yet Americans. Their segregated neighborhoods were temporary hubs of cultural adjustment.

With these points in mind, the 1958 study drew on this contrived analogy between blacks and immigrants to develop the view that blacks were the problems of society. To support this understanding, the report called upon Asian Americans to model the solution of assimilation. In so doing, it tapped into a sociological tradition that relied on Asian Americans to relate the concerns of ethnic whites with those of black Americans.[22] As Asian Americans were racialized in U.S. society as both nonwhites and as the foreigners-within, this racial formation effectively enabled sociologists, especially those from the Chicago School of sociology, to apply to black Americans the model of assimilation that was developed to explain the process that ethnic white immigrants underwent to adjust to the ways of dominant society. Within this framework on race and immigrant assimilation, the experiences of Asian Americans were pitted against those of black Americans. The differences between the social standings of these two racialized groups worked to highlight the areas where blacks needed to improve upon so as to be on par with normative standards of dominant society.

The 1960 report *Race and Residence* translated this understanding to statistical data that assigned to whites the attribute of normalcy and to blacks the property of social deviance. Asians were analyzed in relation to the black/white divide such that any deviation away from blacks and toward whites functioned to affirm assimilation as a viable cure for the inequities of society. Within this framework, the rising social status of Asian Americans effectively showed assimilation's capacity to overcome the color line, as Chinese and Japanese were found to be closing the gap with whites in family composition and in occupational, income, and educational levels from 1940 to 1950.[23] These gains importantly earned Asian Americans the distinction of being the "nonwhite exceptions." This designation came about following an interesting finding: the percentage of Japanese twenty-five years or older who had completed at least four years of high school at 57.7 made the Japanese the "best-educated racial group, ... leading the white population [at 36.4 percent] by a wide margin."[24] Notably, this standout figure did not compel the 1960 study to reframe its racial schema and make Japanese Americans the benchmark of educational attainment or to explain why this high educational attainment did not lead to comparable rises in their occupational and income levels. Instead of redefining the normative status of whites, the report dubbed the Japanese, together with the Chinese (whose percentage at 30.2 fell slightly below that of whites), nonwhite exceptions. The exceptional status of Asian Americans importantly allowed the study to take note of the social disparities between whites and nonwhites while advancing the solution of assimilation.

As the 1960 study related, educational achievement was a key measure of assimilation, and as such, it worked to determine the cultural competency of immigrant and racialized groups with the ways of dominant society as well as their desire to upgrade housing.[25] In noting that "except for Chinese and Japanese," the educational attainment of minority groups was far below that of the white population, the 1960 report sought to convey that the majority of nonwhite groups have yet to learn the ways of dominant society. Findings that showed how one in eight black, Native American, nonwhite Hispanic, and Puerto Rican adults completed high school, compared to one in every three white adults, did not thereby generate a discussion about the need to develop a culturally relevant educational curriculum or programs to mitigate racial tensions in schools so as to create a safe learning environment for kids of all backgrounds.[26] Rather, the low educational achievement among blacks, Native Americans, nonwhite Hispanics, and Puerto Ricans was juxtaposed with the high educational attainment of Chinese and Japanese to address only the solution of assimilation. The status of Asian Americans as the nonwhite exceptions thus functioned only to justify the need to direct resources to help racialized minorities adjust to the American way of life. In so doing, it effectively kept under wraps the impact of structural racism and the fact that the differential ways nonwhite groups were racialized had charted an uneven course for their social mobility.

As the 1958 study noted, Chinese Americans emerged as a "striking example" of assimilation's capacity to establish equal housing opportunities.[27] To demonstrate the remedial effects of assimilation, the report drew on the mass exodus of Chinese Americans out of Chinatowns from 1940 to 1950. Given that the 1958 study had failed to consider any other factor besides assimilation to account for this change, its reading of the drop in the population of San Francisco's Chinatown from 70.2 percent in 1940 to 40.2 percent in 1950 worked to attest foremost to the benefits of assimilation, as did the drop in the population of New York's Chinatown, from 50.2 percent to 31.0 percent.[28] According to the report, what had brought about this shift in residence was the reformation of the Chinese American family:

> Reference was made earlier to the depressing effect of the high proportion of female-headed families on the housing demand of Negroes. The Chinese, during their long period of segregated immobility, had a conspicuous absence of women and hence of families. Their remarkable exodus from the Chinatowns followed the lowering of immigration barriers, which permitted the entry of thousands of Chinese women as wives of American citizens and the consequent formation of many new families.[29]

With these remarks, the 1958 study established the importance of family structure for enabling the movement of Chinese out of Chinatowns while confining blacks to segregated ghettos; it also illustrated what had changed in the popular imagination of Chinese Americans to convert them from an unassimilable to an assimilable population. In the case of Chinese Americans, cultural membership in the nation involved transforming the segregated immobility of bachelors into heterosexual nuclear families, fit for desegregated mobility. This transformation hinged upon the arrival of Chinese women, particularly as wives of American citizens. The arrival of Chinese women crucially showed how notions of gender and sexuality shaped the desirability of Chinese Americans and more broadly, of Asian Americans in Cold War America.

Gender, Race, and the Cultural Citizenship of Asian Americans

As the historian Elaine Tyler May detailed in her study on postwar families, the early Cold War period marked a return to the domestic ideal that was left in doubt following increases in women's labor force participation during the Great Depression and World War II.[30] In an era characterized by anticommunist hysteria and the atomic bomb, the rise of heterosexual nuclear families tucked away in suburban homes not only helped to buffer Americans from these political uncertainties, it also provided Americans a vision of abundance and fulfillment.[31] While May noted that "suburbia was not part of the black experience, since blacks were systematically excluded from postwar suburbs," she nevertheless neglected to consider how this exclusion limited the capacity of the domestic ideal to fully capture American Cold War culture.[32] In fact the domestic ideal was used as a tool to determine who counted as an American. Rather than describing the American reality, the domestic ideal described the ways cultural legitimacy was established and maintained, and showed how the norm of heterosexuality was constructed in Cold War America through the deviance of homosexuality, particularly through the designation of homosexuality as an internal communist menace. As the cultural critic Robert G. Lee remarked in his examination of Asian American representations in popular culture, the need to contain homosexuality was "not merely psychological or metaphorical. In the atomic age, reproducing the nuclear family was understood to be the key to national survival."[33] This belief importantly prompted the federal government to launch a systematic baiting of homosexuals, also known as the lavender scare.[34] Thus the prevailing images of homosocial Chinese bachelors and sexually unrestrained Chinese prostitutes were at odds with the heterosexual domestic order. Assimilating the Chinese into Cold War America thereby necessitated a reworking of the popular representations that had grown out of the exclusionist movement of the late nineteenth century.

Between 1940 and 1960, changes in U.S. immigration and naturalization policies greatly altered the demographics of the Chinese. The sociologist Rose Hum Lee analyzed their impact in two articles. The first article, published in the *American Journal of Sociology* in 1949, focused on the decline of Chinatowns across the United States during the 1940s. Lee explored how the larger social and economic changes taking place in the surrounding cities affected this shift, and how the out-migration of residents who looked to assimilate into mainstream society or sought better job opportunities led to the decline of Chinatowns. But superseding even the effects of Chinese out-migration were strict immigration policies, particularly policies that prohibited the entry of Chinese women. Lee pointedly noted that despite the passage of the 1943 Magnuson Act, which repealed the Chinese exclusion acts and set an annual quota of 105 Chinese, the actual number of new immigrants permitted each year was only 79. The entrance of 79 new immigrants plus the natural rate of increase failed to generate any growth in population, since these figures were offset by the number of Chinese departing the United States.[35]

According to Lee, the only Chinatowns that would remain were those located in San Francisco and New York, since they operated as critical seaport and commercial centers linking the United States with Asia. Apart from these exceptions, Chinatowns would inevitably "decrease almost to the vanishing point." But rather than viewing this as a cause of concern, Lee considered the diminishing Chinese population, along with the eventual disappearance of Chinatowns, to be a useful step toward the full amalgamation of the Chinese. Assimilation, she argued, accelerated more "for 'marooned families' or isolated individuals than for concentrated populations."[36] Like the sociologists from the Chicago School who preceded her,

Lee accepted and promoted the benefits of assimilation to solve the "Oriental problem."[37] Given this framework, it was surprising that Lee began her 1956 article lauding the Magnuson Act as "heralding a new era in our treatment of Mongoloid minorities."[38] Instead of emphasizing, as she did in her 1949 piece, its inability to alter significantly the Chinese population in the United States, Lee celebrated this act for being the first in a series of policy revisions that lowered restrictions against Chinese immigration. Thus, growth rather than decline signified the potential for assimilation. Lee stressed how the government, in an effort to promote family unity, had in 1946 amended the Immigration Act of 1924 to permit the entry of alien wives of American citizens to the United States on a non-quota basis. On July 22, 1947, the federal government lifted racial restrictions that had previously barred persons of Asian descent from the provisions of the 1945 War Brides Act and the 1946 Fiancées Act. Lee estimated that before the War Brides Act expired in 1949, more than 6,000 Chinese men returned to China to get married, resulting in the entry of 5,132 adult Chinese women to the United States. Of the 12,151 newly immigrated Chinese between 1945 and 1953, 89 percent were female.[39]

The growing presence of Chinese women importantly altered not just the demographics of the Chinese in the United States, it also changed the way they were thought of and written about, as seen in Lee's renewed optimism that a growing population and not a diminishing one would lead to greater amalgamation for the Chinese. In other words, Chinese women were embedded within an ideological system that maintained and developed their ability to determine the status of the Chinese. Their entrance as wives and mothers, while structurally brought about through immigration policies, became culturally significant as it signaled, in Lee's words, "a new era in the treatment of Mongoloid minorities." The presence of Chinese women as wives and mothers enabled, in this respect, the cultural enfranchisement of the Chinese as Americans. As the heterosexual domestic ideal dominated the terms of assimilation during the early Cold War period, the role of Chinese women as a stand-in for the formation of new families shaped the emergent Chinese population into subjects capable of being successfully assimilated. The presence and recognition of Chinese women as wives and mothers, rather than reversing the trend of declining Chinatowns by rejuvenating its diminishing population, functioned to fix what a declining Chinatown was primarily to signify, namely, an ethnic enclave housing only aging and dying men. The very disappearance of such "old" segregated Chinatowns spoke to the Americanization of the Chinese, who were now recomposed as heterosexual nuclear families headed out to the suburbs.

The historian Betty Lee Sung's 1967 *Mountain of Gold: The Story of the Chinese in America*, one of the earliest historiographical studies of Chinese in the United States, also employed Chinese women to signify the opening up of U.S. society during the early Cold War years. As a former writer for the Voice of America, a key media outlet for U.S. propaganda in Asia during the Cold War, Sung maintained that the most successful Voice of America program featured a series on the treatment of Chinese in the United States. She discovered during her research for this broadcast that even though the Chinese from 1950 on had "enjoyed an unprecedented degree of acceptance among the American people," they nevertheless endured a racist past characterized by stereotypes of the hatchetmen and the yellow peril. She wrote *Mountain of Gold* to bring these images "up to date" and to educate white readers on how the Chinese, like blacks, were a significant group worthy of academic study.[40] Sung recounted her shock upon learning after a lecture that she gave on minorities in the United States that only one student had ever come in contact with a Chinese. This eye-opening incident prompted Sung to devote a chapter, "Counting Heads," to establishing the visibility of Chinese in the United States through a demographic survey.[41]

To her dismay, the U.S. census revealed that the Chinese composed only 0.1 percent of the total population in 1960, and constituted one of the smallest nonwhite minorities. Unable to let these numbers indicate the relative significance of the Chinese in the United States, Sung remarked, "Though few in numbers, the Chinese should not be dismissed as inconsequential, insignificant, and unworthy of note. The Chinese, too, spice the potpourri that makes up the American people."[42] She proceeded to graph the distribution of the Chinese in all fifty states and in the key metropolitan areas of San Francisco, Honolulu, New York, Los Angeles, and Sacramento in hopes of heightening their visibility in the United States. But once again, Sung found the results troubling, especially the data that showed that nearly three-fourths of the total Chinese population in the country resided in a few select cities. Considering this the wrong kind of visibility, Sung noted,

Sociologists contend that such visibility tends to retard the acceptance and perhaps even provoke antagonism by the majority group toward the minority. At the same time acculturation is retarded. When the minority group is sizable, individual members are less likely to give up their speech and their ways.[43]

Like Lee, Sung looked for an assimilable population to secure a growing acceptance of Chinese within mainstream U.S. society. This search led her to see high concentrations of Chinese not only as impeding their progress toward assimilation but also as triggering white resentment against them. Additionally, this pursuit caused her to regard the "scarcity of females" to be the most "abnormal aspect of the Chinese population," which further worked to prevent their acceptance in white society.[44]

Using a graph that mapped the ratio of Chinese males to females from 1860 to 1960, Sung showed that the period from 1860 to 1890 was the worst of these abnormalities. After 1890, however, each successive decade saw a steady increase in the number of women until a near equilibrium in the male-female ratio was reached in 1960. Sung commented,

A more balanced ratio will enable the men to get married and have a normal family life, thus stabilizing the Chinese communities. The offspring of these unions will be native-borns who will swing the makeup of the Chinese population from a predominantly foreign-born one to native-born. Because native-borns find it easier to adapt themselves to the larger American society and to find acceptance within it, the rate of acculturation will be speeded up. The increased opportunities for Chinese men to find mates among Chinese women mean that intermarriages may decrease. When Chinese families are based in this country large sums formerly remitted to China will remain here.[45]

The sex ratio graph importantly charted, in this view, the terms of assimilation. The mapping of the advancement of the Chinese toward greater acceptance by dominant society was thus predicated on the waning imbalance of the sexes, pointedly expressed through the arrival of Chinese women. The perceived sexual availability and marriageability of these Chinese women not only underscored the compulsory heterosexuality driving the cultural citizenship of Chinese in the United States, it also made tenable heterosexual unions and mitigated the threat of interracial couplings. The formation of families in the United States, as opposed to transnational families, further secured the productive and reproductive labor of immigrants and their native-born offspring for the benefit of the nation. In her espousal of this kind of visibility, Sung qualified its constructive potential, noting that in many regions of the United States the Chinese sex ratios remained largely unbalanced and that significant portions of Chinese "women" in the United States were in fact infants and children. But these setbacks, Sung argued, were temporary, given how the coming decade promised a more assimilable Chinese population.

Popular newspapers and magazines also took note of the changing demographics among the Chinese. In 1951, *Life* magazine featured a look at "America's Chinese" with its depiction of a New York Chinatown that was internally fractured and polarized between the East and the West.[46] To capture this social and cultural rift, the article ran a photographic spread highlighting various segments of the Chinese population. This spread, which centered on a sequence of three photographs, depicted an elderly Chinese bachelor smoking alone in a dark apartment, a beaming war bride surrounded by her children, and lastly, a plump eight-year-old boy. Organized in part by the age of its subjects, these pictures generated a temporal narrative in which the passing of the old ushered in the new. Their accompanying captions also underscored the cultural difference separating the elderly bachelor, who "spoke nothing but Chinese," from the eight-year-old boy, who was "completely Americanized by the New York public school system."[47] As these characterizations followed this temporal arrangement, the contrast of cultures emerged into a narrative of progress wherein a new generation presumably moved away from the culture of the East only to advance into the culture of the West. Their nationality shifted, accordingly, from Chinese to American. Notably, sandwiched between the two representative male figureheads was the war bride; her central placement reinforced her symbolic role in mediating the passage of time and in bringing about a new generation of Chinese Americans. As wife and mother, she made possible the cultural citizenship of the Chinese in the United States.

Similarly, the *Los Angeles Times* in a 1959 article examined the cultural division of the city's Chinese population.[48] It notably relied on spatial designations to map the social and cultural differences among the Chinese in

Los Angeles. The article had thereby juxtaposed its caricature of an elderly Chinese man shuffling down the drab sidewalks of Old Chinatown with an image of an eight-year-old Chinese boy holding hands with his sister and skipping down Mei-Ling Road, one of the main thoroughfares of New Chinatown. The two Chinatowns highlighted in this way not only the disparity between the young and the old but also the change from the old to the new. The *Times* did not, however, limit its analysis of this transformation to the confines of the two Chinatowns. It also set New Chinatown in Los Angeles in contrast with the suburbs in order to highlight the perceived differences in culture, race, and nationality between the two sites.

The *Times* cautioned its readers not to be deceived into thinking that New Chinatown in Los Angeles was actually the place of residence for this new generation. New Chinatown was merely "a glittering façade, a place dressed up" for the tourists' amusement, and a smoke screen that obscured the fact that the actual place of residence for this new group was the suburbs, far removed from this tourist trap. According to the *Times*, "of a population of 22,000 only a few hundred remain in Chinatown. The others have moved to the suburbs." It further insisted that "there is nothing startling about this," for the Chinese "are Americans. As such, they wish to live as Americans—to own homes and breathe the fresh air of the suburbs, where there is greenery for their children to play."[49] While the *Times* may not have found this change "startling," it nevertheless recognized the significance of this resettlement for distinguishing the Chinese as Americans. But just as this transformation hinged upon the movement of the Chinese out of Chinatown, it also necessitated the suburbs to be a place that worked to establish its residents as Americans. Moreover, this shift tapped into the ability of Chinese women to mediate the terms of assimilation, given how this new generation of Chinese consisted not of bachelors but of heterosexual nuclear families. The Chinese were in this way like other white Americans and possessed the same desire to own homes with yards for their children to play in. Assimilation or conformity to the domestic ideal thus successfully overcame racial differences to convey both the sense of possibility and the attainment of social equality between Chinese and white Americans. The diminishing population in Los Angeles Chinatown attested to the effectiveness of Americanization. It revealed how the terms of becoming an American entailed not just the ability to live as an American but to live where Americans lived.

Sing Sheng and the Test of U.S. Democracy

In January 1952, Sing Sheng, together with his wife, Grace, and their two-and-a-half-year-old son, Richard, decided to move out of their apartment in San Francisco and placed a $2,950 deposit for a house in the Southwood suburb of South San Francisco.[50] Shortly after, Southwood residents instructed Sheng and his family not to move into this restricted neighborhood. They claimed that their decision stemmed not from any personal prejudices against Sheng but from a desire to maintain the economic viability of their suburban tract. They also insisted that it was in Sheng's best interest not to take up residence in Southwood, since neighborhood kids would only target him and his family for acts of vandalism.[51] Undaunted by these remarks, Sheng decided to appeal to his neighbors' sense of democracy and equality and petitioned for their consent to live in Southwood. For many weeks the Sheng case captivated the public's attention both nationally and internationally. Given the way the media portrayed the Shengs as a model postwar family, Sheng's battle to reside in Southwood provided a telling look at the ability—or more specifically, the inability—of cultural assimilation to cross the color line. It further showed how U.S. Cold War efforts in Asia had increased the stakes of efforts to secure the rights of Asians in the United States.

Given its racial restrictions in housing, South San Francisco was a prime location for white working-class families. Since 1895, South City, as this area was commonly called, had established an image as a working-class family town whose livelihood depended on the area's factories, the main one being the Western Meat Company. At the turn of the twentieth century, the town became known for its ethnic diversity, consisting of Irish, Portuguese, and Italian immigrants. Chinese settlers were also found at the edge of town, but a fire destroyed this small settlement in 1912.[52] During World War II and the immediate postwar years, South San Francisco experienced a population boom as well as a rise in the number of industries, thus living up to its self-proclaimed moniker, "The Industrial City." Residential tracts subsequently proliferated.[53] The *San Francisco Chronicle* in its coverage of the Sheng case provided a window on the effect of racial restrictive covenants on the racial makeup of South San Francisco. The *Chronicle* reported that during a neighborhood meeting over Sheng's petition to reside in Southwood, the homeowner Belmar B. Shepley voluntarily confessed to being a "hapa haole," or a half Hawaiian, and his wife, a Polynesian. While this racial outing had incited the *Chronicle* to headline how "Southwood finds out it isn't an 'all-white' community, after all," it nevertheless exposed how the white ideal regulated residential patterns in South San Francisco and more importantly, the various attempts to bypass the whites-only restriction in housing.[54]

For about two weeks in February 1952, the Sheng case made headlines in various media outlets across the nation. The broad appeal of the Sheng case captured in part the growing interest that Americans had in Asia, Asians, and Asian Americans following the nation's involvement in the Korean conflict.[55] This was because the expansion of U.S. Cold War efforts in Asia helped call attention to the social status of Asian Americans as a measure of the credibility of U.S. democracy. Given the popular perception that Asian Americans were representatives of Asia, the fight for residential freedom for Sheng was seen as a testament to "free countries" in Asia that U.S. democracy was credible and superior to communism. The need to ensure housing rights for Sheng was in this way connected to the fight against communism in Asia.

The manner in which Sheng went about challenging his exclusion from Southwood also contributed to generating public interest in his case. While Sheng in 1952 could have settled this matter in the district courts of San Francisco, especially since the U.S. Supreme Court ruled in 1948 that state enforcement of racial restrictive covenants was unconstitutional, he nevertheless opted to abide by the social judgment of Southwood residents. Sheng asked Southwood to administer a vote whereby residents could choose through a democratic process whether they wanted to admit a nonwhite family into their neighborhood or not. He further sought to rally support by distributing a letter that explained to Southwood residents why they should vote on his behalf. Sheng stated in this appeal,

> Before you reach any decision as to how you will vote in this ballot, allow us to tell you our opinion. The present world conflict is not between individual nations, but between Communism and Democracy. We think so highly of Democracy because it offers freedom and equality. America's forefathers fought for these principles and won the independence in 1776. . . . We have forsaken all our beloved China and have come to this country seeking the same basic rights. Do not make us the victims of false Democracy. Please vote in favor of us.[56]

In thus stating, Sheng sought to convey that the legitimacy of U.S. democracy was relevant to world politics. He appealed to Southwood residents to use this vote to counter Soviet propaganda and show before an international community the superiority of U.S. democracy over communism. With this aim in mind, Sheng maintained that the best way to combat communism was not through the exclusion of Chinese from the United States or even the rejection of communist China. Rather, by accepting Chinese into the suburbs, the nation could not only attest to the superiority of the U.S. political system but also sway China away from the influence of communist ideologies. The movement of Chinese into the suburbs therefore extended beyond mapping a national and cultural shift from China to America and from Chinese to American; it also marked a political progression from communism to American democracy. As Sheng sought to use his battle to reside in Southwood to assess the credibility of U.S. democracy, his appeal pitted the ideal of whiteness against a racially inclusive model of national belonging. Sheng's fight demonstrated the contestations that were taking place in Cold War America over which racial ideal was to speak to the benefits of the American way of life.

Newspapers dubbed this vote "a test of democracy," revealing that the Sheng case was calling into question U.S. democracy's superiority to communism. Despite these appeals to the broader political implications of Sheng's petition, Southwood residents voted on February 16 to prohibit Sheng and his family from living in Southwood: 174 people voted against Sheng, 28 for, and 14 had no opinion.[57] The outcome of this vote, however, did little to resolve the issue. Instead, the vote against Sheng incited a public dialogue over the meaning and validity of U.S. democracy. As the *San Francisco Chronicle* noted, after the public heard the outcome of the Southwood decision, they began to bombard the newspaper with a "floodtide" of telephone calls, letters, and telegrams that on the whole expressed "their indignation at such a desecration of democracy and American principles." In response to these many correspondences, the *Chronicle* decided to run a full-page editorial to highlight the public dismay at the outcome of this vote, especially the vote's damaging impact on the U.S. Cold War effort in Asia. As noted in the *Chronicle*'s editorial,

> The ultimate effects cannot yet be known—but, like ripples in a pool, the effects of the Southwood plebiscite seem likely to spread to the

outermost corners of this cold-war-torn globe. Already, public and private groups that spend great treasure and labor in wooing Asia to the side of the free world are complaining that Southwood has undone the long and tedious work of the Voice of America, of Radio Free Asia and even of American men who have been fighting in Korea. They say: "We cannot sell freedom to Asia unless we can deliver freedom at home."[58]

As the editorial underscored the need for America to deliver freedom at home, it participated in the nation's Cold War effort to restore the credibility of U.S. democracy abroad. Its push to have Sheng admitted into Southwood thus looked to authorize the United States as the leader of the "free world" by showing before an international community the nation's commitment to safeguarding the freedom and equality of all people.

The *Chronicle* also took note of how newspapers in Asia reacted to the Sheng vote. For instance, an editorial in the *Hong Kong Standard* had deemed Sheng's actions reckless given the assault of communist propaganda against the United States in Asia. The *Standard* maintained that one can never "test democracy," since its espousal, likened to "one's faith in religion, has to be intuitive and not lightly put to the test." Interestingly, the *Chronicle* responded by stating that it did not share in the *Hong Kong Standard*'s judgment of Sheng. Instead, the *Chronicle* blamed white Americans who were swayed by the unfounded fear that nonwhites depreciated the property values of their suburban homes. The *Chronicle*, however, considered the failings of these Americans to be ultimately beneficial, given the way they imbued the nation with a "resolve to do better."[59] As the *Chronicle* juxtaposed its interpretation of Sheng's actions with that of the *Hong Kong Standard*, it depicted the desired political relationship between Asia and America as one in which Asia supplied the nation with its faith while America provided Asia with its resolve. By refusing to add to the *Hong Kong Standard*'s criticism of Sheng, the *Chronicle* further bolstered the moral superiority of American democracy, which refrained from blaming others for its failings but rightfully took responsibility for its own mistakes.

Besides drawing on the U.S. Cold War effort in Asia to advocate the extension of civil rights to Asian Americans, popular periodicals such as the *San Francisco Chronicle* highlighted attributes that Sheng had in common with white Americans in order to construct him as fit for residence in the suburbs. While the majority of these accounts called attention to the fact that Sheng was a veteran of World War II, only a few mentioned that his veteran status had stemmed from his service in the Chinese Nationalist Army. The reason for this oversight may be that China was an ally of the United States during World War II. However, it may also be due to the way this distinction exposed Sheng as a foreign-born immigrant. The desire of mainstream news accounts to portray Sheng as a full-fledged American was apparent in the repeated references to the fact that Sheng's wife, Grace, was born, raised, and educated in the United States and that their son was also American-born. Popular news features further highlighted how Sheng had completed college in the United States and worked as an airline mechanic for Pan-American Airlines, to bolster its argument that the rightful place for Sheng and his family was in the nation's suburbs.[60]

But what worked above all else to cast Sheng as similar to other white Americans was a widely circulated photo that showed Sheng sitting with his wife on their living room couch, staring lovingly at their son. His role as father and husband, more than his identity as a middle-class, college-educated veteran, narrowed the gap that separated him from white Americans. Sheng's American-born wife, Grace, and their son, Richard, facilitated this cultural enfranchisement by distancing Sheng from popular representations of the lone, aged Chinese bachelor whose inability to procreate had ghettoized him within the confines of Chinatown. Depictions of Sheng properly performing his assigned gender role also helped to establish his Americanness. According to the *Chronicle*, Sheng expressed the impact that the Southwood vote had on him and his family by saying, "You know how women are. She [Grace] had it all worked out in her mind how she was going to decorate the house." Noting that Sheng said this "with an understanding smile," the *Chronicle* likened Sheng to the typical family man who not only labored on behalf of his family's interests but was also clued-in to the frivolous ways of women. The purchase of the suburban home was therefore not for his benefit but for that of his wife, so that she could fulfill her role as the typical suburban housewife and spend her days dressing up their home, and for his son, who needed a backyard to play in.[61] The portrayal of Sheng as the head of this heterosexual nuclear family thus functioned to cast him and his family as fully assimilated into the American way of life.

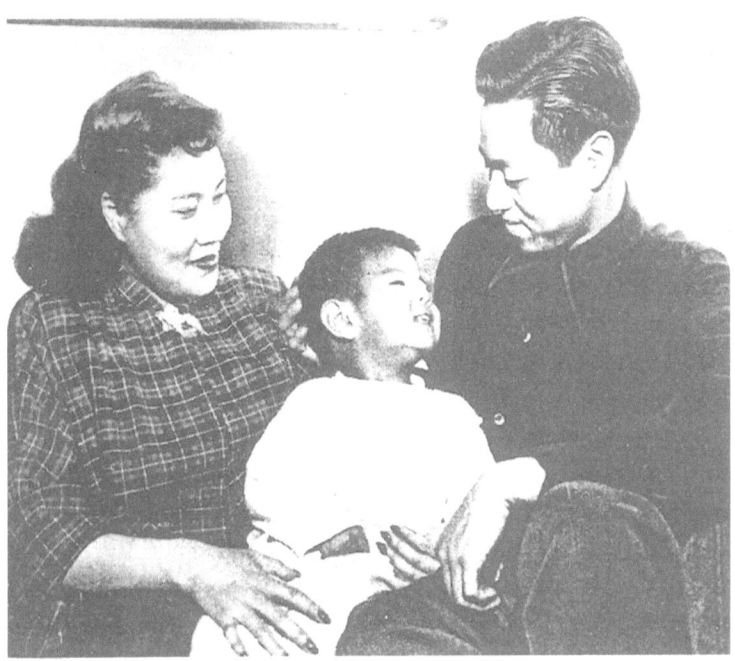

Fig. 2.1. Sing Sheng with his wife, Grace, and their two-year-old son, Richard, in South San Francisco, 1952. Courtesy of Associated Press/*San Francisco Chronicle*

Depictions of Sheng as a fully assimilated American were conceived to generate public support for his admittance into the restricted neighborhood of Southwood, and his case importantly showed that cultural assimilation functioned foremost to make racial integration desirable in Cold War America. Rather than being the missing key that would ensure the crossing of all racialized minorities past the color line, cultural assimilation worked in these accounts to detail the advantages of breaking down the color divide. In this view, the presence of Asian Americans in whites-only locales not only functioned to bolster the believability of the American Dream, but also promised not to alter in any way the postwar suburban lifestyle. Portrayals of the assimilability of Asian Americans thus effectively demonstrated that because of U.S. involvement in the Korean War, the social status of Asian Americans had been turned into a measure of the credibility of American democracy. The effect of U.S. Cold War politics on the social standing of Asian Americans was notable especially since Asian immigrants had always been undergoing the process of assimilation, even during the mid-nineteenth century, when they were deemed unassimilable by exclusionists who sought to bar the immigration of Asians to the United States. What brought the assimilation of Asian Americans to light was the Cold War, in particular the way U.S. foreign affairs had connected the battle against communism to the battle against racial segregation.

Notably, Chinese periodicals in the United States also tapped into the nation's desire to establish the legitimacy of U.S. democracy abroad in order to advocate for the extension of civil rights to Asian Americans. Dai-Ming Lee, editor of the English section of the bilingual Chinese daily the *Chinese World*, used his editorial column to express support for Sheng and his fight to reside in the restricted neighborhood of Southwood. For Lee, the Southwood situation was damaging because it exposed the nation's "vaunted democracy to be far from perfect" while providing the Soviet Union more fuel for its campaign against the United States. Lee further contended that racial inequality in the United States had hurt the effort of "free countries" abroad, especially those engaged in fighting for American democracy with their "blood and treasure."[62] But while Lee praised Sheng for putting American democracy to the test, other Chinese periodicals in the United States were less sympathetic to the approach that Sheng adopted to challenge race-based restrictions in housing. An editorial in the San Francisco–based newspaper *Chinese Pacific Weekly*, for example, argued that Sheng had called undue attention to his situation, for without "this strange voting procedure, the Western newspapers would not be interested in covering this story." It also criticized Sheng for subjecting himself to the judgment of Southwood residents and asserted that "we [the Chinese in the United States] need to have more confidence in the belief that we have the right to choose where we want to live. . . . Sing Sheng should not have suggested that a vote be administered. Does he not already have this right? Why allow others to determine his right?"[63]

Dai-ming Lee responded to this critique by shifting the blame away from Sheng and onto the 174 Southwood residents who voted against him. Lee sought to show that Sheng, unlike those who voted against him, was the true exemplar of democratic principles. Lee further expressed his admiration for the way Sheng yielded to the majority opinion in Southwood. He called this a "selfless decision," one that demonstrated "amazing self restraint." As Lee contended, Sheng had broken no laws when he made a down payment for a house in Southwood. The residents who voted against him, in contrast, had violated the U.S. Constitution. With this in mind, Lee praised Sheng for not exercising his right to take legal action, as this undertaking would only add to the damage that was already inflicted on the credibility of U.S. democracy. For unlike the 174 residents who fed the Kremlin with their racial prejudice, Lee believed that Sheng had acted to protect the image of the nation. In so doing, Sheng had "put those voting against him to infinite shame."[64] The only culprits of this debacle, in Lee's view, were those who voted against Sheng.

The *Chinese Pacific Weekly*, despite expressing its dismay with Sheng's actions, saw a beneficial result. It was heartened by the way the Sheng case had revealed the "gradual liberalism of the American press and the gradual liberalism of public opinion against discrimination."[65] This observation was well substantiated by the proliferation of press coverage of the Sheng case. Stories appeared in the *San Francisco Chronicle*, the *New York Times*, the *New York Herald Tribune*, the *Chicago Tribune*, and *Time* and *Newsweek* magazines, to name a few. National radio and TV stations also took an interest in this story. Outside the United States, the Sheng case was reported in the *Manila Chronicle* and in Hong Kong newspapers. The vast majority of these accounts were not only sympathetic with Sheng's efforts to live in a racially restricted area, but also related Sheng's fight to live in Southwood to the fight against communism abroad. Additionally, key state and political leaders, along with national and community organizations, issued public statements in support of Sheng and their belief that U.S. democracy was superior to communism. They included the San Francisco City Council, the city attorney, the mayor, California governor Earl Warren, U.S. senators, the national Committee for Free Asia, and local church and community groups. The *Chronicle* further documented the pervasive public dialogue over the Sheng case by publishing numerous letters from across the nation that responded to this issue. It even administered its own vote, mimicking the one Sheng issued before Southwood residents. The result of this vote, gathered from tallying up the number of letters for and the number of letters against Sheng between February 16 and 23, indicated a landslide victory for Sheng supporters. The *Chronicle* headlined the results, "266 for Sheng, 16 on the Other Side." In doing so, the *Chronicle* effectively minimized the ability of Southwood residents to reflect public opinion and showed how the broader reading public supported Sheng's efforts to break race-based restrictions in housing. The

Chronicle also noted that "more letters were received on the Sheng affair than on any other single issue in many months," and that only the Shengs had received more letters than the *Chronicle*. The missives that the Shengs received were all sympathetic except for one unsigned letter.[66]

Against this overwhelming display of support for Sheng, the American Homes Development Company of Burlingame issued one of the few public statements that called on homeowners to remain steadfast in upholding the practice of race-based restrictions in housing. It maintained that racial restrictive covenants had "set forth salutary and beneficial restrictions on the land for those purchasers desiring ownership in a community where they would welcome their neighbor and live in equality."[67] The American Homes Development Company portrayed the whites-only rule as a fair decree and tapped into understandings about social equality to justify the systematic enforcement of racial segregation in housing. Notably, these efforts revealed an ongoing conflict over whether a racially inclusive model or a whites-only model was going to represent the superiority of the American way of life.

This battle over race and housing rights saw the pro-Sheng faction of Southwood call for a second town hall meeting to allow for a new vote to take place.[68] A bitter debate ensued, and the town hall meeting ended with those who opposed Sheng soundly defeating the call for a second ballot.[69] The result of this meeting left Dai-ming Lee of the *Chinese World* so incensed that he wrote the following about the anti-Sheng faction:

> This stubborn group clamored that it was doing everything within its right when it voted to bar Sheng, and that the cause of democracy would not be furthered by reconsidering the decision or subjecting the issue to a second ballot. The arrogance and the smugness of this group showed clearly that the anti-Sheng Southwood residents had no desire to learn from their previous mistake. . . . It is unfortunate that bigotry and obstinacy still exist in the world.[70]

While the Sheng case left many disappointed with the results, it also incited another reaction. It prompted Chinese newspapers in the United States to feature on a regular basis news stories about other cases of race-based restrictions in housing. This continued for many months after the Sheng debacle. For instance, the *Chinese World* ran a feature on the attempts of the Rolling Woods district of Richmond, California, a neighborhood on the East Bay of San Francisco, to force Wilbur D. Gary and his seven children to relocate just days after he had purchased a home in that area because Gary and his family were black.⁷¹ The Richmond incident led Dai-ming Lee to decry the intolerance of Rolling Woods residents, who were reported to have hurled rocks and bricks at the Gary house.⁷²

The *Chinese World* also went in search of other "Southwood" or "Sing Sheng" incidences across the United States in which the targets of race-based restrictions in housing were of Chinese origin. The bilingual daily located a Southwood incident in Dayton, Ohio, where a young Chinese American couple sought to have their down payment refunded after receiving numerous threats from neighbors.⁷³ It also found a Sing Sheng incident in Spokane, Washington, where the prospective neighbors of Mr. and Mrs. Quay Fong Chung successfully blocked this Chinese American couple from purchasing a home in their neighborhood.⁷⁴ The *Chinese World* further tracked down a case of housing discrimination in Des Moines, Iowa, where a Hawaiian-born couple of Japanese and Chinese descent had their down payment returned to them following the protests of neighbors.⁷⁵ In addition to these stories, the *Chinese World* featured personal testimonies of Chinese Americans who shared their struggles with finding homes and related their experiences to that of Sing Sheng and his family.⁷⁶

These numerous stories revealed the impact of race-based restrictions in housing on the residential patterns of nonwhites even after the U.S. Supreme Court ruled unconstitutional the judicial enforcement of racial restrictive covenants. Although Chinese newspapers in the United States tended to relate accounts in which white residents successfully blocked racialized minorities from living in their suburban tract, the *Chinese World* did take note of a few cases where racialized minorities were welcomed by their white neighbors. One such occurrence took place in Sonoma, California. As reported in the *Chinese World*, Freddie Wing, upon moving into a whites-only neighborhood of Sonoma with his wife and son, had decided to host a housewarming party.⁷⁷ Much to Wing's surprise, about two hundred residents showed up to welcome him and his family into their neighborhood. The *Chinese World* duly noted how this scenario was in stark contrast with the experiences of Sing Sheng and his family in Southwood. It further drew on this difference to point out that the recent lifting of the naturalization barriers against all Asian groups had worked to generate these conflicting accounts.[78] The *Chinese World* sought in this way to connect the struggle over housing rights to the broader struggle over who counted as an American in Cold War America. Notably, even Sheng's struggle for residential freedom produced mixed results: his exclusion from Southwood was followed by his inclusion in Sonoma, where he, like Wing, successfully purchased a home in a previously restricted neighborhood.[79]

Sheng's exclusion from Southwood did not necessarily point to the failure of U.S. democracy, but neither did his admission into the suburbs of Sonoma indicate its success. Rather, the Sheng case documented the negotiations that were taking place in public discourse over the meaning of American democracy. The relevance of the Sheng case was not that it tested the credibility of U.S. democracy, but that it historicized contestations over just how race would denote the benefits of the American way of life in Cold War America. Notably, these conflicts manifested in the way the popular press fluctuated between portraying Asian Americans as assimilated subjects to be integrated into postwar suburbs and portraying them as nonwhites to be excluded from whites-only locales. Asian Americans emerged from this contestation as assimilable subjects, as U.S. Cold War politics helped to turn racial integration into a desirable ideal.

CHAPTER 3

Asian American Firsts and the Progress toward Racial Integration

Jennie Lee earned the distinction of being the first Chinese and one of the first women to be a certified army-navy welder at the Douglas Aircraft Company.[1] During World War II, Lee's accomplishment was featured in newspapers throughout the greater Los Angeles area, as it captured the values and aspirations that the nation sought to promote. As a female welder, Lee personified the popular wartime propaganda about Rosie the Riveter, who fulfilled her patriotic duty by daring to work in a trade that was previously restricted to men. As Lee was also noted for being a Chinese Rosie, her participation as a racialized minority further affirmed how the nation was in need of and truly welcomed all able-bodied workers to contribute to the war effort. Lee's distinction as the first Chinese Rosie illustrated how World War II had opened up the nation's workplaces to women and to people of all racial and ethnic backgrounds. Unlike the Aryan supremacist ways of Nazi Germany, which led to the mass extermination of Jews throughout Europe, Lee's certification as an army-navy welder showed the United States to be progressing toward the full realization of its democratic principles.

As the mainstream media celebrated Lee's accomplishment in relation to the nation's war effort, the recognition it gave Lee helped to generate an ideal image of racialized minorities, especially those who were to be integrated into dominant society. News accounts drew on Lee's personal interests (besides being the first Chinese Rosie, she was an avid fan of both

Madame Chiang Kai-shek and the Brooklyn Dodgers) in order to advance the needs of the state. The media coverage suggested that Lee's espousal of the Chinese Nationalist government, a political ally of the United States during World War II, and her familiarity with U.S. popular culture showed her loyalty and belonging to the United States, proof of the nation's ability to secure broad-based support for the war effort. Thus Lee, as the first Chinese Rosie, was established as a model for the terms that made racial integration not just possible but also desirable.

The postwar period saw a proliferation of celebrations of the first of a particular racial or ethnic group to achieve a level of social and professional distinction. The widespread attention that popular media paid to these pioneers marked the early Cold War years as a defining era that cultivated the culture of the first. Among the notable trailblazers was baseball legend Jackie Robinson; the signing of the Los Angeles–bred infielder to the Brooklyn Dodgers in 1947 distinguished Robinson as the first black athlete to achieve major league baseball status in modern times. The list also included Judge Albert Armendariz Sr., founder of the Mexican American Legal Defense and Education Fund, who in 1947 became the first in his immediate family to pursue graduate study and the only Mexican American to be enrolled in the University of Southern California Law School. Like stories on the first that appeared prior to the postwar period, mainstream news features of the early Cold War years drew on the achievements of racialized minorities to shed light on the values and aspirations of the nation. These stories not only emphasized the importance of cultural assimilation for bringing about racial integration, they also showed that portrayals of racialized minorities as both willing and able to prove their desirability to dominant society helped to make desegregation a necessary goal. The sheer number of stories that adopted this approach imbued a sense of normalcy and expectedness to these viewpoints.

In Robinson's case, his success as the first black player in modern major league baseball entailed that he refrain from public drinking, smoking, and partying. It also required that Robinson be the one to always turn the other cheek when players dug their spiked cleats into his leg and when players as well as fans shouted racial slurs at him. As the *Time* magazine cover story on Robinson contended, these constraints were crucial because they not only garnered Robinson the respect of his peers, they also enabled his talent as a ballplayer to be the main thing that the public focused on and the main thing that would ultimately win them over. Accordingly, even though the *Time* feature believed that Robinson's athletic abilities were enough to make him rookie of the year, it nevertheless considered it an offense to celebrate his talents apart from his ability to carry out the terms that gained him mainstream acceptance.[2]

Time's coverage of Robinson exemplified one of the most appealing aspects of stories on the first: they depicted racial injustice as foremost a personal and not a societal problem for racialized minorities to overcome. This was also apparent in the way the oral history of Judge Albert Armendariz Sr. accounted for Armendariz's successes. This feature related how Armendariz, as the only Mexican American at USC Law School, had stuck out like a "sore thumb" and how administrators, professors, and fellow students made him feel he did not belong. It further noted how Armendariz came to terms with this alienation by reminding himself that he had enrolled in law school to earn a degree, not to make friends.[3] The oral history credited Armendariz's future accomplishments to the way he worked out his feelings of social isolation, thus advocating a specific solution to the problem of racism: racialized minorities could move forward in society by changing their attitudes and not demanding a change in the attitudes of those around them.

The use of the first as a model of assimilationist ideologies conveyed the message that individual resolve on the part of racialized minorities was key to bringing about institutional change during the postwar period. But the dictates of assimilation in this era also brought to the fore something even more fundamental than the desire of racialized minorities to improve their social standing in dominant society. As the Cold War turned hot in Asia with the outbreak of the Korean War in 1950, stories on the firsts increasingly depicted the drive of racialized minorities to live and work in areas previously restricted to them as indications of their unwavering belief in the superiority of U.S. democracy, rather than just their personal desire to improve their lot in life. Thus the achievements of racialized minorities worked to attest to the credibility of U.S. democracy during a time when the Cold War had escalated into open conflict. Given how the legitimacy of U.S. democracy had a much bigger impact on world affairs during the Cold War than it had in World War II, stories on the first were vital to showing an international community that the United States was superior to communist countries.

This chapter will focus on three individuals whose professional distinctions made headlines during the early Cold War years. Whereas the popular press routinely carried stories on the successes of various racialized groups in the United States, this chapter examines only the stories on Asian Americans. It does this in order to underscore the way U.S. Cold War efforts in Asia had turned the social status of Asians in the United States into a measure of the credibility of U.S. democracy. The three figures of interest are Sammy Lee, who, in addition to being a major in the U.S. army and a medical doctor (an ear, nose, and throat specialist), became the first Asian American to win an Olympic gold medal, a feat that he achieved in platform diving in 1948 and in 1952; Jade Snow Wong, who became the first Asian American to pen a nationally acclaimed book, her 1950 autobiography, *Fifth Chinese Daughter*; and Delbert Wong, who became the first Chinese American judge following his 1959 appointment to the Los Angeles municipal court by California governor Edmund G. Brown.

The attention to Asian Americans further stems from a scholarly interest in tracing the stereotype of Asian Americans as the model minority to the early Cold War years. Scholars of Asian American studies have generally concentrated on the late 1960s as the time when the image of Asian Americans as the model minority first appeared in the popular press, but this study examines the discourse on the first to show that Asian Americans began to assume the role of model minorities during the early Cold War years.[4] It argues that portrayals of Asian Americans as the model minority worked not just to verify the state's adherence to assimilationist ideologies, but also to bolster U.S. efforts to rally non-Western countries away from the influence of communism. The U.S. State Department sent distinguished Asian Americans to East, Southeast, and South Asia to bear witness that U.S. democracy strove to treat all people and countries equally. But the state's reliance on the success stories of racialized minorities to establish the legitimacy of U.S. democracy was not a one-sided affair. Rather, a transnational exchange took place between the United States and communist China, as China was also releasing English-language accounts on the social advancement of Chinese women and of China's minoritized populations in order to showcase the capacity of communism to bring about gender as well as racial equality. Moreover, despite the U.S. government's attempts to propagate stories that demonstrated the superiority of the American political system, it could not fully secure the consent of the nation to this endeavor, as counternarratives emerged to expose the limits of U.S. democracy. This chapter examines the concept of tokenism and how it worked to unsettle the ability of the first to signify the nation's steady progress toward racial equality.

Constructing a Role for the First

The postwar era is generally regarded as a time when the nation relaxed its racial barriers and in so doing, carried forward some of the changes that took place in World War II. Various historians recount how the war against Nazi Germany together with the nation's postwar aspiration to be the leader of the "free world" made racist practices increasingly difficult to justify at home. The passage of the 1944 G.I. Bill of Rights was also significant for providing a sizable number of black, Asian American, and Mexican American veterans the means to obtain a college education, while the lifting of racial restrictions in the job market granted racialized minorities access to professional jobs.[5] As labor unions moved to do away with racial barriers to union membership, the admission of people of color into the rank and file further boosted the employment of racialized minorities in trade jobs.[6] With these changes in mind, the historian Brenda Gayle Plummer described the rise of a Cold War liberalism that catered to an acculturationist mindset and made radicalism suspect. Black popular magazines, Plummer argued, exemplified this way of thinking as they bought into the promise of postwar opportunities and routinely ran features that promoted the ideal of the white middle-class suburban lifestyle. The proliferation of stories on the victories of blacks over the color line effectively turned the early Cold War years into the age of "Negro firsts."[7]

Notably, stories on the firsts did not merely detail how easing racial barriers helped boost the social status of racialized minorities and their subsequent adherence to the status quo. As the United States engaged in an ideological battle with communist countries over which form of government, communism or U.S. democracy, was superior, this rivalry prompted the federal government to not only support desegregation measures but also to use the rising status of racialized minorities to attest to the benefits of the American way of life. As the cultural critic Christina Klein has argued, when the Cold War escalated into armed conflict with the outbreak of the Korean War, the shift fueled the American public's fascination with Asia, apparent in the upsurge of news articles, novels, and films on Asians and Asian Americans.[8] The rise of the culture of the first thus saw Asian Americans figure centrally in the creation of an ethos around the credibility and superiority of U.S. democracy. Besides being the subject of news features, Asian Americans became the storytellers whose testimonies helped to authenticate the superiority of the American way of life.

Sammy Lee was among the notable firsts. The recognition he enjoyed as the first Asian American to win an Olympic gold medal illustrates the political shifts that took place during the Cold War, as the government drew on his accomplishments to rally the support of non-Western countries for the U.S. Cold War effort. Lee earned his distinction during the 1948 Olympic games in London, when he won the gold medal in platform diving; at that time, mainstream news outlets that reported on Lee's win did little to draw attention to his race, other than noting that Lee, who was born in Fresno, California, was an American of Korean descent.[9] However, this changed in 1952, when Lee qualified for the Olympic games in Helsinki. Lee repeated his win in platform diving and earned a second gold medal at the age of thirty-two, but his skills as a diver were not the only thing that earned attention. As the United States was in the midst of fighting the Korean War, Lee's racial designation as a Korean American became a newsworthy trait.

The importance of Lee's racial heritage came to light following an incident that occurred during a preparatory meeting with swimmers and divers at the 1952 Olympic games. As the *New York Times* reported, several Russian swimmers and divers approached Lee at the event and attempted to strike up a conversation with him. Although Lee initially regarded the interaction as a friendly exchange between athletes who were curious about each other's diving techniques, he soon learned that there were political motivations behind the meeting. This realization came about after one of the Russian swimmers pinned an ivory rendition of Pablo Picasso's peace dove on Lee's swimming jacket—a gesture that Lee regarded as routine and welcoming until a U.S. reporter drew his attention to the nature of the pin. Upon grasping what he was wearing, Lee was described to have immediately ripped the dove off his jacket because, as the *New York Times* detailed, the "dumpy dove had become almost as much a Communist symbol as the hammer and sickle."[10]

The exchange between Lee and the Russian athletes displayed to an American audience just what the Cold War was about, and specifically, what was so menacing about communists. It showed how the Russian athletes had purposely approached Lee, whom they tagged as an unsuspecting minority, and attempted to brainwash him into thinking that communist countries were the true harbingers of peace and equality. The Russian athletes, as the *New York Times* argued, even went as far as tricking Lee into wearing a communist symbol. Lee affirmed this view as he was quoted to have said, "I might have slipped on that peace dove thing, but I already know what that guy wants to ask. It goes like this: Are you discriminated against because you are an Oriental? They never get tired of trying I guess."[11] With this remark, Lee revealed what was truly noteworthy about the incident. His response showed how the United States had the upper hand in this ideological battle with the Soviet Union, given how, unbeknownst to the Russian athletes, Lee was not the impressionable minority that they thought he was. Rather, Lee was a major in the U.S. army and an American of Korean descent who was privy to the tactics of the Russians. His ripping of the communist dove from his jacket attested to the ability of U.S. democracy to secure the loyalty of the nation's racialized minorities and to instill in them a clear sense of the world. Lee's subsequent actions also displayed the appropriate attitude that racialized minorities should assume when confronted with communist propaganda. As the *New York Times* noted, Lee refused to meet privately with a Russian newspaperman and opted instead to pay a social call to the South Korean team, even though he did not speak Korean.[12] The story about Lee's exchange with the Russian athletes illustrates the role of the first in providing proof that U.S. democracy offered equal opportunities to all and that racialized minorities were worthy of being treated equally.

Following his win at the 1952 Olympic games, Lee was chosen by the U.S. Amateur Athletic Union to be the recipient of the prestigious James E. Sullivan Memorial Trophy, an award given to amateur athletes displaying exceptional sportsmanship and citizenship. Lee was recognized as "the oldest athlete, the first diver, and the first athlete of Oriental descent" to win the trophy.[13] The honor, however, also carried with it the political entanglements of the Cold War, given how five months prior to the announcement that Lee was the winner of the Sullivan, the United States under the auspices of the United Nations Command together with North

Korea and China signed the armistice to end the Korean War. Lee's win thus incited *Pravda*, the official Soviet paper, to question the timing of the award and to remark that Lee won only because he participated in "the capitalistic, bourgeoisie sport of war in Korea" by staging diving exhibitions in the Republic of Korea.[14] True to form, Lee, as the first, responded to this attack by declaring that "only in the United States can athletes of all colors, races, and religion get the chance to be world champions."[15]

The mainstream press in the United States further advanced the sentiment that the selection of Lee for the Sullivan indicated how the United States, unlike the Soviet Union and China, was actually committed to treating all people and countries equally. Despite the widespread support for Lee's win, some legitimate questions were raised about the choice of Lee for the Sullivan. This was because Lee did not compete in a single national championship in 1953; he was stationed at the U.S. army's 121st Evacuation Hospital in Seoul, where he worked as an ear, nose, and throat specialist.[16] However, Lee's time in Seoul did present the opportunity to put his diving skills to use. Notably, the president of the Republic of Korea, Syngman Rhee, not the U.S. government, initiated this opportunity. In an oral interview conducted by the Amateur Athletic Foundation of Los Angeles in 1999, Lee recounted how he received notice during his stay in Seoul that President Rhee had an ear infection and was in need of a specialist. When he arrived, Lee identified himself as the son of Soon Kee Rhee, a lifelong friend of President Rhee who had died during a political meeting in Los Angeles defending Rhee's right to be the president of Korea after World War II ended and the Japanese were ousted from the Korean peninsula. Because of these ties, Rhee embraced Lee and arranged for a diving exhibition to be held in Seoul.[17] The event sought to make use of Lee's immense popularity in Korea to boost not just the morale of a people who witnessed the division of their country along the 38th parallel, but also their confidence in Rhee's leadership to one day reunify Korea.

Lee, for his part, drew on his distinction to support the political aims of both the United States and the Republic of Korea. In his acceptance speech for the Sullivan, Lee reaffirmed how this win spoke to the superiority of U.S. democracy. Radio stations and newsreels throughout the United States widely broadcasted Lee's witty remark that "only in the United States could a trophy founded in memory of an Irish-American like James E. Sullivan go to a Korean-American named Samuel O'Lee." President Rhee of the Republic of Korea proclaimed the award a testament to "the people in Korea that Americans have their heart in the right place to honor one of us." Lee's racial and national designations had thus permitted his accomplishments to promote not just the U.S. Cold War effort but also the political ambitions of Rhee. More importantly, they allowed Lee to carry out his own transnational political affinities. As Lee detailed in his oral interview with the Amateur Athletic Foundation of Los Angeles, his commitment to promoting the benefits of the American way of life was tied to his desire to see a "free" Korea. He recounted how his father had taken him as a child to an event in Los Angeles commemorating the 1919 March 1 uprising in Korea, when Korean students were killed for marching against Japanese colonial rule. The commemoration made such an impression on Lee that he went to his Japanese American neighbor's house, the Watanabis, with a butcher knife, seeking revenge. He also pointedly made clear that all of his achievements in middle and high school were done to best his Japanese American classmates. But despite his support for a sovereign Korea, Lee refused an invitation by President Rhee and opted not to compete in the 1952 games on behalf of the Republic of Korea. As Lee stated, "since I was an American first, I will take my chances and try to make the American team and do justice both to my ancestral background and to my Americanism."[18] Lee's choice to represent the United States thus showed how he identified foremost as an American and how this identification during the Cold War supported as well as aligned with his backing of the Republic of Korea as the representative regime of a sovereign Korea.

Following Lee's receipt of the Sullivan award, the U.S. State Department made Lee an official sports ambassador to Asia. Prior to taking on this official role, Lee had unofficially represented the United States in diving exhibitions in the Republic of Korea and in Japan. As the sports ambassador of the 1954 Far East goodwill mission, Lee traveled all over East, Southeast and South Asia to places such as India, Pakistan, Turkey, the Philippines, Hong Kong, Burma, and Vietnam. As Lee recalled, he was expected to lead a discussion on racial prejudice in U.S. society after each diving exhibition. This task importantly documented the rise of Asian Americans as the official storytellers of American democracy, who joined other notable African Americans commissioned by the State Department to bear witness to how American democracy worked to ensure freedom and equality to all people in all countries. The firsts thus emerged as a valuable government resource during the Cold War. Lee recounted how he developed a clever way to talk about race and U.S. democracy and would tell those who came to see him dive that Americans did not always practice what they preached, for if they did, he would not be standing before them as a two-time Olympian, doctor of medicine, major in the U.S. army, and winner of the James E. Sullivan award.[19] According to Lee, this witty speech always worked to silence the cynics, given how it affirmed the existence of racial prejudice in the United States only to call attention to its waning influence.

Notably, Lee's role as the model minority also required that he continually work to assure his fellow Americans that the nation was progressing toward the full realization of its democratic ideals and was not fundamentally racist. This role was played out publicly after Lee decided to resign from the army and return to southern California to set up a medical practice in Orange County. As was widely reported in mainstream newspapers throughout the nation, Lee's attempt to transition to civilian life was stalled when the West Orange County Real Estate Board twice thwarted his efforts to purchase a home in Garden Grove. The board maintained that it was a huge financial risk to allow Lee and his family to move into their all-white suburban tracts, as this would only encourage the flow of racialized minorities to West Orange County. The *Los Angeles Times* and the *New York Times* fired back by reciting Lee's long list of accomplishments in order to establish how Lee's residence in Garden Grove would only bring prestige to the city. They especially called attention to the fact that Lee had just returned home from a goodwill tour in East, Southeast, and South Asia, where he served as a living example of the credibility of U.S. democracy.[20]

While mainstream newspapers drew on Lee's many accomplishments to show the injustice of denying residence in the suburbs to one so worthy, Lee, as the first, persisted in modeling the appropriate reaction that racialized minorities should demonstrate in the face of racism. He responded to being barred from the restricted neighborhoods of West Orange County by reiterating his belief in the American people and by delivering the same rhetorical sound bites that he issued while on tour in Asia. What Lee's activities showed was that racialized minorities could fight against racist practices only if they simultaneously assured the nation that its democracy was superior and legitimate. His affirmation by a nation that also marginalized him had in this way restricted his ability not only to discuss the realities of racism in the United States but also to combat its racist practices. This was a stark transformation for Lee, given his reputation as a feisty individual before becoming an Asian American first. As Lee recounted in his 1999 oral interview, he had never backed down against those who discriminated against him and was constantly getting into fistfights growing up with classmates who directed racial slurs at him. Lee also shared that the main driving force behind his 1948 Olympic win was to prove wrong "the bigots in my own country who said that I couldn't do it."[21]

Interestingly, in his oral interview with the Amateur Athletic Foundation of Los Angeles, Lee noted that after he won the Sullivan, he struggled with the question of how to go about protesting against racial discrimination in the United States. Lee recalled that upon hearing of his win, he wrote a letter to the Amateur Athletic Union requesting that he receive the award in Pasadena, California, or at any other club besides the New York Athletic Club; he had been thrown out of the New York club "because they knew me as a Chinaman."[22] But as Lee recalled, after he mailed out the letter, he immediately contacted a friend in the army to retrieve the missive and prevent it from being sent. Lee subsequently expressed deep regret that he had ever written such a letter. The tension that he displayed showed how he continually struggled with the contradictions of U.S. democracy. Although winning the Sullivan had made him reconsider the efficacy of staging a protest against the discriminatory practices of the New York Athletic Club, this shift also shed light on how his promotion of the superiority of U.S. democracy may have also been an appeal to the American public to move past its racist ways. In this view, these articulations were not merely blind espousals of the greatness of the American way. They illustrated how the first worked not just to affirm the credibility of U.S. democracy but also to petition for it to be credible.

The Exchanging of Cultures

When the U.S. State Department contacted Lee to be the nation's sports ambassador in Asia, it extended a similar request to the author Jade Snow Wong. Wong's national and international acclaim rested on her highly successful 1950 autobiography, *Fifth Chinese Daughter*. Although not the first published book-length work written by a Chinese American in English, *Fifth Chinese Daughter* was the first nationally acclaimed commercially successful book written by a Chinese American.[23] Publishers estimated that Wong's autobiography had acquired at least a quarter of a million readers by 1975.[24] Scholars of Asian American studies, moreover, consider *Fifth Chinese Daughter* a foundational text of the field; the literary critic Amy Ling has called Wong the "Mother of Chinese American literature."[25]

Shortly after its U.S. release, the State Department acquired the rights to translate *Fifth Chinese Daughter* into various Asian languages and made the book accessible in Japan, Hong Kong, Malaysia, Thailand, Burma, East India, and Pakistan. It further released Wong's autobiography in England and in Germany. As Wong noted in *No Chinese Stranger*, the 1975 follow-up book to her 1950 autobiography, the story of how a Chinese American woman went to college and became a working professional had generated an "unexpected impact on foreign readers." The State Department, in its attempt to capitalize on this interest, sought to "produce the author in the flesh" and commissioned Wong on a four-month speaking tour to forty-five different locales throughout East and Southeast Asia.[26] In taking on this assignment, Wong consented to be the living proof that a female born to poor Chinese immigrants could emerge fully assimilated and accepted in mainstream U.S. society.[27]

Wong's autobiography expressed key ideologies that the state sought to promote through Wong's retelling of her lived experiences. Moreover, despite the fact that most of the events of *Fifth Chinese Daughter* took place prior to the postwar period, Wong's story contained an underlying message about the benefits of the American way of life that made this autobiography useful for the federal government during the early Cold War years. As with Sammy Lee, what distinguished Wong in the eyes of the government was that her acclaim as the first commercially successful Chinese American author together with the message of her book could work to rally the support of Asian countries behind the U.S. Cold War effort. In the wake of the communist revolution in China and the division of Korea, the State Department considered the testimonies of Wong and Lee critical, for they showed the failure of the Soviet Union to obtain the full backing of the Chinese and Korean people. Moreover, the State Department relied, as it did for Lee, on Wong's shifting racial and national designations to lend credibility to her espousal of U.S. democracy. Interestingly, Wong found that in Asia, despite the popularity of her book, her Chinese American heritage did not bolster her ability to illustrate the benefits of the American way of life. Rather, Wong's dual heritage often hindered her capacity to relate to the people in the countries that she visited.

As pointed out by many literary scholars, most notably Frank Chin, much of *Fifth Chinese Daughter* reads like an anthropological text. Wong sought to bring readers into the confines of San Francisco Chinatown and used this locale to signify the place where Chinese culture remained unaltered long after the arrival of the first group of Chinese immigrants to the United States during the mid-nineteenth century. Wong's portrayal of Chinatown reinforced in this way its image as an insulated and foreign site waiting to be discovered and explained.[28] It further portrayed cultural differences, rather than race-based land use segregation, as the main reason the Chinese were separated from the rest of society. Wong's departure from Chinatown to attend Mills College became her symbolic entrance into dominant society. Notably, Wong's movement out of Chinatown showed that her assimilation did not entail that she disavow her Chinese heritage. Rather, her Chineseness heightened her social worth, as it allowed her to play the part of the cultural ambassador introducing her white friends to the foods and habits of the Chinese. But what this bridging of the two worlds laid bare was not an equal exchange of cultural practices. Rather, it exposed the social unevenness that existed between Chinatown and dominant society: Chinese culture was visible only insofar as it served to fulfill the curiosity of white Americans. Wong's willingness to play the role of the native informant further revealed how this exchange of cultures was but a means to prove the Chinese worthy of being accepted by mainstream society.

Fifth Chinese Daughter offered a quintessential look at how assimilation worked to overcome the color line. As Wong attributed her ability to gain acceptance in dominant society to her willingness to learn the ways of white Americans and to share with them the ways of the Chinese, her story importantly downplayed the ways racism had structured and shaped this interaction. Specifically, it sidelined the way racial discrimination against the Chinese stemmed not just from lack of knowledge about them but from the ability of dominant society to determine what that knowledge was. Instead of revealing that there was nothing essential about Chinese culture that would allow it to be reduced to one or two characteristics, Wong's 1950 autobiography promoted the importance of personal resolve on the part of racialized minorities. She offered a compelling example of how this tenacity enabled her to overcome roadblocks in her life. As Wong recalled, her career counselor at Mills College had issued her the following advice:

> If you are smart, you will look for a job only among your Chinese firms. You cannot expect to get anywhere in American business houses. After all, I am sure you are conscious that racial prejudice on the Pacific Coast will be a great handicap to you.

To which Wong responded,

> Stung and speechless, Jade Snow felt as if she had been struck on both cheeks. The numbness gave way to the first anger she had felt against any of the college staff. She had been told because she was Chinese, she could not go into equal competition with Caucasians. Her knowledge that racial prejudice existed had never interfered with her personal goals. She had, on the contrary found that being Chinese had created a great deal of favorable interest, and because of its cultural enrichment of her life she would not have traded her Chinese ancestry for any other.
>
> No, this was one piece of advice that she was not going to follow, so opposed was it to her experience and belief. She was more determined to get a job with an American firm.[29]

As Wong took it upon herself to combat racial injustice, the internalization of this task turned the struggle against institutionalized racism into a personal challenge. While this form of agency provided the minoritized a sense of control over their circumstances, it overlooked the importance of collective struggle for equal rights and the need for society as a whole to change in order to bring about racial equality. It further made race-based social disparities an indication that racialized minorities were not trying hard enough to be incorporated into mainstream society. During the early Cold War years, the story of how a Chinese American woman refused to see her Chinese heritage as a social handicap and trusted instead in the goodness of white Americans to give her a chance to prove her worth found a ready audience. Equally as appealing was Wong's portrayal of U.S. society as being not so much racist as it was unfamiliar with the cultures of Asian countries. The resulting commercial success of her work not only prompted the State Department to send Wong to Asia to help quell the growing anti-American sentiment, it also imbued in Wong a moral obligation to use her dual heritage as a Chinese and an American to foster better East-West understanding. As Wong noted in her 1975 autobiography, *No Chinese Stranger*, she believed that her dual heritage had authorized her to "interpret what she knew of the U.S. to her fellow Asians."[30]

Given Wong's focus on the importance of cultural exchange, her accounts of her time in Asia differed significantly from those of Sammy Lee. Unlike Lee, Wong did not consider it her role to talk about race and U.S. democracy. She was actually taken aback during one of her speeches in Kuala Lumpur when an East Indian asked whether she was implying that there was no racial prejudice in the United States. According to Wong, it was the first time she was ever asked such a question; she considered the inquiry disrespectful, noting that the "uninvited" guest "was not trained in Chinese courtesy."[31] Wong responded by echoing the views that she developed in *Fifth Chinese Daughter* and stated that it was a greater crime to let racism keep people from trying to improve their lot in life and from striving to create better understandings between groups. With this reply, Wong reiterated her adherence to assimilationist ideologies and deemed racism to be foremost the result of the lack of awareness and respect of each other's cultures, rather than the ability of the dominant group to create knowledges about the other and to deny to them equal access to state resources. Wong's espousal of assimilationist views fueled her desire to talk about culture and not about race.

Despite what appeared to be a deep commitment to cultivating cultural affinities between the United States and Asia, Wong's accounts of her time in Asia were replete with ruminations about the fact that there was not a coherent Chinese or Asian culture to speak of. In almost an about-face from her 1950 account, which had forged a unified sense of Chineseness in order to show how it differed from and could enrich white America, Wong's 1975 account was hesitant to posit any essential quality to being Chinese. Her first stop, Hong Kong, afforded her the chance to establish herself as an authentic Chinese, as she showed reporters that an American-born

Chinese could not only speak Cantonese without an accent but was just as fluent as native speakers. However, Wong's subsequent trips to Singapore, Malaysia, Burma, and Thailand made her question the existence of a real Chinese. These trips further pushed her to realize that a unified Asian sensibility did not exist either. This understanding resulted from her experiences with anti-Chinese hostilities in these countries. Wong detailed how the Chinese had controlled the majority of these countries' resources and exploited the labor of native populations.[32] She was thereby not fully welcomed by the natives of those countries. The deep distrust that these nations harbored against the United States further contributed to the uneven and lukewarm reception of Wong. Wong recounted how reporters would constantly badger her to prove that she was "truly Chinese" and not just a puppet of the United States with an Asian face.[33] Her time in Rangoon, moreover, produced another disconcerting experience. Wong recounted how her hosts had taken an interest in her because they had thought that Wong, being from San Francisco's Chinatown, would be privy to the dealings of the Kuomintang, which had retreated to Taiwan to establish a "free" China following its defeat by communist forces in China. This led Wong to express her dismay that many Asians did not see her as an American citizen but as a Chinese representative.[34]

As the historian Ellen D. Wu has described, the mixed reception that Wong encountered led many U.S. officials to question the benefits of sending a Chinese American to Asia.[35] But for Wong, the issue went deeper than just the inability of Chinese Americans to relate fully to people in Asia. As Wong noted in her 1975 autobiography, her trip to East, Southeast, and South Asia taught her the importance of not consigning people "to convenient mental slots." Wong remarked that just as it was a mistake for Asian communists to believe that all Americans were out to exploit the masses, it was also wrong for the United States to use "communist" as "a catch-all, scapegoat term."[36] Moreover, she argued that cultural categories, like political ones, were not only unstable but also not the best measure of an individual's worth. While the mixed reception that she received in Asia certainly attested to this view, Wong also drew on the plight of mixed-race Asians in Asia to underscore in an even more nuanced fashion the constraints of cultural categories. Given the discrimination that mixed-raced Asians endured in Asia, she contended, it may appear that being pure Chinese would grant to those who did not intermarry a sense of social legitimacy. But Wong's attempts to follow her mother's teachings and make white friends but secure a Chinese husband did not secure her acceptance among the Chinese in the United States. Since Wong chose an unconventional career for a Chinese American woman, her family and community ridiculed her even though she was pure Chinese.[37] In light of this effect, Wong pointedly asked, who benefited from the notion of pure Chinese?

By posing this question, Wong sought to highlight the way Chinese patriarchy and nationalism worked to police the behaviors and activities of the Chinese people. The cultural category of "pure Chinese" provided in this view a sense of belonging and social legitimacy to those who conformed to that status quo. Besides making known how Chinese patriarchy dictated the terms of social acceptability, Wong also called attention to the way U.S. Cold War politics governed the notion of social and political belonging. As Wong noted, her career as a ceramic artist, instead of being a subject of ridicule, had emerged as a distinguishing trait during her service as a U.S. cultural ambassador, for it allowed her to show the people in Asia how U.S. democracy worked to extend equal opportunities to women and not just to racialized minorities. The State Department's enlistment of Wong to model this benefit of the American way of life was significant, as it went against all popular portrayals of women in Cold War America, most notably the archetypal image of the assimilated Asian American woman as suburban housewife and mother. A key reason that may have accounted for the State Department's use of Wong in this manner was that Wong had directed most of her feminist critiques against Chinese patriarchy. For Wong, mainstream U.S. society, in contrast to Chinatown, had afforded her the opportunity to prove her worth as a woman. An example of the constraints of Chinatown life was the refusal of her father to support her college education. As Wong detailed in her 1950 autobiography, *Fifth Chinese Daughter*,

> It is the sons who perpetuate our ancestral heritage by permanently bearing the Wong family name and transmitting it through their blood line, and therefore the sons must have priority over the daughters when parental provisions for advantages must be limited by economic necessity.[38]

By recounting her father's rebuff, Wong revealed that her venture outside Chinatown was also driven by her desire to show her Chinese father that a Chinese daughter was just as valuable as a Chinese son. As Wong detailed in her autobiography how she had managed to live out her dreams in the white world, her story worked to enhance the advantages of being assimilated into American society. Not only did it show Wong's resolve to cross the color line, it also manifested her endeavor to prove the worth of Chinese daughters.

Another key factor that may have accounted for why the State Department selected Wong to be the first Chinese American delegate in Asia was the growing influence of communist China. As China was rising in prominence as a major world power, it claimed the superiority of Chinese communism because of its capacity to improve the livelihood not only of the poor but of women as well. As the scholar of Chinese history Gail Hershatter has argued, women in twentieth-century China were the preeminent symbols of national modernity. The prevailing belief among Chinese intellectuals and revolutionaries was that "if Chinese women are liberated, the Chinese nation will be strong, leaving behind both feudalism and the precarious sovereignty of semicolonialsm."[39] Even though strains of this belief were apparent in China before the founding of the People's Republic of China, the Chinese communist government did much to popularize this belief, as it relied on Chinese women to exemplify the nation's social and economic progress and its superiority to Western countries. Thus communist propaganda not only incited the U.S. government to rely on the successes of racialized minorities to model the benefits of the American way of life, it also prompted the State Department to send a Chinese American woman to Asia for the purpose of showcasing the rising status of women in U.S. society.

Communist China actively disseminated accounts of Chinese communism's capacity to ensure gender equality; a telling example was the publication of the English-language magazine *Women of China*. First launched in 1939 at the Chinese communist revolutionary base in Yan'an, China, by the Women's Movement Committee of the Chinese Communist Party, *Women of China* became in 1949 the official publication of the All-China Women's Federation, a group dedicated to improving the international image of China. Though it was published in Beijing, the intended audience for this English-language periodical was the Western world. The magazine thus found its way to the United States, Europe, and Latin America. In the decade after the communist revolution in China, *Women of China* generated numerous articles that sought to debunk popular perceptions of the role of women in China. The articles described how the Chinese communist government encouraged peasant women to work in farming cooperatives and in industrial factories and also opened schools to help them get an education. Accounts of the advancement of Chinese women worked in this way to bolster the broader national narrative about how communism was effectively working to raise agricultural and industrial production in China while reducing rates of illiteracy. Additionally, this English-language periodical sought to make known how the 1950 Marriage Law was pushing the nation to break from its long-standing social conventions. Specifically, it wanted to highlight how China was moving away from arranged marriages in favor of individual choice and romantic love. Stories on the progress of communist China all followed the same narrative pattern that drew on the 1949 communist revolution to distinguish a pre-liberated from a post-liberated China. This distinction showed how the Chinese communist government had freed the nation from the oppressive rule of Japanese colonizers and the corruption of the Kuomintang. Stories were almost all told from a first-person perspective so as to foreground the agency of Chinese women as builders of their own image and tellers of their own experiences.

The *Women of China* magazine also ran stories that underscored that communist China was leading the way in establishing gender equality and was in this way more socially advanced and progressive than its Western counterparts. To that end, the periodical prominently featured Chinese women as political delegates who attended and organized world conferences to protest against the atomic bomb and to promote world unity. Chinese women were, moreover, shown as high-ranking professionals who worked as doctors and engineers. The magazine also contained accounts of how the Chinese communist government devoted considerable resources to ensuring that Tibetan women and women who resided in the remote parts of Inner Mongolia received the same benefits as other Chinese women. Chinese communism was thus shown to work for the benefit of all Chinese women regardless of ethnic differences.

One approach the magazine took to show China as more socially advanced than Western countries was to feature testimonies by women who had previously lived in Western countries but had come to China to witness and take part in the advancement of the Chinese communist regime. Included among these testimonies was one penned by a Chinese American woman, Lee Ming-Hua, aptly entitled "What I Have Seen in My Motherland."[40] In this first-person account, Lee talked about how she had always kept a close eye on the rising status of China while living in the United States. Lee, along with her husband and two children, finally decided to leave the United States and returned to China via Europe in 1954. Given that Lee grew up in China but spent a good part of her adult life in the United States, her story allowed her to attest to how life in communist China differed greatly from the days of the anti-Japanese war, as food and basic household goods were now plentiful. Her story also allowed her to speak about how China fared in comparison with the United States. With this latter goal in mind, Lee shared how her decision to become an engineer was met with numerous questions in the United States, where no one had understood her desire to take part in national construction. Lee rationalized that this reaction was understandable, given that it was also the response of "Old China." Thus Lee effectively grouped the United States with a past that the Chinese communist regime had moved away from, since such a question was ridiculous in this newly formed China, where women were encouraged to work in all fields. Lee used her experience to back this claim, as she was able find work upon her return to China at the Institute of Mechanics of the Chinese Academy of Sciences, where she headed a plastics group.

In addition to detailing the ways communist China afforded greater opportunities to women professionally, Lee sought to show how living under a communist regime had improved her personal life. Lee noted that teachers in China, unlike the United States, treated her children as if they were their own. She also remarked that despite the appearance that women in the United States were treated as equals, American women actually resembled Chinese women of pre-liberation days and were almost wholly dependent on their husbands for social and economic sustenance. As women under the Chinese communist regime were encouraged to take on high-ranking positions, their rising status enabled them to forge relationships with men based on mutual care. While Lee conceded that there were still many areas of Chinese life that could be improved, she nevertheless professed her unwavering belief in the ability of Chinese communism to bring about greater social and economic advancement in China. Lee's testimony demonstrated how stories about Chinese communism, like those on American democracy, conceived China as the country that was on the actual path toward social progress. Accounts about the superiority of communist China, by focusing on the growing social standing of women in Chinese society, further pointed to an aspect of societal life that it believed outperformed capitalist nations.

In light of the Chinese government's attention to the role of women, the story of Jade Snow Wong and her success in U.S. society held great political significance for the U.S. Cold War effort in Asia. Specifically, the tale of a college-educated Chinese American woman who was also a working professional effectively illustrated the capacity of U.S. democracy to extend equal opportunities to racialized minorities as well as to women. The transnational exchange that took place between the United States and communist countries over which form of government was superior, U.S democracy or communism, had in this way detailed how the concept of "working women" was becoming a measure of the preeminence of the American way of life. Together with the growing status of racialized minorities, the increased presence of women in high-ranking professional positions would function for decades after the early Cold War years as a measure of national progress.

The First as a Token

The appointment of deputy attorney general Delbert Wong as the nation's first Chinese American judge by California governor Edmund G. Brown marked yet another history-making event. It served, as the *Los Angeles Examiner* declared, as an added tribute to the nation's democratic process.[41] The nationwide coverage of Wong's appointment, which included mainstream papers as well as ethnic periodicals such as the *Chinese World*, the *Pacific Citizen*, and the *Pan American Chinese Weekly*, further worked, as the *Hollywood Citizen News* observed, to foster goodwill in Asia where communists "spread the impression that Americans persecute minority groups."[42] This was because the coverage of Wong's distinction as another first did not dwell on the singularity of this national accomplishment. Rather, it spoke to an overall increase in the number of distinguished Asian American professionals in California.[43] Even more noteworthy, contended the *New York Times*, was how Wong's appointment along with the election results in Hawaii had turned 1959 into a year that saw Asian Americans obtain on a national scale a foothold in American political life.

When voters in Hawaii picked Daniel K. Inouye and Hiram L. Fong to be their state representatives in Congress in 1959, they made Inouye the first Japanese American elected to the House of Representatives and Fong the first Chinese American elected to the Senate.[44] The *Pacific Citizen*, a national newspaper published by the Japanese American Citizens League, noted that the election of Inouye and Fong worked not just to foster better understanding and tolerance between the East and the West, it also served as an example to the world of American democracy at work.[45] In thus stating, it echoed the sentiments of state-generated narratives that frequently drew on the "firsts" to model the progress and credibility of U.S. democracy. The *New York Times* further detailed how the situation in Hawaii had built on similar results in California and Arizona, where voters had elected notable Asian Americans to local office. More importantly, the paper noted that the election of Inouye and Fong had come after California voted Dalip Singh Saund, an immigrant from India, into Congress in 1956, making Saund the first ever U.S. congressman of Asian descent.[46] Moreover, Wong's judgeship followed the appointment of John Aiso as the first Japanese American judge to the municipal and later, the superior court of Los Angeles.[47]

In this context, Wong's distinction as another Asian American first became a resounding testament to the progress of American democracy. As Wong figured in popular imaginations as both a nonwhite and as a representative of Asia, the mainstream press drew on Wong's distinction as the first Chinese American judge to speak not only to the nation's triumph over the color line but also of its goodwill toward all people in Asia. Despite the popularity of this signification, stories on the first did not always promote the nation's Cold War agenda. An interesting example is the *Pacific Citizen*'s discussion of John F. Aiso's 1953 appointment as the first Japanese American judge to the Los Angeles municipal court. As this paper had strongly opposed Japanese internment during World War II and had argued that the portrayal of Japanese Americans as the direct extension of people in Japan had brought about this mass incarceration, it argued that Aiso's appointment was a necessary move to establish Japanese Americans as full-fledged Americans. It further noted that California governor

Fig. 3.1. Sammy Lee (center) with gold medal at the 1952 summer Olympics. Also pictured are P. J. Capilla (left) of Mexico, who finished second, and G. Haase (right) of Germany, who took third. Courtesy of the Associated Press

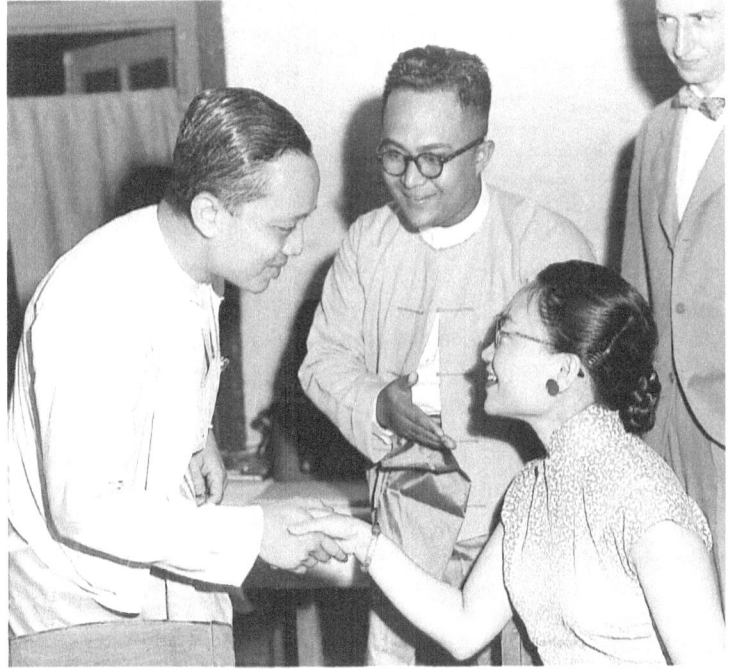

Fig. 3.2. Jade Snow Wong at a reception in Rangoon, Burma, with U Thant, minister of information, 1953. Courtesy of the Jade Snow Wong family

Fig. 3.3. Municipal Judge Delbert Wong with his wife, Dolores, and their children, Kent, Shelley, and Duane, 1959. Courtesy of Los Angeles Public Library Photo Collection

Earl Warren had benefited from making this appointment, for it quelled the negative publicity that surrounded his "anti-Japanese actions" during World War II. The *Pacific Citizen* thus declared Aiso's judgeship to be an essential demonstration that Japanese Americans, and more broadly Asian Americans, were finally being accepted into mainstream American life.[48] It sought thereby to recognize only the Americanness of Asian Americans, so as to correct the misconception that Asian Americans were representatives of Asia.

Besides revealing the circumstances where race and nationality were at odds with one another, the publicity surrounding Asian American firsts illustrated the nation's anxiety around its unmitigated attention to race as a symbol of American democracy at work. This was because the use of race to show that U.S. democracy functioned to reward personal merit also suggested the contrary—that race and not personal merit had determined an individual's access to state resources.[49] The danger that racial issues would expose how the nation remained deeply divided along racial lines and that American democracy did not work to treat all people equally prompted the *Hollywood Citizen News* to declare,

> Judge Wong was appointed and Congressman Saund was elected because they had proved their fitness for the offices they fill. They were not successful because of their race or in spite of it. They were successful because Americans do not believe that the question of race should arise in determining the fitness of anyone for office. That attitude is the best way to combat Communist propaganda. The worst way would be to attempt to select people for office on the basis of race or in proportion to the percentages of their race in the community. That would magnify the question of race instead of minimizing it.[50]

The discussion on Asian American firsts in the *Hollywood Citizen News* reveals that the nation was engaged in an ongoing struggle to reclaim the legitimacy of its democracy during the early Cold War years. In this view, Asian American firsts did not necessarily work to signify the nation's triumph over the color line, given how the *Hollywood Citizen News* had to make a case that Wong and Saund were actually qualified for the positions that they obtained. The firsts illustrated the double bind of using the accomplishments of racialized minorities to signify the credibility of American democracy. Asian American firsts worked not only to show how the nation was no longer rewarding whites based on race rather than merit; they also revealed the state's attempt to use the accomplishments of racialized minorities to deflect charges of racism.

Notably, Judge Wong called attention to the ways the first demonstrated that the nation remained deeply divided along racial lines. He developed this point of view during a 2000 interview, where he reflected on his life's accomplishments and especially his 1959 appointment as a judge of the Los Angeles municipal court. As Wong detailed, his service in the air force during World War II was a meaningful undertaking that he believed altered not only his life but also the lives of the many Chinese Americans who had enlisted. As Wong recalled,

> The service enabled the Chinese to broaden their horizons. In other words, they met and associated and lived with people who were

non-Chinese. For example, in my bomb group, I was the only Chinese flier. I was the only Chinese of the 640 flying combat members. Many of my colleagues, my fellow servicemen have never seen a Chinese, certainly have never lived with one and never fought with one. I mean we flew thirty missions together, so they got to know me and I got to know them.[51]

Service in World War II was in this view significant because it brought together a racially divided nation to interact and get to know one another. Wong's emphasis on his status as the only Chinese among the 640 combat members was further notable, given how it identified him as the racial minority in these interactions. The status of being the only Chinese thereby bestowed on Wong the task of showing dominant society how Chinese Americans were fit to be integrated. Moreover, it became Wong's preferred way of describing almost all of the key events in his professional life. The rank of being the only Chinese effectively captured how Wong saw himself in relation to dominant society.

In his discussion of his time at Stanford Law School, Wong stressed that he was the only Chinese and the only Asian in a class of fifty, with only three women and no blacks or Latinos.[52] The construct of "only" also shaped his discussion of his job as a nonpartisan civil service staff lawyer for the California state legislature and his experiences in Los Angeles, where he worked as a state employee starting in 1951. Wong noted that when he came to Los Angeles, he was only the second Chinese American attorney in Southern California. He recalled that there were about a dozen Chinese lawyers working in San Francisco, but most of them practiced immigration law and, like the lone Chinese lawyer in Los Angeles, had offices in Chinatown with a Chinese clientele. There was no Chinese lawyer working in mainstream society except him.[53] As Wong employed the notion of the only to describe his time in law school as well as his early career experiences, he took a less celebratory approach to discussing his achievements, and chose instead to use the singularity of his experiences to convey that the nation was deeply divided along the lines of race during the early Cold War years. In taking the identity of the only rather than the first, Wong further looked to convey how the opportunities that were afforded him in dominant society had also brought with them a level of social and cultural isolation.

Wong also noted that there was a productive side to being the only. As Wong recalled, this distinction had helped to set him apart from other members of his profession:

> That's [being a Chinese] an interesting aspect in that many of the counties, they have never seen a Chinese lawyer before and I was kind of a curiosity. But the plus factor was that people always remembered me. I had a name like Wong and a face to match, so when I went to different cities to try a case, lawyers would meet me for the first time and they remember me and the judges would remember me. I think that was helpful because when Pat Brown was campaigning throughout the state and I was told that he would go to some community and they would say, "Oh, you have a Chinese deputy general, and yes he has been in our court before, he has been in our city before," so it was very helpful.[54]

The fact that he was the only Chinese American had allowed his peers, and ultimately Governor Brown, to remember him. Wong believed that this was why just two weeks after Governor Brown took office, he received a call from the governor offering him the judgeship.

Notably, what Wong confirmed in this interview was that the state had actively sought to recognize and promote notable racialized minorities. As Wong recounted,

> Normally you know a judge is appointed and there is an announcement in the newspaper. But for my appointment, he [Governor Brown] asked me to fly to Sacramento. I was in Los Angeles and he asked me to fly to Sacramento and I did. And he had a press conference and he appointed me. So in fact, there is a picture of Pat Brown swearing me in.[55]

With this recollection, Wong revealed how his recognition as the first was a planned affair. Elected officials and news organizations were aware that race worked to establish the credibility of U.S. democracy, and that their support of a racialized minority's advancement showed that they were doing their part to help the nation's Cold War effort. Interestingly, it was also in this retelling of the widespread recognition that he received for his judgeship that Wong abandoned the use of the only to describe his status in mainstream society and remarked, "It was really a significant event because I became the *first* Chinese judge in the United States" (emphasis mine).⁵⁶ Public discourse on the first provided a means for Wong to use his distinction to speak to how the nation was on its way to becoming a more inclusive society. Moreover, the status of the first provided a way for Wong to situate himself as a pivotal figure and one of the pioneers who helped to make racial integration desirable.

What was therefore striking about Wong's account of his judgeship was that he did not stick to the narrative path laid out by popular discourses on the first. Unlike Jade Snow Wong, he did not use this distinction to show that hard work and individual resolve were the secrets to his success and to the successes of all racialized minorities. Judge Wong further refused to draw on his distinction as the first to let it be wholly a sign of how the nation was moving to provide equal opportunities to all. Rather, Wong sought to show how being the first did not always imply that he was the first of many. This was seen in the way he continued to draw on the notion of the only to recount his experiences as a judge. As Wong stated,

> In the earlier years anyways, every day when I went down to the courthouse I would realize that I was the only Chinese person in this room. For a time, I was the only Chinese judge in this state, for a long time. I think that I was the only Chinese at the Judges' Association. I was the only Chinese to go to the Judges' Conferences.⁵⁷

Wong also recalled,

> I think that the people who invited me to speak, and I knew that the reason, one of the reasons why I was being invited to come and make a talk was that I was Chinese and that they wanted to get my point of view. You know that we have over 200 judges in this country and specifically, why me? For example, I was invited to join the Hillcrest Country Club, which was a very exclusive club and it was mostly Jewish. It was a Jewish country club. But they wanted to broaden their base and invited me to join. But I could not because it was so expensive. I mean, on my judge's salary, I would never be able to afford that.⁵⁸

In both these accounts, Wong drew on the singularity of his distinction to problematize the notion of the first as signifying the nation's inevitable move toward social progress. As he remained the only Chinese in the courthouse for a long time after his appointment, Wong relied on his status as the only to call attention to how the first had evolved into the token. Wong attempted in this way to show how the first functioned largely to give the appearance of diversity. More importantly, he sought to make known his attempts to resist becoming a symbol of social progress. His recounting of his refusal to join the Hillcrest Country Club was thereby notable, because it demonstrated his awareness of why he was even asked to join. As Wong suggested in his recollection of this event, the Hillcrest Country Club was more invested in warding off critiques of exclusivity and elitism than expanding the racial makeup of its membership. Wong's insistence on assigning himself the distinction of being the only thus showed how he wanted to make use of this status to point to the problem of racism and to express his desire to see more efforts made to mitigate the racial divide.

As his wife, Dolores Wong, shared, following Wong's appointment as the first Chinese American judge, they were bombarded with dinner invitations from the Chinese community in Los Angeles. Even though these social engagements proved to be quite taxing, Judge Wong always accepted the invitations and rarely missed an event because he understood that the community took pride in his accomplishments and wanted to be in on the rising status of Chinese Americans in mainstream society. According to Dolores Wong, Judge Wong knew that he was a model for "what the Chinese community would aspire to become, . . . what the Chinese community would want more of." Besides taking on the role of living example of the aspirations of the Chinese American community, Judge Wong endeavored to help other Asian Americans enter the legal profession. As Dolores Wong recalled,

> I think he must have written fifty to seventy-five letters of recommendation for aspirants to law school. So we recognized that along with the recognition came the responsibility and also the responsibility to give back to the community what the community had given to us personally.[59]

Dolores Wong thus acknowledged another role that the first played. Besides working to assure the nation as well as the international community that U.S. democracy was indeed legitimate, the first served as proof for his or her community that social advancement was a viable goal. Her account reveals that many of these firsts were also actively working to help mitigate the racial divide.

During the fifteen years after Sammy Lee won his second gold medal in platform diving, the nation witnessed a proliferation of accounts that attested to how the United States was moving toward becoming a more racially integrated society; but it was also bombarded with stories about bus boycotts, sit-ins, and marches that undercut the nation's professed commitment to ending racial segregation. As civil rights activists staged protests against racist practices in the United States, they highlighted how structural racism and the inaction of government officials had led to the growth of a black underclass and argued that the nation was not moving toward the creation of a racially inclusive society. In the face of these charges, mainstream media such as *U.S. News and World Report*, *Newsweek*, and the *New York Times* ran stories that featured the successes of Asian Americans, particularly Judge Wong and Judge Aiso, for the purpose of discrediting the claims of black civil rights leaders.[60] According to a 1966 article in *U.S. News and World Report*, during "a time when it is being proposed that hundreds of billions be spent to uplift Negroes and other minorities, the nation's 300,000 Chinese-Americans are moving ahead on their own—with no help from anyone else."[61] It further argued that Asian Americans "faced even more prejudice than Negroes today. We haven't stuck Negroes in concentration camps, for instance, as we did the Japanese in World War II."[62]

In the same year that the *U.S. News and World Report* article utilized the successes of Asian Americans to attack the claims of civil rights activists, the Los Angeles Unified School District released a three-part children's book series that highlighted the accomplishments of racialized minorities in the United States, including Sammy Lee, Delbert Wong, and John Aiso. But instead of denying the realities of racism, this grade school resource sought to use the successes of notable Angelinos, Californians, and Americans to correct the effects of racism. Specifically, it hoped to "assist children of minority races in developing feelings of greater personal worth and dignity as they identify with those members of their group who have contributed to the development of our city and country."[63] Besides the attempt to address the needs of minoritized youths, the LAUSD believed that this publication could encourage white children to respect the contributions of racialized minorities to the development of this nation.

The recirculation in popular discourse of the successes of Lee, Wong, and Aiso made clear the contradictory terms through which Asian American firsts were conceived during the early Cold War years. On the one hand, the accomplishments of Asian Americans were supposed to attest to how the nation had moved away from its racist past. Civil rights activists had in this view exaggerated the effects of Jim Crow laws in keeping blacks down. They should instead redirect their attention and learn from Asian Americans so that they could help blacks get ahead in society. On the other hand, the accomplishments of Asian Americans were supposed to show how the nation was actively working to overcome its racist ways; in the case of the Los Angeles Unified School District, this entailed helping grade school children rise above the negative impact of racism. In this context, the successes of Lee, Aiso, and Wong were supposed to help minoritized children develop a healthy sense of self-esteem while prompting white children to recognize the contributions of racialized minorities to the growth of the nation so that they could move past their racist views. Notably, what both these examples reveal are the various ways Asian American firsts became vehicles to promote state agendas. These notable pioneers had revealed a continuing struggle to define the credibility of U.S. democracy through racial progress; Asian Americans figured centrally in these attempts.

CHAPTER 4

McCarran Act Persecutions and the Fight for Alien Rights

When David Hyun and Diamond Kimm were arrested as part of a nationwide sweep of aliens suspected of subversive activities after the 1950 McCarran Act went into effect, their detention illustrated how the outbreak of the Korean War intensified the nation's fear of an internal communist subversion that threatened to overthrow the government from within. The rise of anticommunist hysteria in the United States not only prompted the federal government to enact measures such as the 1950 McCarran Act for the purpose of monitoring the nation's political activities, it also led federal agents to identify the foreign-born, especially those from countries that had become communist, as most susceptible to communist infiltration. The arrest of Hyun and Kimm, two immigrants from Korea, revealed this increased scrutiny along with the fate of those who refused to acknowledge the American political system. This was because the path to Americanization that required immigrants to affirm the American way of life as the good life and the most desired in the world applied to all in the nation. The arrests of Hyun for his labor activism and of Kimm for running a pro-communist newspaper revealed which activities the federal government believed undermined the superiority of American democracy, activities it deemed "un-American." Their arrests further revealed how the federal government maintained the legitimacy of the American political system during the early Cold War years by suppressing viewpoints that called into question the capacity of U.S. democracy to ensure freedom and equality for all.

Notably, the political dealings of Hyun and Kimm also brought to the fore an understanding of "subversive activities" that differed from the state's conception of this term. As Hyun and Kimm related their fight against unjust practices in the United States to the fight for an independent Korea, they built on the nationalist activities of Koreans in the United States who had endeavored since the turn of the twentieth century to liberate Korea from the colonial rule of Japan. Following Japan's annexation of Korea in 1910 and its suppression of the 1919 March 1 demonstrations for Korean independence, many Koreans fled the country and sought refuge in places such as Shanghai, Manchuria, and Hawaii. Those who came to Hawaii joined a small but growing community of Korean immigrants who had been recruited by planters to work on the sugar plantations. These early immigrants in Hawaii coalesced with those who settled in California and in other parts of the United States to work for the liberation of Korea from Japanese rule. Despite trying to remain united in their support for the Korean Provisional Government in Shanghai, Korean nationalists in the United States were deeply divided over the political structure of an independent Korea and over which leader was to head the liberated country.[1] During World War II, the vast majority of Korean Americans backed the U.S. efforts to defeat Japan. Many, however, opposed the subsequent establishment of the American military government in Korea in 1945 and especially the unilateral decision of the Allied powers to divide the Korean peninsula along the 38th parallel. While this imposed division epitomized the strained relationship between the United States and the Soviet Union, it also spoke to the political and ideological differences of the Korean nationalist movement that had been at play since the first two decades of the twentieth century.

The historians Alice Yang Murray and Lili Kim have effectively shown in their respective studies of the political activities of Koreans in the United States that Korean American women were the backbone of the Korean nationalist movement and the principal fundraisers for nationalist activities.[2] Although this chapter will not expand on these important insights, it nevertheless seeks to highlight through an examination of the Hyun and Kimm cases an aspect of Korean nationalist activities that is rarely if ever touched upon by scholars of Asian American studies. This chapter will examine how the Cold War effectively transformed into "subversive activities" the nationalist efforts of Korean Americans to establish an independent Korea that did not cater to the interests of the wealthy landowning Korean elites. This transformation was significant, for it explained why the federal government was unable to comprehend that Hyun and Kimm's communist activities did not advocate the expansion of a Soviet empire or the overthrow of the U.S. government. Rather, they were undertakings that looked to create a Korea that was free of its colonial and feudal vestiges and that sought to challenge discriminatory practices in the United States. As the historian Bruce Cumings has argued in his comprehensive study of the origins of the Korean War, the inability of the federal government to transcend its nationalist understandings of communist activities and heed the demand of the Korean people for a full restructuring of colonial legacies captured the "essence of the American failure in Korea."[3]

Besides charting the increased efforts of the federal government to monitor the political activities of the foreign-born, the arrests of Hyun and Kimm importantly documented the rise of progressive organizations that fought for the rights of aliens and racialized minorities. Specifically, the Los Angeles chapter of the American Committee for Protection of Foreign Born (LACPFB) led a campaign to obtain stays of deportation for both Hyun and Kimm. In championing Hyun and Kimm's right to due process, the LACPFB notably adhered to an understanding of civil rights that refused to distinguish between alien rights and citizen rights. It thereby endeavored to rally public support behind the Hyun and Kimm cases by releasing a series of circulars that drew on the classic immigrant tale of struggle and assimilation to show that Hyun and Kimm were like American citizens and thus deserved equal protection under the law. Besides overcoming economic hardship on their path to realizing the American Dream, Hyun and Kimm, as these circulars revealed, refused to allow racial discrimination to deter them from believing in the advantages of the American way of life. They had become fully assimilated Americans who aspired after the same things that other Americans sought. As the LACPFB drew on these caricatures to present Hyun and Kimm as similar to other Americans, it demonstrated how the timeless tale of immigrant struggle and assimilation could be deployed to advocate for the rights of the disenfranchised and not just to affirm the benefits of the American way of life.

The Menace of Aliens and of Alien Ideologies

The federal government's conviction of the eleven leaders of the Communist Party in 1949 for teaching and advocating the forceful overthrow of the U.S. government importantly established the legality of imprisoning people, both citizens and aliens alike, for their political beliefs. This conviction not only prompted the rise of attacks against second-string leaders of the Communist Party, it also paved the way for the passage of the 1950 McCarran Act, which further stripped away the rights of those the government designated as disloyal to the U.S. Cold War effort. The trials of the Communist Party leaders, popularly known as the Smith Act trials, revealed some key reasons that the federal government found Hyun and Kimm and their political activities so menacing. Specifically, the Smith Act trials revealed how attacks against communist ideologies had built on xenophobic sentiments. The fear of the foreign not only stigmatized communist teachings, it also worked to bolster the belief that the foreign-born were likely communist agents. Additionally, the Smith Act trials showed how the federal government endeavored to frame antiracist politics as the schemes of outsiders who sought to disrupt national unity and plant the seeds of an internal communist revolution. By framing antiracist activities in this way, the federal government effectively discredited the political activities of Hyun and Kimm and presented them as evidence of how Hyun and Kimm had conspired to overthrow the U.S. government.

When the U.S. Supreme Court in 1951 backed the verdict against the eleven leaders of the Communist Party, it upheld the constitutionality of the 1940 Smith Act to limit freedom of expression. The Court also used the stigma of the foreign to distinguish the menace of communists and of communist ideologies. This was apparent in the way the Court voided the clear and present danger test used to safeguard freedom of speech by arguing that the eleven had acted as fifth column agents and not as political leaders.[4] The Court's designation of the eleven as foreign agents thus turned their ideas into the dictates of enemy regimes; the meetings they conducted no longer qualified in legal terms as discussions about communism but as evidence of the intent to forcibly overthrow the government.[5] As the historian Michal Belknap has argued in his study of the Smith Act trials, the U.S. Supreme Court was compelled to rely on the foreign stigma to identify the threat of the CPUSA because the Justice Department could not prove that the CPUSA was controlled by the Soviet Union or was engaged in military activity. If the Justice Department could have, it would have tried the leaders for sedition under the Voorhis Act.[6] In upholding the Smith Act, the Court singled out "foreign agents" and "foreign ideas" as menaces to society. In so doing, it also sanctioned government prosecutors to draw on the foreign stigma to criminalize the activities of the Communist Party as they turned their attention to legally suppressing the dealings of second-string party leaders.

As FBI agents embarked on a nationwide sweep of second-string leaders of the CPUSA, their pursuit resulted in the arrests of twelve California communists in July 1951 and of three more in August, along with the severance of one case due to the defendant's illness.[7] The Smith Act arrests in California capped off previous efforts made by federal agents to obtain the names of California's communist leaders. Three months after charges were brought against the eleven party leaders in New York, a total of twenty-one Los Angeles residents were subpoenaed, detained, and ultimately released after refusing to name the names of local communist leaders before the grand jury.[8] What distinguished the California fourteen from the other Smith Act cases that followed the trial of the eleven was that it successfully fought for the right to reasonable bail. The case of the California fourteen further gained national prominence after the U.S. Supreme Court in 1957 reversed the 1952 conviction of the fourteen, a decision that effectively restricted the capacity of the Smith Act to convict communists for sedition, as the Court called for a distinction to be made between the advocacy of an abstract idea and an action taken to forcibly overthrow the government. In addition to putting an end to the harassment of progressives under the Smith Act, the case of the fourteen showed how the initial conviction of communist leaders in California rested not on their advocacy of the violent overthrow of the government but on their supposed exploitation of blacks and the issue of racism to undermine the credibility of U.S. democracy. While this charge cast blacks as the unwitting victims of communist infiltration, it also made antiracist politics appear as the schemes of outsiders and not as the real concerns of those within the nation.

In the trial of the California fourteen, the issue of race, of why there was a prevalence of blacks in the CPUSA, entered the proceedings in a noteworthy fashion, given how none of the fourteen defendants were black.

The issue of race nevertheless became the centerpiece of the trial after government prosecutors called to the stand three black witnesses whom the government had paid to spy on the CPUSA and to testify to how the party used the fight for racial equality as a means to rally the support of blacks for the goal of Soviet expansion.[9] In addition to the testimonies of these star witnesses, the government submitted as evidence the findings of the 1954 HUAC study *The American Negro in the Communist Party*. According to this report, the international body of communist leaders had been plotting since the 1920 Second World Congress of the Communist International to use blacks to create national disunity and to incite a socialist revolution in the United States.[10] The study contended that the CPUSA, as an extension of this alien enterprise, not only aimed to "infiltrate and control the Negro population" but was also well "schooled in the techniques and tactics of achieving such control." It further urged the federal government to take seriously the capacity of the foreign to corrupt the native, given how blacks were easily duped by the lures of alien ideologies."[11]

Interestingly, when the 1954 HUAC report shifted its attention away from detailing the menace of communism and toward showing how the United States will ultimately prevail against the schemes of Soviet agents, it did so by recasting blacks as agents of their own livelihood who possessed the ability to see past the deceit of communism. To back this claim, the report cited FBI findings that among the 5,395 leading members of the Communist Party, the vast majority, or 4,555 members, were either foreign-born or born to foreign parents, while only 411 members were black. This small number confirmed, according to the study, that the "American Negro was not hoodwinked by these false messiahs."[12] The HUAC report generated in this way two competing understandings of blacks. These understandings revealed the role that blacks needed to play not only to establish the credibility of U.S. democracy, but also to establish their own legitimacy. Notably, whether blacks acted as unwitting victims of communist schemes or as discerning agents who saw through the lies of party members, both of these caricatures worked to identify aliens and alien ideologies, rather than racism, as the real threat to national security. The HUAC report further noted that "no group within the United States or elsewhere . . . realized the solution of its problems by embracing the Communist ideology." By discrediting the capacity of communist ideologies to bring about social equality, the 1954 study presented American democracy as the most effective way to mitigate the racial divide in the United States and rectify the social injustices of the world.¹³

As the CPUSA prepared to counter the government's attempts to imprison party leaders, it hired Leo Branton Jr., a black lawyer, to represent three of the fourteen defendants and, more importantly, to contest the claim that the party exploited blacks for its own gain.¹⁴ To that end, Branton performed his role as the only black person in the trial in a compelling fashion. He used the media attention to explain why blacks, because of their commitment to civil rights, had a special interest in the Smith Act trials. He also drew on his racialized identity to authenticate the charge that the federal government was the real user of blacks.¹⁵ Branton challenged the jury to consider why the government regarded blacks as qualified only to be stool pigeons. He argued that if the government was truly committed to achieving racial equality, it would have appointed a black person to the counsel table, as a U.S. attorney general, or even as an FBI agent. But as Bratton retorted,

> Maybe they can't find any who were qualified. But then again maybe I am naïve. Maybe the Communist Party has really used me. Maybe they didn't get an attorney whom they felt capable of conducting a defense for them. Maybe they got me for an attorney because they felt that they could further their scheme to use the Negro people.¹⁶

In thus stating, Branton effectively drew a comparison between the charge of how the CPUSA had used him as a lawyer and the indictment that the federal government had used blacks as informers. But as Branton highlighted, the job of defending white clients afforded more social responsibility and prestige to blacks than the job of testifying against whites. Branton sought in this way to counter the government's accusation and to emphasize that the government, not the CPUSA, had exploited blacks for its own gain.

To unsettle further the government's charge against the fourteen, Branton relied on his noncommunist affiliation to align himself with those who opposed the tenets of communism. He thus addressed the three petitioners whom he defended during trial:

> I don't believe that socialism is inevitable, and I don't believe that communism will solve all the ills of the world, but there is one thing on

which we can agree, and that is that all the effort should be put forth to treat all people with dignity, and in that part of your fight, I am with you ... and I say if that is using Negroes, then more power to you."[17]

With this remark, Branton sought to give jurors the option of being against communism while supporting the right of communists to freely express their beliefs. His attempt to authenticate how communism, like U.S. democracy, was concerned with ensuring social equality further worked to lessen the threat of communism by making familiar the foreign.

Like the Smith Act trials, the McCarran Act persecutions of David Hyun and Diamond Kimm importantly illustrated that the anticommunist hysteria of the early Cold War years was entrenched in the fear of the foreign. But in the federal government's persecution of the foreign-born, it endeavored to purge the nation of unwanted ideas by deporting—not just imprisoning—those whom it believed had engaged in subversive activities. Notably, in the Hyun and Kimm cases, as in the trial of the California fourteen, progressive organizations challenged the government's appropriation of the fight against racism to discredit the teachings of communism. The Hyun and Kimm cases not only sought stays of deportation, they also contested the government's endeavor to make the fight for racial equality seem foreign.

The McCarran Act and the Rise of the Los Angeles Committee for Protection of Foreign Born

The escalation of anticommunist hysteria following the entrance of the United States into the Korean War in June 1950 led to the passage of a measure that further curtailed the rights of aliens and citizens in the United States. The 1950 McCarran Act, otherwise known as the Internal Security Act or the Subversive Activities Control Act, passed on September 23, 1950, over President Truman's veto. It went into effect on October 22, 1950. Introduced by Senator Pat McCarran, this measure built on the 1940 Alien Registration Act (which later became known as the Smith Act), the 1918 Immigration Act, and the 1940 Nationality Act to impose stricter sanctions on the activities of aliens and of progressive organizations so that the nation could better brace itself for what Senator McCarran called the "black era of fifth-column infiltration."[18] The 1950 act connected in this way the anticommunist hysteria of the early Cold War years to the first Red Scare that had followed World War I and to the incarceration of Japanese residents on the West Coast during World War II. Together these events limited alien rights as a means to regulate political activism.

The McCarran Act mandated the registration of communist organizations with the U.S. attorney general. It instituted the Subversive Activities Control Board to review and investigate organizations that the attorney general suspected of engaging in subversive activities. The 1950 act also sanctioned the withholding of passports to alleged communists. It further bestowed on the attorney general the power to arrest aliens suspected of engaging in subversive activities, to detain them without due process, and to initiate the deportation of the accused. The attorney general was also afforded the power to suspend orders of deportation at his discretion. The 1950 act ruled that aliens charged with subversive activities could not be naturalized, while naturalized citizens could have their citizenship revoked. As the law stated, those who chose to participate in the world communist movement had "repudiated their allegiance to the United States, and in effect transferred their allegiance to the foreign country."[19] While a handful of those arrested under the Smith Act or the 1940 Alien Registration Act were aliens and were issued orders of deportation as authorized by this law, it was not until the passage of the 1950 McCarran Act that a mass drive to deport aliens and denaturalize citizens took place. One report estimated that from 1949 to 1950, the number of persons flagged to be deported jumped from 290 to 3,400.[20] While the government was unable to obtain the backing of state and federal courts to denaturalize citizens based on their political beliefs in the majority of trials that took place over this matter, the 1953 annual report of the Immigration and Naturalization Service noted that the Foreign Service of the State Department had successfully revoked the citizenship of six naturalized citizens for "fraudulent concealment of subversive membership" and two more for "bad moral character." For the remaining 327 cases of revoked naturalization, the State Department had invalidated the citizenship of naturalized citizens on the grounds that they had established permanent residence in other countries.[21]

In the month between when the McCarran Act was passed and when it went into effect, the acting commissioner of the Immigration and

Naturalization Service requested that the district director of the INS in Los Angeles submit from its confidential files a list of names of aliens in Los Angeles who were active members of the Communist Party and who were undergoing deportation proceedings. David Hyun was among the eleven aliens named. Hyun's order of deportation stemmed from his arrest on July 25, 1949, for engaging in "subversive activities." After posting a $2,000 bond, he was released the same day.[22] But just as federal agents used the time between when the McCarran Act passed and when it went into effect to compile a list of names of aliens who were party members, David Hyun banded together with other progressives in the Los Angeles area to start an organization to fight for the rights of aliens.

Prior to October 1950, those working to protect the rights of aliens met as an informal committee supported by the Los Angeles chapter of the Civil Rights Congress (CRC). The CRC was a civil rights organization that formed in 1946 and became widely known not just for its backing of key civil rights cases in the postwar era but also for its communist affiliations. On October 8, 1950, just two weeks before the McCarran Act was to go into effect, an organizing conference took place with Hyun serving as the chairman of the organizing committee to create a Los Angeles chapter of the American Committee for Protection of Foreign Born. In early 1951, Rose Chernin, who was a former CRC membership director, became the first executive director of the Los Angeles Committee for Protection of Foreign Born (LACPFB).[23] The LACPFB organized around one fundamental principle—in matters pertaining to civil rights, there should be no distinctions made between aliens and citizens. Over the next fifteen years, the LACPFB would assist in hundreds of cases of deportees who resided in the Los Angeles area. It dedicated the bulk of its resources to protesting the mass deportation drives of Mexican workers suspected of unlawful entry to the United States during the early Cold War period.[24] Although the majority of those who were served with deportation orders and sought the help of the LACPFB were from Mexico and from countries all across Europe, the committee also came to the aid of four immigrants from Japan and Okinawa, one from the Philippines, and three from Korea.[25] When the McCarran Act went into effect in October 1950, the Hyun and Kimm deportation cases were among the first handled by the LACPFB.

The Case of David Hyun

On October 21, 1950, the day before the McCarran Act was scheduled to go into effect, the acting commissioner of the INS in Washington, DC, sent a radiogram to call for the re-arrest of David Hyun, who was first held under custody and released in July 1949.[26] To ensure that Hyun remained locked up until he was deported, the INS reissued to Hyun a warrant of arrest on October 31, 1950, that overrode all previous warrants for the sole purpose of denying to Hyun the right to bail.[27] The deportation case against Hyun took place over a period of sixteen years and generated much media attention. Not only was the Hyun case the subject of radio talk shows and featured in TV news broadcasts, but numerous newspapers and magazines from across the United States also took an interest in this case. Drew Pearson, a well-known newspaper columnist and radio journalist of the early Cold War era, devoted an entire radio broadcast to discussing "the Korean Communist cell in Los Angeles" and denouncing Hyun and Kimm.[28] Despite this negative coverage, popular as well as alternative presses typically depicted Hyun in a sympathetic light. Ushering in the barrage of media attention on the Hyun case were the dramatic midnight raids staged by immigration officials who sought to arrest aliens from across the nation the minute the McCarran Act went into effect. As reported in the *New York Times*, David Hyun, age thirty-three, resident of Los Angeles, native of Korea, and citizen of China, was among the twenty arrested and served with an order of deportation that evening.[29] Together with Frank Carlson, Miriam Christine Stevenson, and Harry Carlisle, Hyun was taken by immigration officials and detained in a facility at Terminal Island, which was a strip of artificial land located in San Pedro between the Los Angeles and Long Beach harbors that prior to 1941 housed a community of Japanese American fishermen and their families, to await deportation.

The case of Hyun, Carlson, Stevenson, and Carlisle, known as the Terminal Island Four, became the first deportation case taken up by the LACPFB. Besides employing a legal team to contest the legality of the McCarran Act, the LACPFB distributed pamphlets, raised funds, and held information rallies to educate the public on the injustice of the 1950 law and to mobilize support for the Terminal Island Four. Many of the bulletins featured letters and poetry written by the four while in detention. They also included etchings that Hyun drew to cast the four as political prisoners.³⁰ Despite this campaign, the four failed to obtain a favorable ruling in the lower courts. But they scored a key victory on April 30, 1951, when the U.S. Supreme Court allowed the four to be freed on bail of $5,000 each while it reviewed whether the McCarran Act denied to aliens their constitutional right to due process. The four were released on May 3, 1951, after six and a half months of detention at Terminal Island. This victory proved to be short-lived as the U.S. Supreme Court in March 1952 upheld the validity of the McCarran Act and affirmed the authority of the attorney general to arrest, detain, and deport aliens without trial or the show of evidence and to deny to aliens the right to bail. In so doing, the Court backed the imposition of stricter sanctions against aliens as a way to police politics in the nation.

Following Hyun's arrest in 1949, the INS began gathering evidence to build a case for his deportation. While the initial hearing took place in Los Angeles, with Hyun and his legal counsel present, the INS scheduled subsequent meetings in Honolulu, Hawaii, where Hyun previously resided, over the objections of Hyun and his attorney. These hearings continued to take place in Honolulu even after Hyun was detained in Terminal Island. Moreover, from the four depositions that were conducted in December 1950, the INS decided to use the two that best supported its claim that Hyun was a member of the Communist Party. Drawing on these testimonies, the INS charged that Hyun had been instrumental in reactivating the Communist Party in Hawaii in 1945 and that in 1946 Hyun had become a member of its executive board. The INS also alleged that between 1946 and 1947 Hyun had participated in recruiting members to join the party and became a strong advocate for the redistribution of wealth in the United States. It noted that Hyun, upon moving to Los Angeles in 1947, formed a branch of the Hawaiian Civil Liberties Committee on the West Coast and in 1949, he became the educational director of the Westlake Section of the Communist Party in Los Angeles.³¹

In light of how the evidence against Hyun was gathered in his and his counsel's absence and without their submission of questions, Hyun and his legal team once again sought to have his deportation orders dismissed on the grounds that he was denied the right to due process after the Terminal Island Four had lost their case before the U.S. Supreme Court. They based their appeal on the *Wong Yang Sung v. McGrath* decision, in which the U.S. Supreme Court ruled that the deportation of aliens needed to abide by the Administrative Procedure Act. But the *Sung v. McGrath* ruling was issued four months before the outbreak of the Korean War, while Hyun's petition came after the U.S. intervention in the Korean conflict and after the Court upheld the constitutionality of the McCarran Act. Not surprisingly, Hyun lost his case before the Board of Immigration Appeals, and his order of deportation was made final on December 1, 1952. After being detained for nearly four months in 1953, Hyun was released on bond when the Ninth Circuit Court of Appeals agreed to hear his case. The Court of Appeals, however, ruled that Hyun did receive a fair hearing, and the U.S. Supreme Court agreed in May 1956. Ironically, the new evidence presented to show how Hyun continued to engage in subversive activities listed all of the events that he participated in since 1950 with the LACPFB to assist the defense of deportees.[32] In a bizarre twist, the INS notified Hyun in 1958 that his case was delayed indefinitely. Despite a few attempts to reopen his case, the Board of Immigration Appeals withdrew Hyun's order of deportation on February 19, 1966. The decision of the Board of Immigration Appeals to suspend orders against Hyun came about after the U.S. Supreme Court ruled in 1963 in a case handled by the LACPFB, *Gastelum-Quinones v. Kennedy*, that the burden of proof rested not on the petitioner but on the government to establish that the accused maintained meaningful membership in the Communist Party.

The seemingly unending series of deportation proceedings against David Hyun, while suggesting the determination of the Justice Department to rid the nation of those who went against the government's Cold War objectives, also demonstrated the resolve of Hyun and his backers to contest this crackdown. But in the struggle for a stay of deportation orders, the fight for alien rights went beyond securing to Hyun the right to free speech and entailed showing how Hyun deserved the right to reside in the United States, and to be released from the sentence of forced exile. Much of this fight involved the concession to as well as the appropriation of the terms that the federal government used to distinguish the loyalty of aliens by Hyun, his family, his lawyers, and progressive organizations as a way to obtain Hyun's release. In the brief submitted on behalf of Hyun for the Terminal Island Four case, the word "communism" was never mentioned, as his legal team endeavored to disassociate Hyun's political activities from the stigma of this enemy ideology. To establish further that Hyun was not a danger to society and was deserving of bail, the brief indicated that since the outbreak of the Korean War and his arrest in 1949, Hyun made no public remarks to indicate his position on the war or the presence of the American military government in Seoul, even though he maintained the right to do so.[33] As Hyun's legal battle against deportation demonstrated, the legitimacy of aliens in Cold War America rested in part on a particular retelling of their lived experiences. Literary critics such as Frank Chin, Jeffery Paul Chan, Lawson Fusao Inada, and Shawn Wong have called attention to the way Asian American authors of the 1950s fostered a readership among white Americans by advancing the construct of Asians as an unobtrusive group that quietly assimilated and modeled the American ideal. While Hyun and his backers definitely drew on this caricature to detail Hyun's life in the United States, they nevertheless did so in order to reclaim Hyun's political legitimacy.[34] Rather than a sign of "selling out," their use of the model minority construct demonstrated the coerced consent of Asian Americans to the American ideal.

The pamphlet entitled *Exile: The Story of David Hyun* was perhaps the most widely distributed leaflet published by the Friends and Neighbors of David Hyun, an umbrella organization composed of Hyun's backers, to rally public support behind the Hyun case.[35] It was for this reason an important piece of literature that revealed the narrative strategy deployed to convey why Hyun was unfairly served with deportation orders. Unlike the circulars generated on behalf of the petitioners of the Smith Act trials, the Hyun pamphlet did not revolve around the need to safeguard Hyun's constitutional protections. Instead, it highlighted aspects of Hyun's life and character that made it desirable to extend constitutional protections to an immigrant. In so doing, the pamphlet worked to mitigate the perceived threat that Hyun's alien status posed to national security by claiming first and foremost his Americanness. The pamphlet established the injustice of his deportation orders by recounting critical moments in Hyun's life. As the circular detailed,

> David Hyun was only seven years when he first arrived on U.S. Territory, where he was to live continuously from then on, having less and less identity with the country of his birth as the years passed, knowing no fellow-countrymen other than Americanized emigrates, and becoming thoroughly English-speaking and American in habit and thought and association.[36]

The pamphlet further conceived of Hyun as a model citizen by emphasizing how Hyun not only excelled in school but was also an active member of his church; his father, the Reverend Soon Hyun, was a prominent Methodist minister in Kauai, Hawaii. Like most Americans, Hyun was depicted as a hardworking individual who paid his way through school by working full-time on sugar plantations and in packing plants as well as by working on occasion as a gardener and a tutor. But what distinguished Hyun, according to the pamphlet, was his love of freedom. This love led him to win the island-wide oratorical contest where he delivered a speech entitled "The Meaning of the United States Constitution."

Conversations with his father were Hyun's only reminders of his early childhood in China and in Korea. The circular detailed how Hyun was first made aware of his alien status the day he enlisted for the ROTC at the University of Hawaii. He was not compelled to serve because of his alien status, but Hyun, eager to do his part, joined anyway. The pamphlet noted that Hyun not only paid for his own uniform and equipment but eventually rose to the rank of cadet captain in the ROTC. And despite being labeled an "enemy alien" during World War II, since Korea was a colony of Japan, and denied the opportunity to serve in active duty, Hyun remained committed to contributing to the U.S. war effort and joined the Hawaii Defense Volunteers. The circular further noted that Hyun never gave up on his dream of becoming a naturalized citizen: he submitted an application to become an American citizen even though he did not meet the racial qualification of whiteness that governed the nation's naturalization policy.

The pamphlet's narration established Hyun as an American by drawing on Hyun's enduring pursuit of the American Dream despite all encounters with racism. The pamphlet's emphasis of this point importantly showed how loyalty to the American ideal could be deployed to override legal dictates in determining the desirability of aliens: the immigrant's unfailing belief in the superiority of U.S. democracy affirmed the benefits and the desirability of the American way of life. Even though the INS rejected Hyun's application for naturalization, his refusal to doubt the validity of U.S. democracy together with his venture into other avenues of enfranchisement, such as becoming a professional and forming a family with his American-born wife, Mary, and their two American-born children, David Kyun and Freeland Than, effectively identified Hyun as an American while affirming the American Dream of upward mobility. Hyun's rise to the middle class and his position as head of a nuclear family thus worked to show the capacity of the heteronormative ideal to further bolster Hyun's cultural citizenship.

According to the pamphlet, Hyun fell victim to a smear campaign spearheaded by the consolidated group of sugar plantation and cannery owners in Hawaii known as the "Big Five." Even when he became a civil engineer and later an architect, Hyun never forgot his days working long hours on sugar plantations and in pineapple canneries for little pay. What Hyun sought to change was the way minorities received less pay than white workers for the same job. Following his appointment to the CIO Council Executive Board, Hyun worked to organize Hawaiian sugar plantation workers in the strike of 1946. The Big Five retaliated by dubbing Hyun's pro-labor activities "subversive" and "communistic." These charges led to Hyun's arrest in Los Angeles in 1949. But just as the circular maintained that the label of "subversive" wrongfully designated Hyun as a communist, it also argued that his alien status belied his true American self. The pamphlet identified Hyun as a fully assimilated American who spent his life believing in the American way, and built a case for why Hyun should be released from the forced separation from his wife and children. Hyun's social and political legitimacy in Cold War America was in this way established through his successful assimilation to the American ideal. His participation in the rhetorical ritual of professing an unrelenting belief in the superiority of American democracy thus revealed how the government's harassment of aliens for their political beliefs generated a selective retelling of their lived experiences. This persecution notably fostered the rise of a singular tale of immigrant struggle and assimilation that worked to affirm the superiority of the U.S. political system over communism.

By taking on this narrative approach, the Hyun pamphlet built on a narrative practice that was developed in the 1920s and institutionalized by the INS in the early 1930s to sway the attorney general to exercise his discretionary powers and suspend the deportation of aliens whose legal terms of residence in the United States had expired. While the procedure of readjustment was extended only to European immigrants during the 1930s, it gave rise to a particular approach to retelling the immigrant life that was later adopted in petitions requesting the suspension of deportation orders against nonwhite aliens. In this retelling, the focus on the undying loyalty of the deportee to the American way of life along with the social and economic toll that the departure of the deportee would exact on family members in the United States became key to prompting a reconsideration of deportation orders.[37]

Following the passage of the 1950 McCarran Act, another proviso was added that granted the attorney general the power to suspend the deportation of aliens to countries that would result in the physical persecution of the deportee. This stipulation significantly provided Hyun and his supporters another avenue to fight his deportation after the cessation of U.S. military involvement in the Korean conflict and the surfacing of reports on the repressive tactics of the Republic of Korea president Syngman Rhee. The bulk of this activism took place between 1954 and 1956. The umbrella organization Friends and Neighbors of David Hyun, in addition to releasing the pamphlet *Exile: The Story of David Hyun*, published a booklet that was submitted as evidence in court and distributed publicly so as to rally the public to petition Attorney General Herbert Brownell to suspend the order of deportation against Hyun. Notably, this booklet contained over a hundred affidavits of signed documents and letters requesting the suspension of Hyun's deportation orders from Methodist ministers, dignitaries of different nations, U.S. labor leaders, leaders of progressive organizations, prominent members of the armed forces, and journalists. It revealed how the immigrant tale worked not only to establish Hyun as deserving of residence in the United States but also to petition the federal government to adhere to the principles by which it professed to abide.

As indicated by the title, *I Am Appealing on Behalf of My Youngest Son . . .* , this booklet was written as the plea by David's renowned father, Reverend Soon Hyun, to have orders of deportation against his son halted.[38] The writing of this circular from Reverend Hyun's perspective was strategic, given his prominence in the Korean nationalist movement and his status as a political refugee in the United States. Reverend Hyun wrote of his past dealings with Rhee and how Rhee's jealousy of Soon Hyun's rising influence in Hawaii together with his criticism of Rhee's dictatorial ways prompted Rhee to dispatch thugs to assault Soon Hyun with threats to kill him if Hyun did not retract his criticism of Rhee. Soon Hyun further shared how two of his close associates, Kim Koo and Lyuh Woon Hyung, were assassinated because of their opposition to Rhee. The elder Hyun reported these occurrences as he sought to describe the fate that awaited his son if he were to be deported to the Republic of Korea. Besides using his personal relations with Rhee to substantiate the claim that David faced execution if deported, Soon Hyun employed his immigrant experience to remind the government that the United States had been a place of refuge for Korean nationalists escaping the political persecution of Japanese colonial rule in Korea. Hyun described how he returned to Korea from Hawaii in 1907 in order to help organize and participate in the 1919 March First Movement for Korean independence from Japanese colonial rule. But the bloody crackdown on this movement by the Japanese government prompted Soon Hyun to retreat to Shanghai and then to Hawaii. At the time of the writing of this appeal, Hyun was seventy-five years old and a retired minister, having served in the Methodist Episcopal Church in Hawaii and Korea for nearly forty years, mostly in Kauai. As the elder Hyun described how he was able to raise his family here, he not only affirmed that the United States was a place of refuge but also beseeched the nation to continue to be that safe haven for freedom fighters.

Despite the overwhelming evidence of physical persecution in the Republic of Korea, the U.S. Supreme Court in May 1956 denied David Hyun the right to be considered for this provision because of his charge for sedition. Attorney General Brownell also withstood public outcry and refused to exercise his discretionary powers and suspend Hyun's order of deportation. As noted earlier, for undisclosed reasons the INS delayed Hyun's case indefinitely in 1958 and withdrew its orders of deportation in 1966. One can only surmise that the reason that the U.S. Supreme Court and the attorney general refused to consider the factor of physical persecution in 1956 and that the INS delayed the deportation of Hyun indefinitely in 1958 was that the U.S. government did not want to verify that Rhee was a tyrant—to do so would be to admit that the U.S. involvement in the Korean conflict failed to spread democracy there. In this view, the upholding of deportation orders for Hyun and their subsequent delay reveal the government's attempts to maintain the integrity of U.S. Cold War objectives. Additionally, the Hyun case was significant for historicizing how the classic immigrant tale had documented in some instances the coerced consent of aliens to model the superiority of U.S. democracy in order to establish their legitimacy in the United States.

Fig. 4.1. Terminal Island, 1950. Etching by David Hyun for the Los Angeles Political Prisoners' Welfare Committee Information Bulletin. Courtesy of the Southern California Library for Social Studies and Research

Fig. 4.2. Diamond Kimm before the House Committee on Un-American Activities, 1955. Courtesy of the Korean American Digital Library, University of Southern California

Fig. 4.3. David Hyun with his wife, Mary, and their children, David Kyun and Freeland Tahn, 1953. Courtesy of the Southern California Library for Social Studies and Research

Fig. 4.4. Diamond Kimm with his wife, Fania Goorwitch, in the Democratic People's Republic of Korea, 1965. Courtesy of the Southern California Library for Social Studies and Research

The Case of Diamond Kimm

While the case of Diamond Kimm did not generate as much media attention as the Hyun case, it nevertheless importantly illustrates that communist teachings allowed Koreans in the United States to connect their struggle against racial inequality to the fight against U.S. military presence in Korea. Kimm first came to the attention of the INS after a warrant for his arrest was issued in 1941 for unlawfully remaining in the United States after his student visa had expired in July 1938. Kimm immigrated to the United States in 1928 to study at the University of Southern California. After he completed his B.S. degree in geology, Kimm obtained an M.S. in the same field in 1933 before accepting a postgraduate position in metallurgical engineering at Colorado School of Mines. His wife and son, who accompanied him to the United States in 1928, returned to Korea in 1934. Although Kimm intended to return to Korea in 1937 before his visa expired the following year, he stayed in the United States after war erupted between China and Japan. In March 1942 the presiding inspector for the INS granted Kimm the right to voluntary departure in lieu of deportation and allowed arrangements to be made within sixty days after World War II ended.[39] As detailed in the legal files for the Kimm case, Kimm made several attempts to contact the INS at the end of World War II but received no reply. Ten days before the outbreak of the Korean War, the INS held a hearing to follow up on Kimm's 1941 warrant of arrest for remaining in the United States after his visa had expired. The stated purpose of this 1950 hearing was to assess whether Kimm qualified for a suspension of deportation orders.

Kimm's next hearing took place the day before the 1950 McCarran Act went into effect. It ended with the INS inspector asking whether Kimm was a member of the Communist Party. Before Kimm could answer, his counsel pled the First and Fifth Amendments on Kimm's behalf. On March 13, 1951, Kimm was arrested under the McCarran Act and served with an order of deportation that overrode the previous order of voluntary departure. The order became final in January 1952. But given that the stated purpose of Kimm's hearings was to assess whether Kimm qualified for the suspension of deportation orders and not the gathering of evidence to substantiate the charge of subversive activities, his legal counsel sought to have the orders revoked on the grounds that Kimm was denied the right to due process. Kimm's attorney also used affidavits from the Hyun case to petition for a stay of deportation orders and to establish that Kimm, like Hyun, faced the threat of physical persecution if deported to the Republic of Korea. Despite these appeals, the U.S. Supreme Court ruled on June 13, 1960, that the burden of proof fell on Kimm to show that he was not a member of the Communist Party and was thereby eligible for suspension of deportation orders. The Court, however, reinstituted the original order of voluntary departure and in 1962, at the age of sixty, Kimm left for Czechoslovakia en route to the Democratic People's Republic of Korea after thirty-four years of continuous residence in the United States.

The hearings that took place in 1950 focused on Kimm's activities with the progressive Korean-English–language newspaper *Korean Independence*, a Los Angeles–based bilingual weekly that was known for its anti-Rhee stance. Kimm helped found the paper in 1943, and in 1948 he left his career as a chemist to be its full-time managing editor as well as the principal writer of its Korean section. During one of Kimm's 1950 hearings, the INS inspector expressed disbelief that Kimm subsided on a meager income of $150 to $200 per month with no public assistance after he devoted his full attention and time to running the weekly paper.[40] Despite operating on what appeared to be a very small budget, Kimm managed to publish two thousand copies of the *Korean Independence* per week and to distribute these copies to progressive communities across the United States as well as in Great Britain, China, Canada, Mexico, and Cuba.[41] In 1948 the California State Senate Committee on Un-American Activities identified the *Korean Independence* as a communist front. In a 1956 HUAC report, the government built on this charge and declared that the *Korean Independence* was a vehicle used to promote the policies of the Soviet Union and the Democratic People's Republic of Korea.[42] Following the outbreak of the Korean War, these charges prompted the FBI to harass not only Kimm but his colleague John Juhn as well, as Juhn was another founding member of the *Korean Independence*. Like Kimm, Juhn left the United States for the Democratic People's Republic of Korea after he was served with an order of deportation in 1955. Another staff member, Sang Rhee Park, was also arrested in San Francisco. Notably, the district judge who presided over Park's case decried the oppressive tactics of the INS and released Park in 1952.[43] The *Korean Independence* folded in 1957 after thirteen years of operation.

Progressive organizations, particularly the LACPFB, protested the federal government's efforts to shut down the *Korean Independence* and to persecute Kimm for his political beliefs. The LACPFB argued that the government, in seeking to suppress dissent against the U.S. war effort in Korea, had violated the freedom of the press. To rally public support behind Kimm, the LACPFB distributed leaflets, as it had for Hyun, which highlighted certain aspects of Kimm's life and character that made the denial of the right to free speech as well as the order of deportation appear not only unjust but also undesirable. But unlike the circulars published on Hyun's behalf, the LACPFB could not show to the same extent that it did for Hyun that Kimm's life mirrored the image of the American ideal. Unlike Hyun, Kimm appeared to be without family in the United States, and despite being highly educated, he was not a distinguished professional in the mainstream labor market but worked during the time of his arrest for an ethnic newspaper. In short, Kimm did not conform to the heteronormative middle-class ideal of the early Cold War years. The circulars that were printed on Kimm's behalf thus drew on his service with the Office of Strategic Services from January to September 1945 to establish Kimm's loyalty to the United States.[44]

During World War II, Kimm had been approached by the OSS to carry out a special mission in Korea. He agreed to the terms of this assignment and resided in Catalina, an island off the coast of Southern California, for nine months. While in Catalina Kimm underwent intensive physical and mental training as the government prepared to have him sent to Korea as an American spy working to obtain Japanese military secrets. Because of this service, the OSS presented to Kimm and to the other Korean volunteers the opportunity to become U.S. citizens. As Kimm explained in a hearing before the INS, he and the other volunteers declined this offer because they deemed it better for the U.S. war effort if they returned to Korea as Koreans.[45] However, they never got the chance to carry out their mission, as World War II ended before the date of their scheduled flight to Korea. Even still, the circulars that were distributed to rally the public behind Kimm's campaign used Kimm's stint with the OSS along with the praise that he received for his service to show that Kimm was loyal to the United States. These leaflets argued that it would be unjust to exile a patriot and likened Kimm's deportation to the Republic of Korea to a death sentence. To substantiate this claim, the circulars called attention to Rhee's track record of disposing of people who opposed his regime. They further noted that a newspaper in the Republic of Korea, the *Dong-Ah Daily*, had identified the weekly that Kimm managed, the *Korean Independence*, as a seditious publication for its anti-Rhee stance. With this in mind, the threat of physical persecution that awaited Kimm if he were deported back to the Republic of Korea was a likely factor that prompted the U.S. Supreme Court to reinstate in 1960 Kimm's original order of voluntary departure.

Following the U.S. Supreme Court's ruling, Kimm began to write letters to the embassies of Czechoslovakia and the Soviet Union requesting permission to immigrate to those countries. Because he was required to show that he was fit for residence there, Kimm submitted with each application a biographical sketch in the form of a sworn affidavit. The submitted life narrative notably presented a version of Kimm's life that differed from the accounts detailed during the many INS hearings before state and federal courts and in the circulars that were released to rally the public behind Kimm's fight against deportation. The multiple renditions of Kimm's life offered a striking look at how the Cold War had structured and dictated Kimm's retelling of his lived experiences.

In the version that Kimm submitted to the embassies of Czechoslovakia and the Soviet Union, he revealed that he was married to Fania Goorwitch, also known as Fania Bernstein, who was an immigrant from Poltava, Russia. Even though Kimm had always maintained that he was married, all of the legal documents and proceedings that were generated up until the issuing of this affidavit to support his voluntary departure listed Kimm as being married to Soon Syuk Cha. Kimm did disclose in an INS hearing that sometime after the departure of Cha and their son, Charles Kimm or Chang Keun Kimm, from the United States to Korea in 1934, he and his wife had decided to part ways because they did not know if they would ever be reunited. One reason Kimm never mentioned his relationship with Goorwitch may have been his desire to keep Goorwitch from being persecuted, since she had helped Kimm manage the *Korean Independence*. Another reason may have been that the interracial coupling of Kimm and Goorwitch—one that was most likely not forged in the nation's courts—could heighten the threat that Kimm, an alien and a racialized minority, seemed to pose to white America. But in this endeavor to secure his and Goorwitch's deportation and admission to a communist country, Kimm drew on the legitimacy afforded to married couples in order to obtain that permission.⁴⁶ It was in this context that he outed his relationship with Goorwitch and disclosed their union in official state records.

The affidavits that Kimm and Goorwitch submitted to Czechoslovakia and the Soviet Union thus provided a different framework through which Kimm and Goorwitch's lived experiences and political activities were to be judged. This new lens importantly shaped the retelling of their life narratives. Even though Kimm's affidavit fell short of confirming that he was a member of the Communist Party, it allowed both his opposition to Rhee and his pleading the Fifth to signify his leftist leanings. The affidavit made no mention of Kimm's service with the OSS but stressed his participation in the struggle for Korean independence from Japanese colonial rule. Because of this shift in focus, the story of Kimm's immigration to the United States also revealed a different beginning. It started not with his arrival in California in 1928 to study at USC, but with Japan's quashing of the 1919 March First Movement in Korea, whereupon Kimm fled to Manchuria to join the resistance efforts there. The affidavit detailed how Kimm returned to Korea to complete his schooling in Seoul before coming to the United States to continue his fight for Korean independence. It further noted that Kimm on two separate occasions had sought to return to Korea, but the political instability in East Asia had kept him in the United States. Goorwitch's affidavit established her leftist leanings by listing all of her union and LACPFB activities. It further disclosed that she had worked closely with Kimm and helped him run the *Korean Independence* from 1951 to 1957.⁴⁷

The Kimm case, besides offering this revealing look at the many ways U.S. Cold War politics influenced the writing of life narratives, illustrated a key issue that was not so evident in the Hyun case. It revealed that U.S. racism undermined the credibility of U.S. democracy in the minds of many immigrants, while fueling the appeal of the Communist Party as the political entity most committed to ensuring freedom and equality for all. The impact of U.S. racism on the political activities of the foreign-born was made explicit during Kimm's 1955 HUAC hearing. In this hearing, HUAC officials presented Kimm with a letter that had been intercepted in North Korea by U.S. officers. Dated November 15, 1948, the letter was addressed to the prime minister and the foreign minister of the Democratic People's Republic of Korea, Kim Il Song (Sung) and Pak Hon Yong, and was penned by Lee Sa Min and Sonu (Sunoo) Hak Won, both from Seattle, Washington.⁴⁸

The missive notably detailed an earlier attempt to deliver a letter to Kim Il Song (Sung) and had named Lee Sa Min, Pyon Chun Ho, Kim Kang (Diamond Kimm), and Alice Hyon (Hyun), who was the elder sister of David Hyun, as the coauthors of this earlier correspondence. It further indicated that the attempt to deliver this other correspondence was made by Alice Hyun's son, Wellington Chong (Chung), who had left for Prague, Czechoslovakia, from Los Angeles.[49]

In addition to identifying Kimm as one of the members of this pro–North Korea contingent, the 1948 letter provided a summary of recent political events in the United States that centered on the election of President Harry S Truman along with a quick assessment of the U.S. State Department's conflicting opinions on the withdrawal of troops in Korea. It also expressed a strong desire to secure a steady correspondence between Korean communists in the United States and their comrades in Korea. The letter requested the exchange of periodicals, newspapers, and other pertinent news information. Besides suggesting the establishment of points of liaison in Eastern Europe, the letter listed two addresses in the United States, one in Seattle and one in Los Angeles, which could be used for the exchange of information. The November 1948 correspondence further devoted a section to detailing the activities of Korean Communist Party members in the United States.[50]

The letter noted the assembly of twenty-six Korean communists in the United States under two front organizations of the CPUSA, the Democratic Peoples Front League and the Progressive Party Support Organization, which were both formed to assist in the liberation of Korea from foreign incursion. The twenty-six consisted of thirteen members in Los Angeles, one in San Francisco, five in Seattle, one in Chicago, four in New York, and two in Washington. The letter recounted a mass meeting held by the two front organizations and listed four organizational points that party members unified under. What was striking about these four points was their transnational scope. The first two points called for the withdrawal of the U.S. army from South Korea, given that the USSR had withdrawn its troops from North Korea, and for the recognition of the North Korean Democratic People's Republic. Point 3 demanded the "abolition of segregation of Orientals in the U.S.," and the final point called for the unconditional release of communist leaders in the United States.[51] Taken together, these four points detailed how the Communist Party provided for some

Korean Americans a way to bridge their fight for a liberated Korea with their struggle for civil rights in the United States. Notably missing from these directives were declarations of support for the expansion of a Soviet empire and intent to conspire for the violent overthrow of the U.S. government.

Since the discovery of the 1948 letter by U.S. officers, one of the letter's principal authors publicly retracted his commitment to organizing for racial equality through the Communist Party. A year before Kimm was called to testify, Harold W. Sunoo (Sonu Hak Won) had testified before HUAC.[52] Unlike Kimm, Sunoo relied on this hearing to reclaim his legitimacy in the United States and adhered to a narrative advanced by HUAC to make known his newly found patriotism. Sunoo's testimony consisted of two essential components. It detailed the event that triggered his disillusionment with the Communist Party and it named names in order to establish his loyalty to the United States. As Sunoo recollected, his eyes were finally opened to the repressive tactics of communist regimes during a visit to Czechoslovakia en route to North Korea, where he witnessed firsthand the disconnect between communist "theory" and "practice." This startling revelation prompted his immediate return to the United States so that he could tell the truth about what he had seen. Sunoo stated that he sought foremost to reach out to Koreans and Chinese in the United States who had been "fooled by the false promises of communism."[53] In addition to detailing this moment of reckoning, Sunoo recounted the process through which he encountered the Communist Party, a narrative that was replete with naming names and places. Interestingly, even though Sunoo identified several key Korean communist leaders in the United States, such as the Reverend Lee Sa Min, Alice Hyun, and Wellington Chong (Chung), none of those named were currently in the United States. All were either in the Democratic People's Republic of Korea or in Czechoslovakia.

According to Sunoo, he did not become affiliated with the Communist Party until he came to Seattle from California in 1943 to teach and to study at the University of Washington, Seattle. Sunoo noted that during this time he encountered an "unpleasant experience in finding [a] house and in the race prejudice problem." When asked by a HUAC official to clarify whether he was discriminated against because he was Asian, Sunoo replied, "That was the thought I had at the time. Of course it was wartime and very difficult to find a house and a room."[54] As Sunoo responded by explaining how he misrecognized the reason behind his inability to find housing in 1943, he looked to suppress the way racism worked to shed a negative light on the American way of life. Instead, he looked to reclaim his political legitimacy in the United States before HUAC. Sunoo further developed this contrived misunderstanding to account for why he strayed from the American way. As he recollected, he had followed the counsel of his friends and joined the Communist Party, believing the party to be a political entity that was committed to fighting against racist practices in the United States. But as Sunoo affirmed, racism was just a tool that communists used to attract members rather than an issue that the party was actually concerned about remedying. Sunoo also noted that the vast majority of Korean intellectuals had favored communist ideologies. Given that he had considered himself an intellectual and did not want to be left out of this circle, Sunoo dedicated himself to the cause of creating a free Korea by joining the Communist Party.[55] By casting his participation in the party as part of an intellectual trend, Sunoo sought to further downplay the fact that communist ideologies provided many Korean Americans a viable way to link their fight against racism to their fight for Korean independence. This framing bolstered the view that racial equality and national sovereignty were the false promises of communism that masked the actual goal of Soviet expansionism.

HUAC officials took turns commending Sunoo for coming forward and sharing his testimony. A remark made by one of the officials tellingly demonstrated how communism had functioned in the United States to mean only one thing:

> All of us recognize that there are inequities and injustice but most of us feel that those things will be better worked out and sooner worked out within the framework of the American Constitution than within the satellite orbit of the Soviet Union.[56]

As this statement indicated, the ritual of communist baiting went beyond fostering a particular way of talking about race and U.S. democracy. It also developed a way of thinking about the Cold War that recognized only two real sides to this war, the United States and the Soviet Union. The HUAC trials were in this respect a social practice that worked to maintain this view of the Cold War; any disavowal of U.S. democracy became a support of Soviet expansion, and the possibility that Korean independence and racial equality could be achieved outside the U.S. political system was ignored.

Notably, Kimm's 1955 HUAC hearing revealed the development of a filter to discern the political leanings of Korean Americans. While the hearing began with the conventional mode of ascertaining Kimm's identity, it nevertheless took a different approach to determine Kimm's political affiliation. The presiding officials did not ask whether Kimm was a member of the Communist Party. They asked him where he was born. Kimm's reply that he was born in Long Chun did not, however, adequately answer the question. When one official clarified that what mattered to them was whether Long Chun was located in North Korea or in South Korea, Kimm retorted, "It is extreme north."[57] What this exchange thus revealed was the development of a geographic nomenclature that worked not only to identify Kimm's activities as subversive but also to fix what that subversion signified. It showed how the political border that the Allied powers of World War II had unilaterally established in Korea along the 38th parallel had in effect turned all those from the northern part of the Korean peninsula into communist adherents who aspired foremost to aid the realization of the Soviet agenda. Since Kimm was born in the northern portion of the Korean peninsula, this fact automatically transformed his lifelong struggle to establish an independent Korea that did not cater to the interest of wealthy landowning elites into "subversive activities" that aided the expansion of the Soviet empire.

The use of this geographic designation to cast Kimm's political undertakings as incompatible with the ideals of freedom and equality was further played out when Kimm maintained that his work with the *Korean Independence* did not break any laws. Rather, Kimm contended that it was the attack on his paper that violated the First Amendment. In response to Kimm's charge, one of the presiding HUAC officials snapped,

> It is strange to me to have a man in this position who said he was arrested for deportation, he is not a citizen, charging us with violating the Constitution, this North Korean.[58]

As the official ended this retort by dubbing Kimm a "North Korean," he affirmed by drawing on this contrived nationality the view that communists worked only to advance totalitarian ideals. Freedom and equality, on the other hand, were American ideals. Denying to Kimm, a North Korean communist, his right to due process and freedom of the press became in this way an essential component to maintaining the credibility of the American political system. It showed that the belief that freedom and equality were essentially American ideals hinged upon the suppression of activities and viewpoints that sought to prove the contrary. Moreover, the dubbing of Kimm as unlawful and alien by the very policies that denied to him his civil liberties bolstered the view that communism was incompatible with American democracy.

As the historian Bruce Cumings has remarked in his comprehensive study of the origins of the Korean War,

> It is extremely difficult for an American, with inbred assumptions about society and the good life, to understand or appreciate Korean political and social conflicts in 1945. An American's understanding of communism in the United States held little relevance for understanding communism in Korea. . . . Communism in Korea in 1945 did not signify a deeply held worldview or adherence to an authority residing in the Kremlin, or a commitment to Marxist internationalism. It was a specifically Korean communism. Its adherents could scarcely be distinguished from nationalists and conservatives in their belief in the uniqueness of the Korean race and its traditions and the necessity to preserve both, or in their understanding that a unique Korea required a unique solution.[59]

Cumings's remark relied on essentialist views of culture, race, and nationality to talk about the social and political impediments that prevented many in the United States from recognizing multiple understandings of communist activities, but his statement nevertheless showed communism to be a culturally and historically specific concept. Communism meant different things to different people; the cultural specificities that shaped the meaning of communism made it difficult to translate ideas across borders, whether political, cultural, or racial.

In the stigma of communism that emerged following the government's crackdown on Communist Party leaders and on the foreign-born, we see how the state used the fear of difference to maintain the status quo by ridding the nation of unwanted ideas and people. This fear informed the construction of a U.S. nationalist understanding of communism that kept government officials from recognizing that Korean communists were striving for the ideals of freedom and equality. The belief that all communist activities aided the expansion of the Soviet empire thus prevented the federal government from recognizing why Hyun and Kimm regarded the American military presence in Korea as another colonial regime. Equally important was that the stigma of communism worked to discredit and to make foreign Hyun and Kimm's struggle against racist practices in the United States. This effect notably revealed how assimilation into the American way of life entailed espousing an unwavering belief in the superiority of U.S. democracy, where the American way was the only way.

The Hyun and Kimm cases also revealed the efforts of progressive organizations to fight against the stigma of communism and of the foreign. An important legacy that organizations such as the LACPFB left behind was the insistence that the struggle for civil rights resist attempts to distinguish between the rights of aliens and the rights of citizens. This particular view of civil rights crucially posited the notion that alien rights did not necessarily work to affirm the social and political legitimacy of citizens. Rather, alien rights exposed the power of the state to regulate the activities and the viewpoints of all in the nation. The insistence that no distinction be made between alien rights and citizen rights looked in this way to limit the federal government's authority to strip people of their constitutional protections. By fighting for the civil rights of Hyun and Kimm, the LACPFB had thus endeavored to safeguard the rights of a nation.

CHAPTER 5

Advancing Racial Equality and Internationalism through Immigration Reform

Writing just six months after the communist revolution in China, the historian Gerald T. White argued for immigration reform that would make the treatment of Chinese equal to that of other groups in the United States as a way to better relations with Asia. In an article penned for the *Far Eastern Survey*, he acknowledged that many deemed the liberalization of immigration policy toward the Chinese "inadvisable," given how the Chinese government had become communist. But White asserted that it was precisely that event that prompted him to call for the repeal of discriminatory measures against the Chinese.[1] White considered upholding the nation's "moral idealism" to be the best defense against communist infiltration, and called upon the federal government to grant the right to family unification to Chinese Americans and eliminate the unfair quota system. He believed that the extension of equal rights to the Chinese could realize the nation's ideals not just by affirming the credibility of U.S. democracy abroad but also by fostering better cooperation between the United States and noncommunist countries in Asia.

Fifteen years would pass before the nation saw the repeal of immigration quotas based on race and national origins with the enactment of the 1965 Immigration and Nationality Act. Nevertheless, White's piece suggests that the call for immigration reform related racial equality to the advancement of the U.S. Cold War foreign policy of internationalism. The federal government's enactment of the 1965 measure illustrates the nation's shift toward an internationalist approach to containing communism, a shift that enhanced the importance of extending equal rights to Chinese in the United States. It further charts the activism of Chinese American organizations and their efforts to obtain equal rights through immigration reform during the decade and a half prior to the passage of the 1965 act.

Following the communist revolution in China and China's entrance into the Korean War, the perceived foreignness of Chinese Americans accounted not only for the federal government's heightened scrutiny of their political activities but also for the efforts taken to secure their civil rights. As the federal government endeavored to carry out the policy of communist containment, the perception that Chinese Americans were direct extensions of people in China cast them as likely agents for subversive activities. But as the cultural critic Christina Klein has argued, the government's endeavor to contain communism through internationalism also importantly turned the perceived foreignness of Chinese Americans into a trait that enhanced their value as Americans.[2] The rise of "two Chinas," the communist People's Republic of China and the noncommunist Republic of China in Taiwan, together with the racialization of Chinese Americans as the foreigners-within, enabled the split in the treatment of Chinese Americans during the early Cold War years. Besides influencing state actions, this racial formation importantly shaped how Chinese Americans went about securing their loyalty to the U.S. Cold War effort and, by extension, their legitimacy in Cold War America by denouncing the Chinese communist government. Notably, many also drew on this transnational political articulation of Chinese loyalty to show Chinese Americans as deserving of equal rights, particularly the right to family unification.

Since the 1905 Chinese boycott of American goods, Chinese Americans had participated in Chinese nationalist activities as a means to improve the social standing of Chinese in the United States. As the historian Shih-shan Henry Tsai has detailed, the boycott, which broke out in Shanghai and spread throughout China, marked the culmination of fifty years of frustrations that the Chinese government harbored against the United States and its restrictive immigration policies against the Chinese.[3] Chinese in the United States and in Hawaii also took part in this sanction as a protest against the unfair stipulations of Chinese exclusion. While the 1905 boycott did little to alter the nation's immigration policy, it did prompt, as Tsai argued, Chinese Americans to channel their efforts into building a strong and modern China in order to obtain greater rights and freedoms in the United States. American racism thus fueled Chinese nationalism.[4] Following the 1905 boycott, the activism of Chinese Americans greatly contributed to the overthrow of the Qing dynasty and the formation of the Republic of China in 1911. During the postwar years, the endeavor to improve the social standing of Chinese Americans through nationalist activities saw many endorse the corrupt Chiang Kai-shek's Chinese Nationalist Party, the Kuomintang, over Mao Zedong's Chinese Communist Party. The nationalist activities of Chinese Americans were in this way intricately connected to their fight for civil rights.

This chapter examines the 1951 Chinese extortion racket and the 1956 Chinese slot racket to show that the nation's expansionist goals in Asia worked together with Chinese loyalty to promote the extension of civil rights to Chinese Americans through immigration reform. These two events illustrated the government's attempts to monitor systematically the activities and loyalty of Chinese in the United States following the communist revolution in China. However, they also revealed the rise of a public discourse over whether a strict immigration policy or a liberal one was more effective to advancing the nation's Cold War objectives. The aftermath of these two rackets saw the increased support of policy makers for an internationalist approach to ensuring national security and for immigration reform that placed Asian Americans on par with white Americans and Asia on equal footing with Europe. It further witnessed the efforts of the Chinese press in the United States to rally public support for such a reform, as well as the activism of the Chinese Consolidated Benevolent Association and the Chinese American Citizens Alliance to get such a measure passed.

When the mainstream press reported in 1951 that Chinese communist officials were holding for ransom the relatives of Chinese Americans who remained in China, the widespread coverage of the Chinese government's attempts to extort money from overseas Chinese alerted the nation to the Chinese extortion racket. News of this racket led the federal government to halt the remittance of money to China and to go after backers of the Chinese communist government. To show that the Chinese in the United States supported the U.S. Cold War efforts in Asia, Chinese American leaders professed their cooperation with state initiatives. They also made use of the government's expressed concern for ransom victims to press for immigration reform that granted Chinese Americans the same right to family unification that was afforded to white Americans. By emphasizing that Chinese Americans were connected to a broader overseas contingent that opposed the Chinese communist government, Chinese American leaders sought to enhance the importance of Chinese support for the U.S. Cold War effort in Asia and the importance of immigration reforms to securing that allegiance.

Five years after reports on the extortion racket first surfaced, mainstream and Chinese news media in the United States focused on another seemingly more dangerous threat. The 1956 Chinese slot racket, a black market in illegal Chinese immigration, was said to threaten national security as it provided a channel for Chinese communist spies to enter the United States. To thwart the federal government's call for a systematic inquiry into the legal status of Chinese in the United States, Chinese American leaders not only reaffirmed the loyalty of the Chinese to U.S. Cold War efforts in Asia, they also called for the repeal of restrictive quotas set by the nation's immigration policy as a way to curb Chinese illegal immigration. Chinese American leaders thus built on previous petitions and argued that immigration reform was a necessary civil rights measure that worked to strengthen ties between the United States and Asia. These efforts, as this chapter details, contributed to the passage of the 1965 Immigration and Nationality Act, which placed Asian Americans on par with white Americans and Asia on an equal footing with Europe.

As the political scientist Daniel J. Tichenor has detailed in his study of the 1965 Immigration Act,

> As much as Cold War competition created new imperatives for ending the U.S. government's long silence on black civil rights, it raised equally compelling concerns about the explicit ethnic and racial biases in national immigration policy.[5]

Tichenor notes that postwar presidents such as Harry Truman and John F. Kennedy "linked the causes of civil rights and immigration reform" and argues that Lyndon B. Johnson signed the 1965 Immigration Act after being convinced that immigration reform promoted the goals of U.S. foreign policy and of civil rights.[6] The legal scholar Gabriel Chin in his analysis of the 1965 measure similarly contends that Congress was driven by the need to bring about racial equality when it voted to abolish immigration quotas based on race and national origin. The historian Mae Ngai also supports this view in her study of this immigration act.[7] But despite arguing that the 1965 reform "was very much akin to civil rights and desegregation," given how both movements against racial discrimination incited mass support and the backing of white liberal elites, Ngai refrains from calling the 1965 law a civil rights reform, because the 1965 act, unlike civil rights reforms, did not advocate on behalf of black Americans or endeavor to ensure rights entitled to citizens.[8]

This chapter unsettles the differences detailed by Ngai and hopes to broaden the scope of what counts as civil rights reforms to include the 1965 Immigration Act. It contends that the reason immigration policies foregrounded the concerns of Asians over blacks was that nationality and not just skin color defined the alterity of Asian Americans. Asians were racialized differently than blacks were, resulting in immigration policies that limited the rights and privileges of Asian Americans, and necessitated that the fight for civil rights for Asian Americans include immigration reform. This study examines how Chinese American leaders saw the rights of aliens as connected to the rights of citizens. It develops the historian Sue Fawn Chung's analysis that the struggle for Chinese civil rights consisted largely of fighting to repeal discriminatory measures against the Chinese that were enacted in the nation's immigration policies.[9] With these points in mind, this chapter highlights the importance of immigration reform to securing the rights of all and to promoting the credibility of U.S. democracy during the early Cold War years.

Establishing Chinese Loyalty in Cold War America

A little over a year after Mao Zedong stood before the hundreds of thousands that gathered at Tiananmen Square and proclaimed the founding of the People's Republic of China on October 1, 1949, the *Los Angeles Times* noted that Chinese in Los Angeles "quietly wondered if and when they will be 'shipped off' to relocation centers."[10] The San Francisco–based English-language Chinese weekly *Chinese Press* similarly reported that many feared the possibility of suffering the "same plight" that Japanese residents on the West Coast had endured during World War II.[11] The *Nation* cautioned against dismissing the rising wave of anti-Chinese sentiments and urged Chinese residents not to trust the assurances of officials in California, given how Japanese Americans were issued similar promises but found themselves in relocation centers.[12] The talk of internment stemmed from concerns over the increased assaults against Chinese Americans after the People's Volunteer Army marched into Korea to fight what Mao called the "War to Resist America and Aid Korea" just three months into the outbreak of the Korean War. As the Cold War turned "hot" in Asia, this shift crucially unsettled the image of the Chinese as allies of the United States and generated doubt over the loyalties of Chinese in the United States.

As the *Nation* reported, after communist China entered into the Korean War, the police in Los Angeles refused to restrain rowdy patrons at Chinese-owned cafés from beating up "Chinese Commies."[13] Moreover, the Chinese embassy described how Chinese shops in the United States were stoned in protest against Chinese aggression in Korea.[14] The *San Francisco Chronicle* further recounted how "Caucasian visitors" to the city's Chinatown openly expressed resentment against the Chinese, while the *Los Angeles Times* noted that a local Chinese merchant, "fearing that his American friends would boycott him," canceled orders for Chinese Christmas cards.[15] But what was perhaps even more noteworthy than this chronicling of incidents of anti-Chinese sentiments was how these stories retold such cases in order to demonstrate why such attacks were unwarranted. For instance, the *Nation* defended the Chinese who were sympathetic to the new government in China by arguing that such feelings did not necessarily translate into their support of "Chinese aggression in Korea" or "subversive intentions" against the United States. It maintained that the real issue was whether the Chinese "were to be castigated as 'disloyal' simply because they may object to certain phases of American foreign policy in the Far East?"[16]

Despite the *Nation*'s attempt to make the case that a group's political leanings should not be the basis for discrimination, the majority of mainstream and Chinese media in the United States looked to assure readers of the loyalties of the Chinese. These articles, written mostly between December 1950 and February 1951, showcased Chinese allegiance in two key ways. While many emphasized how Chinese in the United States denounced the communist takeover of China and supported the Republic of China in Taiwan, other reports, such as those that appeared in the *Chinese Press*, quelled talk of Chinese internment by arguing that just as the nation realized how Japanese evacuation "was not only unnecessary but an affront to a loyal segment of Americans," it needed to recognize the same for the Chinese. The English-language Chinese weekly verified Chinese loyalty by pointing out that the vast majority of Chinese in Los Angeles in 1950, like the Japanese in 1942, were Americans, as an estimated 75 percent of the city's ten thousand Chinese were American-born.[17] It further looked to show how the Americanness of Chinese was founded not just on their legal status as citizens but on their similarity in lifestyle and taste with Anglo Americans.

In its attempt to substantiate the successful assimilation of Chinese Americans, the *Chinese Press* relied on the findings of an editorial published by the *Des Moines Register* that was written from the viewpoint of an Anglo American. As the editorial made clear, its push to see the Chinese as Americans aimed to deter the nation from repeating the blunders of World War II by calling for the internment of Chinese on the West Coast. The author drew on his observations of a trip to California to argue that "San Francisco's Chinatown just isn't very Chinese any more." According to his inspection, this locale had transformed into a place that was known for its award-winning recipe for zucchini and shrimps and that brought together youths of different cultural backgrounds to listen to the Cal-Washington game at soft-drink parlors. The Americanness of the Chinese was further evident as Chinese families were spread out all over the city and resided in some of the wealthiest neighborhoods.[18] In view of these changes, the *San Francisco Chronicle* noted that it "hurt" the Chinese to hear their fellow Americans making cracks at them on streetcars and condemned such behavior as "boorish" for displaying "a lack of respect for American citizenship."[19]

Besides advocating the recognition of the Chinese as Americans, news features sought to establish loyalty to the U.S. Cold War effort as a distinguishing feature of one's Americanness. The *Los Angeles Daily News*, for instance, framed the visible presence of Chinese at rallies across California for the U.S. Defense Bond campaign to be a "cheering verification" of their Americanness.[20] Similarly, the *Chinese World* drew on the participation of Chinese Americans in the armed forces in both World War II and the Korean War to identify them as Americans.[21] It also looked to prove Chinese Americans' loyalty to the U.S. Cold War efforts in Asia by printing an excerpt of a letter from an injured soldier, which exemplified what it believed to be the "general attitude of Chinese-Americans":

> I have no regrets in fighting the Chinese Reds in Korea.... Although the soldier across from me may be distant cousin, the important thing is that the northern Chinese choose to believe in Communism and I believe in the American way of life.[22]

As the paper likened the participation of Chinese Americans in the Korean War to their desire to "come out of Chinatown," it further employed this comparison to underscore how the willingness to fight a "distant cousin" spoke to the disidentification of Chinese Americans with their culture of ancestry and to their identification as Americans. Their support for the U.S. Cold War effort in Asia was in this view a defining feature that made them part of the nation.[23]

As these accounts show, the recognition of Chinese as Americans became linked to the promotion of the U.S. Cold War efforts in Asia. Stories that focused on Chinese Americans' ties to their homeland politics did not discredit accounts of the successful assimilation of Chinese in the United States. Rather, they worked to enhance the display of Chinese loyalty. Interestingly, even though news features took note that the majority of Chinese Americans were well aware of the corrupt Chiang Kai-shek regime, they also made clear that in this Cold War the clearest expression of anticommunism was support for Chiang. For instance, the *Los Angeles Times* explained that the reason the Chinese in China backed Mao was that they lost faith in Chiang's leadership. It refrained, however, from applying this rationale to Chinese Americans. Instead, the *Times* argued that the "majority of Chinese in the U.S. still support Chiang, mainly because he was not a Communist." Other news features similarly contended that if a vote were to be taken among Chinese Americans, Chiang would carry 99 percent of the vote.[24]

The *New York Times* noted this display of Chinese loyalty in its December 3, 1950, report on the banding together of representatives of Chinese American civic, business, and cultural organizations in New York City to protest the Chinese communist government's intervention in the Korean conflict. The resulting proclamation, delivered by the president of the Chinese Consolidated Benevolent Association (CCBA), bore the signatures of sixty organizations with a combined membership of forty thousand Chinese. Besides opposing the entrance of China into the Korean War, the statement denounced the People's Republic of China as a puppet regime of the Soviet Union and as an extension of Russian imperialism. It also declared the support of New York's Chinese American population for Truman's decision to send naval forces to Taiwan. The proclamation backed the government's assurance that this deployment was a protective measure initiated to support the recognition of Taiwan as the true representative of the Chinese people rather than a covert attempt at territorial expansion.[25]

Days after the publication of the *New York Times* article, the *Los Angeles Times* reported that the city's ten thousand Chinese residents also came forward to denounce communist China as a "Russian stooge." Once again, the protest statement issued through the CCBA pledged the loyalty of the Chinese to the U.S. Cold War effort through their support of the U.S.-backed Chinese Nationalist government in Taiwan. The proclamation made clear the opposition of Chinese Americans to the seating of communist China in the United Nations.[26] Taken together, these accounts established that the ties that Chinese Americans maintained to their "country of origin," which now included Taiwan, did not call into question their Americanness just as long as these ties promoted the U.S. Cold War agenda. Chinese complicity with the terms of national loyalty bolstered in this way their legitimacy in Cold War America while preventing the internment of Chinese Americans as a means to ensure national security.

The Chinese Press in the United States

A year after the initial wave of concerns over the impact of China's entrance into the Korean conflict on the social standing of Chinese Americans, reports surfaced that Chinese Americans were receiving letters from relatives in China requesting money in order to secure the release of family members held captive by officials in southern China. The Chinese extortion racket became the first of two rackets that prompted the U.S. federal government to initiate a systematic monitoring of the political activities of Chinese Americans during the early Cold War years. This racket also incited the two leading national organizations representing the interests of Chinese Americans, the Chinese Consolidated Benevolent Association and the Chinese American Citizens Alliance, to step forward and protest such scrutiny. Besides revealing the activities of these two organizations, a study of the Chinese extortion racket reveals the influence of the Chinese press in the United States. One such newspaper, the *Chinese World*, deserves special attention because in 1949 its editor, Dai-ming Lee, started an English section for the express purpose of shaping mainstream media coverage of the viewpoints of Chinese Americans following the communist revolution in China. Lee sought in this way to prevent the Chinese Nationalist government from being the sole voice of overseas Chinese.

As the historian Him Mark Lai has argued, Chinese news media in the United States from the late nineteenth century to the mid-twentieth century were best categorized by the political views that they espoused. Since they lacked sufficient funds to employ full-time reporters in China and the United States, they relied heavily on cable news sources based in China and Hong Kong and carried translations of stories from English-language dailies. What therefore distinguished one paper from the next were the editorial materials and the political beliefs that each paper upheld. Editors of Chinese newspapers were often leaders of the Chinese American community.[27] During World War II and the Cold War, Chinese politics heightened the importance of the Chinese press, especially the eighteen dailies in the United States and Canada.[28] While both the Kuomintang (KMT) and the Chinese Communist Party (CCP) sent agents to organize the support of Chinese Americans, the operatives sent over by the CCP were few in number and never established a formal political organization in the United States. The advancement of views espoused by the CCP was largely undertaken by progressive organizations such as the Chinese Hand Laundry Alliance, the Chinese Youth League, the Chinese Workers Mutual Aid Association, the Chinese American Democratic Youth League, and to a lesser extent, the CPUSA. The New York–based

China Daily News served as the only significant news organ for Chinese progressive organizations.[29]

The KMT, in contrast, had a formal political base in the United States. After the communist takeover of China, KMT operatives actively suppressed any show of support among Chinese Americans for the Chinese communist regime and more importantly, any criticisms launched against the Chinese Nationalist government. Pro-Chiang factions infamously deployed hooligans to crash the twelfth-anniversary celebration of the Chinese Workers Mutual Aid Association on October 9, 1949, when it became apparent that the association intended to use its annual event to commemorate the founding of the People's Republic of China. Despite receiving threats a few days before, the Chinese American Citizens Alliance (CACA) honored its agreement to rent its San Francisco auditorium to the Mutual Aid Association.[30] As a result, the CACA headquarters was subjected to unlawful search and seizure by an unspecified group of "outsiders." Following this incident, Y. C. Hong, president of the CACA, issued a statement affirming not just the anticommunist position of the CACA but also the organization's belief in the freedom of assembly.[31] Meanwhile, KMT supporters amplified their scare tactics and created a hit list of fifteen people.[32] They bought out the majority of Chinese newspapers in the United States, which were often fledging businesses, and exerted pressure on papers that they did not control in order to deter them from criticizing the Chiang regime. Although the *China Daily News* bore the brunt of such attacks, as ruffians hired by adherents of the KMT manhandled vendors that sold this paper, the liberal bilingual nonpartisan *Chinese Pacific Weekly*, the *China Weekly*, and the *Chung Sai Yat Po* were also negatively impacted.[33]

In the midst of these events, the *Chinese World*, one of two leading Chinese dailies in San Francisco, did not refrain from antagonizing KMT supporters.[34] For instance, it exposed the Anti-Communist League headed by the Chinese Six Companies, the San Francisco chapter of the Chinese Consolidated Benevolent Association, to be a front for Chinese Nationalist activities and accused the Six Companies of funneling to the KMT money that was raised to support American soldiers in Bay Area hospitals. In retaliation, the KMT-controlled newspapers dubbed the *Chinese World* a supporter of Mao and charged that it hid its support for communist China only after China entered the Korean War against the United States.

Fearing an assault on its premises by pro-Chiang factions, the *Chinese World* hired armed Pinkerton Detective Agency guards to keep a twenty-four-hour watch over its offices while the San Francisco Police Department Subversive Detail came to assess the situation, only to rule the matter an in-house dispute.[35]

The *Chinese World*'s opposition to both the KMT and the CCP stemmed from the paper's longtime support of constitutionalism. Since its inception in 1891, the founder, Tong King Chong, used his weekly paper, the *Mon Hing Yat Bo* (the predecessor to the *Chinese World*), to denounce autocracy in China. Tong was deeply influenced by the teachings of the philosopher Kang Youwei, who traveled to the United States in 1905 to promote the creation of a constitutional monarchy in China. This rivaled the efforts of Sun Yat-sen, who also sought the support of Chinese Americans for the establishment of a Chinese republic. The *Mon Hing*, which was one of the most influential papers among Chinese in the United States, became a daily in 1906 and changed its name to the *Chinese World*.[36] The paper continued its espousal of a constitutional government in China and backed the Chinese Democratic Constitutionalist Party, which was founded in the United States in 1927. This political leaning prompted the *Chinese World* to oppose not just the rise of communism in China but also the one-party dictatorship of Chiang's Nationalist regime. Thus the *Chinese World* was one of the few papers that was not a mouthpiece for the KMT or the CCP. Multiple forces worked to limit the political activities of Chinese Americans, and there were various motivations behind Chinese American support for U.S. Cold War efforts in Asia. What set the viewpoints of the *Chinese World* in dialogue with those of mainstream media was the outbreak of the Chinese ransom racket. Following mainstream attention to this matter, the *Chinese World* ran daily editorials as well as news features on the extortion racket from approximately November 1951 to April 1952.

The Chinese Ransom Racket

On November 10, 1951, the *San Francisco Chronicle* reported that an international ransom racket operated by the Chinese communist regime was affecting hundreds of Chinese families in the United States and throughout the world.³⁷ The *Chronicle* charged the Chinese government with extortion, reprinting as evidence excerpts of telegrams and letters that Chinese families in San Francisco received from relatives in China with requests for money to secure the release of their kin from torture at the hands of communist officials. According to the *Chronicle*, extortion appeals generally ranged from $500 to $10,000; the highest known ransom, $100,000, was purportedly extracted in six installments from a family that ran a grocery business in Phoenix, Arizona. The paper maintained that these requests emerged after the U.S. government set limits on the amount of voluntary remittances sent to China, causing a shortage of the foreign currency the Chinese government needed for the purchase of Malayan rubber, petroleum, and other essential materials to support its involvement in the Korean War.

The bulk of these appeals originated from Toishan, a city in the Guangdong province of southern China, from which the vast majority of Chinese in the United States immigrated; the *New York Times* reported, however, that the actual sending of letters to overseas Chinese and the handling of money transfers were processed in Hong Kong. It estimated the amount extorted from Chinese Americans to be in the millions, with over 60 percent of Chinese in New York, San Francisco, Boston, Chicago, and Washington having received letters. However, the *Times* noted that extortion appeals made up only a fraction of the 1.5 million letters received from China per week and that Chinese progressives in New York believed the racket to be the concoction of Chinese Nationalist propaganda.³⁸ Despite these insights, U.S news media reported on the far-reaching effects of this shakedown and detailed how it impinged on the lives of Chinese in Canada, Japan, Southeast Asia, Taiwan, and Hong Kong. The racket was also shown to have affected Chinese residents in every state, including families in Wichita, Kansas, and Madison, Wisconsin.

The proliferation of reports on the Chinese extortion racket following the *San Francisco Chronicle*'s feature, besides generating national interest in this issue, increased the influence of the Chinese press in the United States. *Newsweek*, for instance, credited the *Chronicle* for being the first to disclose the racket to the "Caucasian world" and duly noted that Chinese newspapers in the United States had spearheaded the reporting of this scandal.³⁹ As *Newsweek* and other mainstream newspapers and magazines relied heavily on editorial materials from the *Chinese World* for details on specific ransom cases along with updates on how Chinese in San Francisco were responding to the crisis, the English-language Chinese daily found itself in an interesting situation. It began to carry stories from newswires that based their accounts of the racket on findings that had first appeared in its own pages. The national and international interest in the Chinese ransom racket transformed the *Chinese World* into a primary source from which mainstream papers extracted information. The attention generated by these media outlets, in turn, shaped how the *Chinese World* reported on this matter.

The widespread coverage of the Chinese ransom racket prompted the federal government to look into the matter. California state senator William F. Knowland reportedly made contact with the U.S. State Department within two days of the release of the *Chronicle*'s feature and was instructed by Dean Rusk, the assistant secretary of state, to compile the names of ransom victims and their stories. As Rusk sought to submit a report to the United Nations asking that China be placed under UN sanctions for extortion, he considered the collection of this data to be essential. Rusk also confirmed receiving news about similar blackmail attempts against the Chinese in Southeast Asia.[40]

In addition to the State Department's request for a systematic gathering of information on ransom victims, the Treasury Department sought to stop the remittance of funds through Hong Kong to China, voluntary and otherwise, proclaiming this act to be "absolutely illegal."[41] It argued that, because payments sent to Hong Kong supported the military efforts of China, they violated the Foreign Assets Control Regulation that was passed just weeks after China entered the Korean War. To get a handle on this issue, the Treasury Department sent over a dozen federal agents to San Francisco, New York, Boston, and Chicago.[42] After a weeklong inquiry, officials confirmed the findings of the State and Justice Departments and of the Chinese embassy, which estimated that fifty thousand Chinese in the United States had received ransom letters.[43] The Treasury Department responded to this report by calling for a mass resistance by Chinese Americans to extortion demands. The ultimate goal was to crack down on the transfer of all funds to China; to this end the two top Treasury officials overseeing the government's investigation set up office in the Federal Reserve Bank of San Francisco and urged Chinese residents to come forward with information not just on ransom requests but on the channels used by those in Hong Kong to remit money to China.⁴⁴ In so doing, the federal government's use of the ransom racket to control the flow of money to China importantly blurred the line that separated remittance requests from extortions.

Following the initiatives taken by the federal government to monitor the activities of Chinese in the United States, the *San Francisco Chronicle* ran a feature that for the first time since its coverage of the ransom racket criticized leaders of the Chinese Six Companies for not pressing Chinese residents in San Francisco to submit information, despite the prodding of Treasury officials and a private meeting with Senator Knowland, who reportedly asked the heads of the Six Companies to facilitate a systematic inquiry. The *Chronicle*'s reproach further built on its understanding that Chinese leaders in Chicago had already conducted a mass meeting to instruct the city's Chinese residents to refrain from responding to ransom demands.⁴⁵ The scrutiny over the inaction of the Six Companies honed in on reports that many were reluctant to submit ransom demands to U.S. officials since they feared that this disclosure would place family members in China in harm's way. As Kenneth K. Lee, ex-president of the Chinese Six Companies, explained,

> We do not plan to make a complaint to the United Nations about it. We think registration (of the racket's victims) cannot take place. If we asked victims to register we feel that many would not come in for fear of reprisals against families behind the Iron Curtain in China. We cannot issue a proclamation against making ransom payments because much as our people respect Six Companies' leadership we doubt that the proclamation would be obeyed.⁴⁶

As a result, it seemed hardly surprising that the *Chronicle* claimed that Chinese leaders in San Francisco were unwilling to support the systematic registration of ransom victims. Even still, the *Chronicle*'s scrutiny of Chinese leaders was notable, given how the paper drew on the anguish of those who fell prey to ransom demands to boost the nation's moral imperative to fight against communist China in the Korean War. Stories on ransom cases that appeared in the *Chronicle* thus focused on the despair of extortion victims in order to publicize the cruelty of the Chinese government, which reportedly killed the wife of a Sacramento man because she was "old and useless" even after he paid three ransoms totaling four thousand dollars. The *Chronicle* reported on extortion victims who "mobilized" against blackmail attempts by taking their own lives because it was "the only way out," and further relied on tales of suicide to underscore how Chinese Americans struggled with ransom demands.[47]

Along with the *Chronicle,* popular magazines such as *Life* and *Time* focused on the anguish of ransom victims in order to portray Chinese Americans in a sympathetic light. The *Life* feature on the Don Mar ransom case, for instance, called attention to the enormous distress that the receipt of ransom demands had exacted on the Chinese. It detailed how Mar, despite living in Wichita, Kansas, with less than a hundred Chinese families, had received ransom demands and was agonizing over the safety of his wife and daughter-in-law, who were being threatened with severe punishment by officials in China. The magazine's focus on Mar's suffering not only looked to generate public understanding of the plight of ransom victims, but also worked to avert the accusation that those who paid ransoms were backers of communist China. But given how the *Life* article also aligned its coverage of the ransom racket with state objectives, it did not use this sympathetic portrayal to foster public support for immigration reforms that promoted family unification as a way to end the racket. Instead, it cast Chinese familial devotion as an obstacle to the cessation of ransom demands and the reason that "Don Mars all over the country will be expecting telegrams for a long time."[48]

Like the Mar case, the Chin Hong incident emerged as one of the most widely covered ransom stories in the United States. Its appeal was based on the racket's tragic consequences for a forty-year-old laundryman from New York. According to *Time* magazine, Hong, who had already sent his entire life savings of seven hundred dollars to buy relatives out of jail in China, was driven into a frenzy after he received a follow-up request for another thousand dollars. The additional request prompted Hong to bolt out of his apartment and attack police officers with a butcher knife. Officers shot and killed Hong in what was reported to be an act of self-defense. According to the *Time* article, the brutality of the Chinese government had brought about Hong's tragic end. Moreover, his attack on police officers was an act of insanity. Notably, the Treasury Department used this incident to bolster its call to enforce the Trading with the Enemy Act.[49] The Treasury Department claimed that the crackdown aimed to protect the welfare of Chinese Americans, but halting the remittance of funds to China was intertwined with the need to distinguish the United States from the cruelty of the Chinese communist government.

The widespread coverage of the Joe Lum Jang case further showed how mainstream media used the ransom racket to demonstrate the superiority of U.S. democracy. The *Time* feature on Jang, for instance, highlighted the ruthlessness of the Chinese communist regime by drawing on Jang's anguish upon learning of the sufferings of his sixty-three-year-old mother, who had returned to China after raising her five "Americanized" sons.[50] As the article reported, shortly after the communist takeover of China, Jang received word of his mother's arrest by communist officials for mistreating her daughter-in-law. The officials reportedly placed a mark on her face, branding her an "unlawful woman," and forced her to stand before the village courthouse without food or water. After a day and a night of this punishment, Jang's mother, Sin-shee Jang, paid a fine of $1,000 and was released. In November 1951, Jang received a cable from his cousin requesting the remittance of $1,750. According to the *Time* report, Jang discovered that his mother was accused of being disloyal to the Chinese government and that she and four other villagers, with heavy chains wrapped around their necks, were forced to kneel on chain links and denied food and water before they confessed to the crime. Until the receipt of money, Jang's mother was to walk around bearing a sign that read "landlord." Jang and two of his brothers decided that "Mother has been tortured enough. We want her to die now." A few weeks after Jang mailed his refusal to pay, he received word that his mother had killed herself by jumping into a well. The subsequent focus on Jang's disgust with "those god-dammed communists" for forcing him to make this decision showed the Chinese regime to be ultimately responsible for his mother's demise, while affirming that the United States acted in the interest of Chinese Americans.[51]

While mainstream coverage of the Mar, Hong, and Jang cases detailed the various responses of Chinese Americans to ransom demands, it nevertheless utilized their plight not just to underscore the cruelty of the Chinese communist government but also to generate public sympathy for the anguish of Chinese Americans. With this in mind, the *San Francisco Chronicle*'s reproach of the Chinese Six Companies for failing to organize a systematic registration of ransom victims did not necessarily seek to discredit the loyalty of Chinese Americans to U.S. Cold War efforts in Asia.

Rather, it reflected the need to alter portrayals of Chinese Americans from anguished victims to agents of mass resistance after the federal government prohibited the sending of money to China via Hong Kong.

In an attempt to show the growing resistance among Chinese in San Francisco to paying ransoms, the *Chronicle* highlighted how Dai-ming Lee, editor of the *Chinese World*, had sent a cable to Mao protesting the persecution of relatives of overseas Chinese and was gathering letters as proof of Chinese extortion.[52] While the mention of Lee's activism aimed to demonstrate how Chinese Americans were acting against ransom demands, it also detailed how Lee had used the English section of the *Chinese World* to generate that understanding. Lee, in so doing, followed in the footsteps of the paper's founding editor, who during the Boxer Uprising had created a separate English-language paper, the *Oriental and Occidental Press*, for the sole purpose of persuading San Franciscans that Chinese in the United States were not affiliated with the Manchus and did not support their campaign to rid China of Christians.[53] As Lee also endeavored to shape public opinion about Chinese Americans, he notably redeployed the narrative strategies used by the mainstream press in his coverage of the ransom racket in order to advance the issues that he believed mattered most to Chinese Americans.

The *Chinese World* ran its first English feature on the racket in June 1951. In early September it reported that the "account clearing" leveled against overseas Chinese had reached a new peak and, according to newspapers in Macau, had generated hundreds of thousands of dollars for Red China.[54] Just days before the *San Francisco Chronicle*'s exposé of the racket, Lee reported on the receipt of numerous inquiries from Chinese residents in San Francisco on how best to handle ransom demands. He also noted that C. H. Kwock, editor of the *New China Daily Press*, had reported a similar situation in Honolulu, where over a hundred families received letters and cables with ransom demands.[55] After the start of the federal inquiry into the matter, Lee asked readers to come forward with ransom letters and advised ransom victims to issue a joint resolution to stop paying ransoms.[56] In addition to wiring a cable to Mao, Lee sent an open letter to Yeh Chien-ying, governor of Guangdong, reminding the Chinese government of its promise of "favorable treatment" to overseas Chinese.[57]

Besides portraying Chinese Americans as resisting ransom demands, Lee employed the expressed concern of the U.S. government for extortion victims to advance the interests of Chinese in the United States. Like leaders of the Chinese Six Companies, Lee noted ransom victims' fear that the disclosure of names of family members in China would result in the Chinese government's retaliation against their kin, but he used this fear to underscore that the federal government could assist victims by allowing their relatives in Hong Kong and even in China to come to the United States. By pressing for changes in immigration policies, Lee emphasized how the State Department, and not just the Chinese, could act to prevent extortions. He thus argued for the need to expedite the processing of visa applications in Hong Kong and for the liberalization of refugee quotas to include those persecuted in China.[58] As Lee contended, the long delays that took place in the handling of Chinese visa applications due to laborious background checks gave the Chinese government more opportunities to issue ransoms. He also beseeched "warm hearted Americans" looking for ways to help ransom victims to urge the State Department to permit the entry of spouses of American citizens of Chinese descent, both husbands and wives.[59]

Lee asserted that the State Department, by taking measures to promote family unification, could deter ransom victims from taking their own lives. He explained that Hong Kong, far from providing Chinese refugees a safe haven, was plagued with overcrowding and offered little hope for a decent living. As a result, many abandoned the idea of fleeing to Hong Kong and sought relief in death. Thus, even though Lee used the Jang and Hong cases to demonstrate the cruelty of the Chinese government, he also showed how restrictive U.S. immigration policies contributed to the problem.[60] Lee also asked the government to consider the ramifications of suspending all remittances, especially because remittance restrictions of $100 a month already caused great financial hardship among those stranded in Hong Kong and Macau.[61] In putting forth these ideas, Lee not only used the plight of extortion victims to defend U.S. involvement in the Korean War, he also advocated for immigration reform. In this view, Chinese allegiance to the U.S. Cold War effort became a means to promote the equal treatment of Chinese Americans by granting to them the same right to family unification that was afforded to other Americans.

Notably, mainstream media did not mention how the nation's restrictive immigration policies enabled the extortion racket to have such a deep impact on Chinese Americans, even though the papers drew heavily on the *Chinese World* for information on the ransom demands. This selective reporting revealed how their use of the racket sought foremost to uphold state objectives. Conversely, the *Chinese World*'s stories on the racket cast Chinese Americans as victims of racist immigration laws, not just of ransom demands. These accounts did not discuss how the disclosing of names, besides endangering the lives of their kin, could reveal the forging of fictive family ties that long functioned as an illegal means of Chinese immigration to the United States, and that accounted in part for the government's discriminatory procedures in screening Chinese applicants for entry to the United States. This explains why Lee, despite having gathered nearly a hundred ransom letters, refused to submit them to the State Department and awaited the decision of the Chinese Six Companies on how best to comply with the government's investigation, even though the *Chinese World* was known to be at odds with the Six Companies for its support of the KMT.[62]

As Lee's push for immigration reform relied on the compliance of Chinese Americans with state directives, the appeal to liberalize immigration policies came on the heels of accounts that the Chinese Six Companies were meeting to discuss the proposals of the Treasury Department and of Senator Knowland. The *Chinese World* also reported a meeting of forty ransom victims to make known how the Chinese were organizing against the racket. It recounted how conferees voted to circulate a petition to be penned by Lee, demanding that Mao and Yeh Chien-ying, the governor of Guangdong, crack down on extortions even though Lee had already wired such letters to Mao and Yeh. The attendees also decided to send an appeal to the U.S. government to seek its help with the racket. This appeal was to be signed by American citizens who were victims of Chinese extortions. A separate petition, however, was to be drawn for alien victims to be submitted to organizations such as the Committee for a Free Asia, which promoted reform and development in Asia. Although participants requested that the government not release the names of relatives in China, they nevertheless signed a declaration stating their full support of the Treasury Department's move to ban remittances in order to show that Chinese Americans were not afraid of public disclosure.[63] On December 14, 1951, the petition, which bore the signatures of 1,101 Chinese Americans, was sent to Mao.[64] Shortly before the sending of the petition, the Anti-Communist League of the Six Companies brought together eighty-six representatives of Chinese associations in the United States to adopt a proclamation that called for the collection of ransom letters and their submission to the State Department for the filing of a UN report. The proclamation also declared plans to start a worldwide anti-extortion movement.[65] The Chinese in Singapore, the Philippines, and Hong Kong responded to the appeals of Chinese in the United States and sent letters to China protesting the ransom racket.[66]

Following this show of Chinese cooperation with state initiatives, the Treasury Department publicly praised the leadership of the CCBA. While the Treasury attributed the activism of Chinese Americans to their understanding that the only way to end the racket was to stop sending remittances and paying ransoms, it also stressed that sending money to China, voluntarily or otherwise, was illegal and carried a maximum penalty of $10,000 and ten years in prison.[67] According to the *Chinese World*, officials in Guangdong also took note of ransom protests and responded by deploying ten thousand communist agents to investigate the matter. The Chinese government further invited Chinese delegates in Hong Kong to survey the situation in China. However, only nine out of the twenty-five associations in Hong Kong responded, as the other sixteen feared reprisals from the Chinese communist government.[68] In view of these events, Lee contended that Chinese American activism had effectively led to declines in the remittance of money to Hong Kong and in the number of extortion attempts from China. He made these claims despite findings that showed that the amount of money wired from Hong Kong to China during the first two weeks of December 1951 was greater than the amount for all of November, and reports that detailed the persistence of unfair imprisonment of relatives of overseas Chinese in China.[69]

As accounts of ransom cases diminished after two months of widespread mainstream coverage of the Chinese extortion racket, this decrease may account for why the State Department never filed a report to the United Nations. But while the state's concern over extortions lessened, the activism among Chinese Americans continued. Following the noted drop in the number of ransom cases, the Chinese Six Companies together with Chinese merchants in San Francisco petitioned the Treasury Department to modify its ban on remittances to China. In backing this appeal, Lee used his column to remind the state of the deep sacrifices that Chinese Americans made to support the U.S. Cold War effort in Asia.[70] Instead of highlighting how communist officials tortured the relatives of Chinese Americans, Lee called attention to how many suffered in China due to the lack of resources to buy food. He even started a petition for those who wanted to help the starving in China to sign, and also asked concerned citizens to mail a letter to their congressmen and senators.[71] On March 11, 1952, the Chinese Chamber of Commerce of San Francisco sent an appeal to the Treasury Department, requesting special permission for Chinese Americans to remit "family maintenance" funds to China, but the Treasury Department turned down the request.[72] In late April, the *Chinese World* reported on the resurgence of ransom demands and described this renewed racket as more aggressive in its demand for foreign dollars to be sent to China. As it contended that the best way to halt these recurrent requests was to allow for the families of Chinese Americans to come to the United States, the paper continued its efforts to appropriate the nation's fight against communism to advance the interests of Chinese Americans.[73]

What brought an abrupt halt to stories on the ransom racket was the report that the government had issued a fifty-three-count federal indictment on April 28, 1952, against the China Daily News Inc. and two of its officers, the president, Eugene Moy, and the former managing editor, Albert Wong, for publishing advertisements of banks in China such as the Nanyang Commercial Bank Ltd. and the Overseas Chinese Service Bank of China. These banks, which had branches in Hong Kong, were known to conduct special investigations for customers trying to locate the whereabouts of relatives in China and to assist in purchasing stocks of Chinese corporations.[74] But the charge against the *China Daily News* for violating the Trading with the Enemy Act did not just seek to end the funneling of U.S. dollars into China. It also sought to shut down the sole news organ of Chinese leftist organizations in the United States, one that was already under the constant scrutiny of FBI agents and KMT supporters.[75] This endeavor, as Moy declared, was in clear violation of the freedom of the press.[76] The federal government was able to draw on the Trading with the Enemy Act over the Smith Act to shut down the *China Daily News* for its political beliefs, demonstrating that immigration restrictions, which resulted in family separation and overseas remittances, increased the ways the civil liberties of Chinese Americans could be infringed upon.

A few days after the federal government issued indictments against the China Daily News Inc., it charged three more, Chin You Gon, Tom Sung, and Chin Hong Ming—who like Moy and Wong, were members of the leftist Chinese Hand Laundry Alliance (CHLA)—with sending money to China. All but Wong were found guilty in 1954. After an unsuccessful appeal in July 1955, the remaining four were forced to pay a collective fine of $25,000. In addition to the fine, Moy was sentenced to two years in jail while the others were given a one-year jail term.[77] The conviction of the four CHLA members illustrated how the federal government used the extortion racket not only to crack down on remittances to China during the Korean War but also to suppress the activities of Chinese American radicals.

Lastly, what Lee's coverage of the extortion racket revealed was an attempt to create a viable political alternative to the KMT and the CCP. Lee used many of his editorials to undermine the efforts of the Chinese Nationalist government to use the extortion racket to rally the support of overseas Chinese behind its leadership.[78] Lee argued that Chiang should have remembered that the KMT originated with overseas Chinese when he opted to disregard their criticism of his decision to militarize the Chinese government under a one-party dictatorship.[79] Moreover, to counteract what even Lee saw as Chiang's first expression of regret for not doing a better job to protect overseas Chinese and their relatives in China from being blackmailed, he questioned Chiang's sincerity, given how Taiwan had turned away Chinese refugees harassed in China. Applicants seeking an entry permit, he contended, ran into "as much difficulty as they might have if they tried to come to the United States."[80] As Lee drew on this example to show how Taiwan was not "free China," he issued a telling critique of not only the KMT but also the United States, whose restrictive immigration policies had compromised their efforts to forge ties with overseas Chinese. With these critiques in mind, Lee looked to heighten the visibility of an overseas contingent that was both anticommunist and non-KMT, whose support could help the KMT and the United States contain communist China.

While Lee often connected Chinese Americans to the larger overseas Chinese population that resided outside China and Taiwan in his writings on the ransom racket, his designation of Chinese Americans as "overseas Chinese" was particularly prominent in editorials that sought to discredit the Chinese Nationalist government. Although much of Lee's reproach of the KMT looked to rally the anticommunist non-KMT Chinese behind the

Chinese Democratic Constitutionalist Party and more broadly behind the Third Force, a group backed by the CIA as a political alternative to the KMT, calling Chinese Americans "overseas Chinese" had another aim. It aspired to develop a transnational sensibility among Chinese Americans, evidenced by Lee's repeated appeals to Chinese Americans to see how they, as overseas Chinese, were the only hope for forging a "free China."[81] The construct of "overseas Chinese" evoked memories of the critical role that Chinese who resided outside China played in the overthrow of the Qing dynasty and the subsequent founding of the Chinese Republic in 1911. The association of Chinese in Cold War America with this historic constituency looked not only to assert the influence of overseas Chinese on Chinese politics but also to establish that effect.[82] Besides verifying and calling forth the existence of an overseas network that endeavored to establish a democratic China, Lee's petitions functioned in the context of the U.S. Cold War agenda to promote the importance of internationalism and to make visible a transnational contingent that could advance the superiority of the United States over communist China. In turn, Lee hoped to use the nation's need for noncommunist alliances to advocate for reforms that would improve the livelihood of Chinese Americans.

As Lee explained in an editorial addressed to the American public, the reason he looked to the United States to alleviate the plight of ransom victims worldwide by liberalizing its immigration policies was that he realized that "help will not come from Moscow's stooge, Mao Tse-tung, nor will it come from Chiang Kai-shek."[83] Lee's appeal to the American public was in this way analogous to his address to Chinese Americans, as it sought to make the United States the only hope for the Chinese who endeavored to create a democratic China. His petition thus worked to promote the image of the United States as the leader of the "free world" and to emphasize that Chinese support could help affirm that claim. By casting Chinese American loyalty to the U.S. Cold War effort as an important resource for furthering the nation's foreign policy in Asia, Lee not only advanced his political agenda, but also disclosed a complex interaction between the racial formation of the Chinese as the foreigners-within and the aspirations of Chinese Americans to impact Chinese politics. Some Chinese Americans were complicit with this racial formation, given how their loyalty promoted their equal treatment in the United States.

Achieving Civil Rights through Immigration Reform

Lee's insistence that immigration reform could help foster better relations between the United States and Asia was part of a broader national dialogue over the importance of immigration laws to advancing Cold War internationalism.[84] Policy makers, for instance, considered the 1948 Displaced Persons Act an important legislation that initiated the nation's uneven shift toward internationalism. What they thereby sought to achieve through this humanitarian gesture of welcoming European refugees to the United States was the rebuilding of a noncommunist Europe. The 1952 McCarran-Walter Act, on the other hand, exposed the clash between isolationists and internationalists that appeared in debates over the issue of immigration quotas based on race and national origins.[85] Whereas isolationists justified the need to keep the existing quota system intact by turning the issue of quotas into a matter of national sovereignty, internationalists deemed racial and national quotas a detriment to U.S. foreign relations. The lesson they learned from World War II was that the need to secure an alliance with China had cut across racial and national preferences and entailed the repeal of the Chinese exclusion acts.[86] The discord over the direction of U.S. Cold War foreign policy went beyond a clash over how ideas about race and nationality were to inform the state's regulation of national borders, and became a conflict about whether or not they should. Given the way immigration policies had relied on both national and racial categories to shape the desired makeup of the nation, the push to institute a more liberal quota system became a means to foster not just better foreign relations but also better race relations.[87]

For the Chinese in the United States, the 1948 Displaced Persons Act marked yet another immigration policy that affirmed that the Chinese were still not among the nation's racially and nationally preferred groups. As China was not granted any quotas for refugee admittance, this exclusion reinforced the stringent immigration policies that had denied to Chinese Americans the right to family unification since 1924. But as this 1948 measure revealed the nation's attempt to advance its Cold War objectives through internationalism, it also introduced an important rationale that Chinese American leaders made use of as they participated in debates over the 1952 McCarran-Walter Act and campaigned for the elimination of racial and national quotas.[88]

Among the legacies of the Immigration Act of 1924 was the emergence of an organized struggle to extend to American citizens of Chinese descent the same right to family unification that was afforded to other citizens. This movement was headed by the Chinese American Citizens Alliance (CACA), a national fraternal organization formed in 1895 to protect the rights and privileges of American citizens of Chinese descent.[89] As the attorney Y. C. Hong argued in a 1925 pamphlet entitled *A Plea for Relief*, which he wrote while serving as president of the Los Angeles chapter of the CACA, the stipulation barring the entry of aliens ineligible for citizenship had exacted an undue hardship on citizens of Chinese descent.[90] In its attempt to ban the entry of Japanese immigrants to the United States, the federal government had also restricted the entry of alien Chinese wives of American citizens. As a result, many Chinese Americans were faced with the prospect of either permanently separating from their wives in China or giving up residence in the United States to reunite with their spouses in China. Hong maintained that no good could come from this exclusion, since preventing Chinese American men from returning to China to marry worked only to promote interracial coupling. More importantly, he contended that this prohibition not only made citizens unequal before the law, but also afforded greater rights to alien Chinese merchants than to American citizens, as the 1924 law allowed for the entry of the alien Chinese wife of an alien Chinese merchant.[91] Hong's plea for relief illustrated how the fight for Chinese American civil rights was linked to the fight for immigration reform. It further showed how the limited rights afforded to Chinese aliens impinged on the rights of citizens of Chinese descent.

Along with this appeal, the CACA garnered the support of sympathetic senators and congressmen to introduce identical bills in both houses of Congress in 1928 to permit the immigration of alien wives of American citizens.[92] In 1929, Hong and Kenneth Y. Fung, executive secretary of the CACA, appeared before the Senate and House Immigration Committee to testify on the hardship that the 1924 law had exacted on Chinese Americans.[93] The culmination of these efforts led to a partial relief to total exclusion when Congress passed the Act of June 13, 1930, to allow for the entry of alien wives who were married to American citizens prior to May 26, 1924, the date of the enactment of the Immigration Act of 1924.

The passage of the 1943 Magnuson Act saw the renewed activism of the CACA. Even though the 1943 measure lifted over sixty years of Chinese exclusion and granted naturalization rights to the Chinese, it placed the immigration of alien Chinese wives under the annual racial quota of 105, whereas during the time of Chinese exclusion, the absence of a quota allowed by default the entrance of alien Chinese wives on a non-quota basis.[94] In contrast, alien wives of non-Chinese descent were permitted to enter the United States on a non-quota basis as stipulated by the 1924 law. To contest this discrimination, Kenneth Y. Fung once again appeared before the House Committee on Immigration and Naturalization to testify on behalf of the needs of Chinese Americans.[95] Following the many efforts taken by the CACA, Congress passed the Act of August 9, 1946, to place Chinese wives of American citizens on a non-quota basis.[96] Not only did this measure finally put citizens of Chinese descent on a par with other citizens with respect to the admission of alien wives, it also allowed all veterans of World War II to benefit from the provisions of the 1945 War Brides Act and the 1946 Fiancées Act.

The biggest threat to this equality came when the House passed the Judd Bill on March 1, 1949, eliminating the non-quota status of alien Chinese and Filipino wives. To prevent the Judd Bill from becoming federal law, the CACA launched what was perhaps its most aggressive campaign to date. As CACA grand president Henry Lem argued in his letter to Patrick McCarran, chairman of the Senate Judiciary Committee, the CACA in its protest of the Judd Bill aimed to "rectify an indefensible injustice to our own citizens."[97] In addition to writing numerous protest letters to elected officials, the CACA worked together with senators to introduce in the Senate a competing bill that preserved the non-quota status of alien Chinese and Filipino wives. These efforts successfully blocked the Judd Bill from becoming public law. They also marked the end to the twenty-five-year battle to ensure that male citizens of Chinese descent were afforded the same right as other male citizens with regard to the admission of alien wives. Before the outbreak of the Korean War, the fight to admit alien Chinese wives of American citizens on a non-quota basis became the CACA's crowning achievement in its effort to advance the civil rights of Chinese Americans. In addition to contesting discriminatory immigration acts, the CACA challenged the disenfranchisement of citizens of Chinese ancestry, the segregation of Chinese children in public schools, and the application of discriminatory regulations on Chinese businesses.[98]

Following the communist revolution in China, the CACA worked with the CCBA to press Congress to permit the entrance of Chinese refugees and to grant permanent resident status to Chinese students stranded in the United States. The CACA further campaigned to ensure that Chinese Americans were afforded the same right as other citizens to sponsor their minor children to the United States on a non-quota basis. The issue prompted the CACA to support the passage of the 1952 McCarran-Walter Act. Interestingly, it also incited the organization to protest the failure of the 1952 law to institute a process of fair review of applications that were filed by foreign-born American citizens for travel to the United States.

The McCarran omnibus immigration and nationality bill presented a mixed bag of stipulations for Asian Americans. While it fell short of placing Asian immigration on a par with European immigration, it nevertheless lifted the ban against Asian immigration by establishing a Chinese quota and a single Asian quota, which were both based on race and not on national origins. More importantly, the 1952 measure granted to all Asian groups the right to citizenship by naturalization. As the bill also allowed for the entry of alien husbands of American citizens and of the Asian children and spouses of American citizens on a non-quota basis, these provisions greatly extended the right to family unification to Asian Americans, particularly Chinese Americans. Prior to this bill, the Chinese child of American citizens entered as a nonpreference quota immigrant, while the non-Asian child of American citizens entered on a non-quota basis.[99]

Of all the Asian American organizations in the United States, the Japanese American Citizens League (JACL) came out most strongly in support of the passage of the McCarran bill. The JACL feared that it would lose concessions granted in this proposal if it backed the competing Humphrey-Lehman bill, which it believed to be too liberal to have a real shot at passing. What drove the JACL to put its full weight behind the McCarran bill was the granting of naturalization rights to Asians. As the JACL underscored in its petition for the McCarran measure, of the approximately 88,000 resident aliens that were ineligible for naturalization, 85,000 were Japanese. It argued that these numbers alone justified the support for the McCarran bill and that it would be a grave disservice to this group, composed largely of elderly Isseis, if the McCarran bill was blocked in order to advance a bill that would altogether eliminate immigration quotas based on race and national origins but might not see the light of day for many years to come.[100] Following the receipt of a personal appeal from Samuel Ishikawa, associate national director of the JACL, Y. C. Hong, who in 1951 was the grand president of the CACA, came out in support of the JACL's efforts to advance the naturalization right of Japanese in the United States and wired a series of letters to influential members of Congress to declare the CACA's support for the McCarran bill. Hong further joined the heads of the JACL, the Filipino Federation of America, and the Korean National Association to form the Four National Organization, which claimed to represent 90 percent of American citizens of Asian ancestry, to call for the passage of the McCarran bill.[101]

As mentioned earlier, the CACA, besides backing the passage of the 1952 McCarran-Walter Act because of its naturalization provisions, had supported the bill for allowing Chinese American parents to sponsor the immigration of their minor child to the United States on a non-quota basis. Despite achieving these gains, the CACA continued to fight for the enactment of an immigration policy that abolished altogether the use of quotas based on race and national origins. Hong thus appeared before the 1952 hearings of the President's Commission on Immigration and Naturalization that were held following the passage of the McCarran-Walter Act to contest the continued use of discriminatory quotas to limit Asian immigration. Additionally, he argued that the McCarran-Walter Act upheld an unfair process of administrative review of applications by foreign-born American citizens for travel to the United States. As Hong contended, the use by immigration officials of a separate and more stringent process to review the applications of Chinese Americans than that used to review the applications of all other groups had unjustly impinged on the right of minor children born in China to American citizens of Chinese descent from immigrating to the United States and in so doing, had inflicted "an inexcusable discrimination against our own American citizens."[102] Immigration officials, for their part, had long justified the strict review of Chinese applicants as a necessary measure to block the illegal entry of Chinese to the United States. As many Chinese Americans upon their return to China had reported fictive births and sold these immigration slots to families seeking to send their child to the United States, this practice led to the rise of Chinese illegal immigration.

Three years after Hong's testimony, the practice of Chinese illegal immigration, or the Chinese slot racket, generated national concern because it was believed to be a channel that Chinese communist spies used to enter the United States. Like the extortion racket, the Chinese slot racket prompted the federal government to initiate efforts to monitor systematically the dealings of Chinese in the United States. Chinese American leaders, however, countered the government's attempts to encroach on their civil liberties while reasserting their loyalty to the U.S. Cold War effort in Asia. They further sought to persuade the nation that racist immigration policies, not a Chinese propensity toward crime, were the real trigger for Chinese illegal immigration. With this in mind, Chinese American leaders continued to petition for an immigration reform that would grant to Asian Americans the same rights afforded to other Americans.

The Chinese Slot Racket

When Y. C. Hong appeared before the President's Commission on Immigration and Naturalization in October 1952, he noted that under state law a person maintained the right to judicial review if his citizenship status was in dispute, provided that at the time of the dispute he was in residence in the United States. That right, however, was denied to American citizens living abroad where the American consul possessed the sole power to deny citizens their right to come to the United States and to prove their nationality before the courts. Hong argued that it was "unfair to grant to one group of American citizens the right to judicial review and deny it to another group on the ground of diversity of residence."[103] He also found it incomprehensible that the State Department as well as the Consular Service maintained, even after the repeal of the Chinese exclusion acts in 1943, special rules to ascertain the identity claims of American citizens of Chinese descent. In contrast to the procedure set up to determine the identity claims of other groups, the testimony of parents was not enough to verify the identity of an applicant of Chinese descent. In the case of the Chinese, they needed also to submit family photos, remittance receipts, and family correspondence. They were further subjected to unfair questioning and required to present results of blood grouping tests to establish paternity and bone examinations to determine age.[104]

The American consul general Everett F. Drumright of Hong Kong had similarly taken note of these regulations in his December 1955 report to the U.S. State Department. But rather than argue that these rules discriminated against foreign-born American citizens of Chinese descent, Drumright argued that they were necessary. He claimed that American male citizens of Chinese ancestry and Chinese merchants following their return to China would report a birth for every year that they remained in China. These births, which were believed to be largely fictitious, resulted in the creation of immigration "slots" that were later sold and sometimes given to a Chinese seeking entry into the United States.[105] Drumright contended that this slot racket justified the need to presume fraudulent the identity claims of all Chinese applicants until proven otherwise, even after the 1943 repeal of Chinese exclusion.

Drumright charged in his report that the criminal practices of the Chinese had evolved into a highly organized industry that profited from brokering Chinese illegal immigration to the United States. He estimated that there were 124 Gold Mountain Companies, or *Kum Shan Jongs*, in Hong Kong, where the manager of each company also worked as a citizenship broker who was constantly on the lookout for buyers of slots. Coaching schools emerged either as a component of or as a separate entity that worked in conjunction with Gold Mountain Companies to help applicants learn the family history of sponsors and to train applicants to talk with consular officers.[106] Drumright claimed that the Hong Kong police, while aware of this underground industry, did nothing to crack down on its dealings.[107] He also implicated immigration lawyers in the United States as being part of this scheme as they routinely fixed the blood tests of clients.[108] According to Drumright, various facets of Chinese culture, such as the practice of plural wives and the lack of understanding among the Chinese of the concept of oaths, propelled the growth of the slot racket.[109] Drumright also noted how citizenship brokers often carried out the interests of their clan associations, further seeking to incriminate Chinese family associations in this scandal.[110]

Drawing on a finding generated from a random selection of two hundred cases from 1953 to 1955, Drumright contended that 84 percent of all applications for entry to the United States based on derivative citizenship were fraudulent. He thus proclaimed that

A criminal conspiracy to evade the laws of the United States has developed into so well organized a system at Hong Kong that almost any Chinese with the proper resources may enter the United States even if ineligible under our immigration laws.

According to Drumright, American citizenship could be bought for a mere three thousand dollars. He urged the federal government to take all necessary steps to stop this illegal flow of Chinese immigrants. He believed this matter to be of utmost significance because communist China was endeavoring to use overseas Chinese to spread communism throughout the world.[111] To bolster further his claim that Chinese illegal immigration was a threat to national security, Drumright noted that applications for entry to the United States consisted largely of men of military age who at some point lived and attended schools in communist China. He believed that the lack of knowledge among the Chinese about their rights in the United States along with the language gap had made them an apt "tool" for sponsors. Moreover, their false claims of identity had made them susceptible to being blackmailed, since officials in China were holders of their true identity. These officials, Drumright argued, already showed what they were capable of in the extortion racket.[112] Notably, in a follow-up report Drumright revealed what he sought to gain from calling national attention to the Chinese slot racket. While he acknowledged that admitting Chinese wives to the United States and preventing Chinese men from returning to Hong Kong and China could help stop illegal immigration, he believed the most effective means was to centralize power so that the consul general could have more authority in decision making.[113]

Following the receipt of the Drumright report in December 1955, the State Department dispatched twenty agents to Hong Kong to investigate reports of false claims of derivative citizenship.[114] On February 14, 1956, the Justice Department impaneled a special federal grand jury to examine evidence of immigration and passport frauds committed by Chinese nationals claiming to be children of American citizens. It alleged that the slot racket was a three-million-dollar-a-year operation.[115] At the time of the impaneling, the U.S. Attorney was reported to be investigating one hundred cases to determine whether claims of derivative citizenship were fraudulent. There were also up to 750 claims awaiting trial in the federal court in San Francisco. Given how the 1952 McCarran-Walter Act had stipulated sixteen as the cutoff age when claims of derivative citizenship could be filed, this proviso had largely accounted for the high number of claims filed by the Chinese during this time.[116] With this in mind, Dai-ming Lee issued a pointed critique about the timing of this investigation and wondered whether the stigma of communism unjustly deprived the Chinese of the "meager hope for a family reunion." He urged the State and Justice Departments not to conflate Chinese illegal immigration with communist infiltration and advocated a fairer administrative review of identity claims.[117]

Lee's concern that the communist stigma had unfairly cast suspicion on the activities of Chinese Americans was not unwarranted. Just two weeks after impaneling the federal grand jury, on February 29, 1956, the Justice Department subpoenaed at least twenty-four San Francisco Chinese family and district associations to turn over the whole of their records within a twenty-four-hour period as the grand jury prepared to begin its inquiry.[118] While twenty-four of the associations handed over portions of their records within the specified time, they obtained a continuance, which effectively prevented their records from being reviewed by the grand jury as the federal court impounded their records pending the court's review. Four days later, the twenty-four Chinese family and district associations filed motions to quash."[119] Under the leadership of the CCBA, these associations invoked the Fourth Amendment to protect them from what they considered the unfair search and seizure of their records. The associations sought in this way to use the investigation to uncover the government's misstep in accusing all Chinese in San Francisco of running an illegal immigration racket and of being a party to a communist conspiracy. They thus banded together to contest the government's efforts to infringe on the civil rights of Chinese Americans.

On March 16, 1956, the day after closing remarks were completed on the motions to quash, the CCBA of San Francisco held a press conference to call attention to the way this blanket investigation had unjustly incriminated the Chinese population in the United States. It proclaimed,

> The subpoenas in question can only be used for the obvious purpose of oppressing and intimidating the entire Chinese-American community in San Francisco and, whether intentional or otherwise, they are having the effect of stigmatizing the social and family status of a respected community with criminal coloration.[120]

The CCBA of New York, which claimed to represent sixty Chinese American civic, cultural, and family associations, also came forward to denounce the criminalization of Chinese in the United States. During the hearings on the motions to quash, the CCBA of New York sent telegrams to vice president Richard Nixon, secretary of state John Foster Dulles, and leaders of both houses of Congress opposing the "blanket summoning" of Chinese organizations in San Francisco. It further decried the harassment of Chinese on the streets of Chinatown in San Francisco by federal agents asking for identification papers.[121] On the day of the press conference, the CCBA of New York sent over a delegation of twenty Chinese to meet with the U.S. Attorney Paul W. Williams to express how they were greatly "disturbed" by and "jittery" about the recent subpoenas. It reiterated the concerns of the Chinese Six Companies that this investigation had led to the severe decline of businesses in Chinatowns across the United States. The U.S. Attorney assured the delegates that no such subpoenas would be issued against Chinese family associations in New York, thus attempting to counter the perception that the subpoenas represented the "wholesale persecutions" of Chinese Americans. The CCBA, however, maintained that the investigation did in fact represent an assault on the entire Chinese community.[122]

The *San Francisco Chronicle* supported the efforts of Chinese family associations: it sought to dispel the belief that the Chinese Six Companies was an organization engaged in criminal activities and emphasized how the Six Companies was instead an agency that cared for the sick and the poor among the Chinese and that advocated on behalf of Chinese Americans by opposing anti-Chinese laws.[123] The leading black newspaper in northern California, the *Sun Reporter*, also expressed its support for the Chinese Six Companies and argued that the infringement of rights of one group constituted a danger for all. It further backed the view that this probe was an act of racism: "We wonder, with the officials of the Chinese family associations, if such a subpoena would ever have been served on an occidental organization."[124] Among the various state officials to come forward against the blanket probe of Chinese family associations in San Francisco was Samuel Yorty, who in 1956 was a former congressman and a Democratic candidate for the U.S. Senate. According to Yorty,

> The free Chinese crowded into Hong Kong live in the shadow of the communist Chinese police state. They are harassed, threatened and

even blackmailed by the Red rulers. Their fate is watched with keen and sympathetic interest by millions of free Chinese in Malaya, Burma, Thailand, Indonesia and other areas where we are anxious to build "good will." Sending Federal agents to Hong Kong under current circumstances is certain to prove valuable grist for the communist propaganda mill.[125]

Like Yorty, Dai-ming Lee drew on the nation's desire to forge ties with "free" countries in Asia to argue that the injustice inflicted on Chinese Americans had worked to turn the opinion of those in Southeast Asia against the United States.[126] He further noted that Chinese in the United States were part of the thirteen million overseas Chinese who had established a foothold in Southeast Asia. Moreover, given that they were familiar with the mindset of Chinese communists and had absorbed American ideals of democracy and freedom, Lee considered Chinese Americans to be "excellent protagonists for the cause of the free world."[127]

Judge Oliver J. Carter dealt a severe blow to the U.S. Attorney's office when he ruled in favor of the twenty-four Chinese family and district associations on March 20, 1956. He made clear that while he opposed the excessive use of the subpoena power, he did not question the authority of the grand jury to investigate a matter that he believed merited inquiry. What Judge Carter found unreasonable was the way the U.S. Attorney's office had requested the entire records of the twenty-four Chinese family and district associations "without any relation to time, place or person." He noted that in his research into this matter, he found no subpoenas that upheld a period for more than twenty-seven years.[128] He thus granted the U.S. Attorney's office a stay of execution rendering void the state's subpoenas in order to give the government time to prepare an appeal but rejected the motion to reopen hearings on the subpoenas once the government specified terms of the subpoenas. He further granted a stay for the release of the impounded records pending the government's appeal.[129]

Following this ruling, the Justice Department impaneled a new federal grand jury on April 4, 1956. However, this new jury opted not to appeal Judge Carter's decision and did the work to bring individual civil and criminal indictments against the Chinese.[130] The State Department reported that following the investigations conducted in Hong Kong and the United States from July 1, 1956, to December 31, 1957, there were 908 civil action cases and 57 criminal cases brought before the courts. Of the 908 civil action cases, 51 were either lost or conceded by the government, while 49 cases were won. The remaining 808 cases were dismissed at request of the plaintiff.[131] Notably, besides waging this legal battle against Chinese illegal immigration, the federal government sought to rally public support behind these investigations, especially after the misstep of the U.S. Attorney's office in subpoenaing the entire records of the twenty-four Chinese family and district associations. Thus, on the same day that Judge Carter handed down his decision, the State Department announced that it would make public the Drumright report.

Dai-ming Lee used this occasion not only to celebrate the court's upholding the right of Chinese Americans against unlawful search and seizure, but also to issue a call for action.[132] Lee urged the Chinese to let go of factional and family disputes and band together to advocate for immigration reform. Following the release of the Drumright report, Lee penned editorials for three straight months challenging the report's claims and showing how the government's probe of Chinese Americans had greatly damaged the image of the United States. But much to his chagrin, Lee was unsuccessful in obtaining the backing of the KMT, as the Chinese Nationalist government did not intend to interfere with the U.S. government's investigations.[133] The refusal of the KMT to speak out against the United States prompted the *Chinese World* to reprint stories from newspapers in Taiwan, such as the influential *United Daily News*, to publicize how the Chinese in Taiwan were greatly dismayed with the U.S. government's probe against Chinese Americans.[134] The *Chinese World* also drew on Chinese media in Hong Kong to show how the U.S. government's investigation resulted in damaging the nation's reputation in Asia. For instance, the *Hong Kong Standard* charged that the U.S. State Department had fabricated the slot racket in order to obtain more funding from the House Appropriations Subcommittee. As the *Standard* reasoned, if Drumright was correct in his assessment that American passports were so easy to procure, the State Department should not have any trouble obtaining the street addresses as well as the names of the 124 citizenship brokerage firms that were ostensibly in operation. It further maintained that the problem with the State Department was that "one cannot tell where politics ends and diplomacy begins." It deemed the U.S. government's espousal of the Drumright report to be a poor way of expressing "one's appreciation for the friendship of a friendly city."[135] The *China Mail* reiterated this censure and asked for a "full and unreserved repudiation of the accusation of the State Department." The Hong Kong government also came forward to deny allegations that its police had turned a blind eye to the racket.[136]

In addition to drawing on this international scrutiny to detail how the harassment of Chinese Americans was not the best approach to solving the nation's immigration woes, Lee sought to counter Drumright's contention that the history of Chinese in the United States consisted of a chain of criminal activities.[137] To that end, Lee revisited the 1906 San Francisco earthquake in order to emphasize the damage that it inflicted on the city's Chinatown and not the devastation that it wreaked on the Hall of Records, which destroyed the state's immigration files. According to Lee, the damage to San Francisco's Chinatown threatened to erase not just the contributions of Chinese Americans to the development of the Far West, but also the evidence that they were survivors of racist assaults since the late nineteenth century.[138] In this view, the practice of subjecting the Chinese to interrogations and blood and clinical tests was evidence of anti-Chinese sentiments that immigration officials used to enforce Chinese exclusion rather than to verify identity following the destruction of the state's immigration files. Lee contended that the slot racket, instead of exposing a history of criminal behavior, had revealed a history of prejudice against the Chinese. The government's harassment of Chinese Americans failed in this way to recognize how they were on the front line in the fight against communist China. Lee concluded by asking whether the government's intent was to deport Chinese Americans back to communist China to support its cause for world domination.[139]

Like Lee, the CCBA, following the release of the Drumright report, looked for ways to secure the legitimacy of Chinese Americans. It thus brought together for the first time 124 delegates from thirty-four Chinese communities in the United States for a three-day conference in Washington, DC, from March 5 to March 7, 1957. The purpose of this conference was to discuss measures that would increase the social standing of Chinese Americans.[140] Shortly before the conferees arrived in Washington, the legal advisor for the CCBA of San Francisco issued a set of recommended guidelines to ensure a successful conference, given the national and international attention that the meeting had garnered. He urged conferees to refrain from voicing attacks against the U.S. government so as to avoid generating a bad impression of the United States before the world. There was, moreover, a standing order to keep partisan expressions of Chinese politics out of the conference in an attempt to preserve unity among the conferees.[141] Organizers further sought to maintain the credibility of the meeting by assuring its attendees that the conference was in no way sponsored by the Chinese Nationalist embassy in the United States, even though the Chinese Nationalist ambassador, Hollington K. Tong, gave the opening address. Other speakers, such as Representative Walter Judd, stressed that the Chinese had an obligation to make Americans understand their culture and anticommunist viewpoints.[142]

Despite the limits placed on what could be said at the meeting, the guidelines did not deter delegates from devoting the whole of the conference to addressing the need for immigration reform. After the final session of the three-day meeting was completed, the attendees issued a statement to declare their support for

1. promotion of the welfare of Chinese in the United States;
2. improvement of conditions regarding Chinese immigration;
3. promotion and spread of Chinese culture to non-Chinese people in America;
4. loyalty to the United States;
5. the United States policy of fostering and supporting all peace-loving peoples and of aid to the free Chinese.

As these five points adjoined the interest of Chinese Americans with that of the nation's Cold War agenda, the list illustrates how Chinese loyalty to the U.S. Cold War effort became a means to obtain immigration reform. The push to secure the legitimacy of Chinese in the United States through immigration reform was further evidenced as delegates passed fourteen resolutions that called for the liberalization of the 1952 McCarran-Walter Act, the setup of a fair administrative review of applications of foreign-born American citizens for entry to the United States, and an increased quota for the admission of Chinese refugees. What the resolutions further make clear is how many Chinese Americans attempted to obtain social acceptance in the United States in the aftermath of the Korean War and the slot racket by promoting positive aspects of Chinese culture.[143]

Finally, the correspondence between the CACA leaders Y. C. Hong and Henry Lem revealed how the CACA was also actively thinking of ways to counter the effects of the Drumright report in addition to lobbying Congress for immigration reform.[144] As Hong expressed to Lem, he was greatly dismayed with the State Department for "rehashing an old theme by making the Chinaman a scapegoat again" as it sought to get more money to feed bureaucrats from the Congressional Appropriations Committee. Hong recommended that Lem, who in 1957 was the grand president of the CACA, go back to the fundamentals of good public relations in order to mitigate the negative perception that all Chinese in the United States were criminals. Specifically, Hong advised Lem to employ the technique of the JACL and "get other people to praise you," as this method proved effective in raising the image of Japanese Americans after World War II.[145] With this in mind, the CACA in its 1957 Biennial National Convention program reprinted an article that first appeared in a local paper in Los Angeles, which drew on a 1956 FBI study to praise the Chinese and the Japanese for having the lowest number of known arrests among all racial groups.[146]

The many efforts of Chinese American leaders to show how Chinese exclusion was the cause of Chinese illegal immigration did not go unnoticed. The government began to implement reforms to rectify the legal and social problems caused by the denial to Chinese Americans of the right to family unification. Specifically, the government relied on a process devised by the INS to reinstate illegal immigrants back into the alien/citizen dichotomy. Considering how the discovery of one fraudulent claim could implicate, for instance, thirty more people spanning multiple generations, the administrative headache generated from the need to investigate each case and to carry out deportation orders prompted the San Francisco district of the INS to institute the Chinese Confession Program in 1956.

Notably, the Chinese Confession Program made use of existing laws to allow for the administrative adjustment of status to confessors. Accordingly, those who entered the country illegally were eligible for suspension of deportation and for permanent status if they resided in the United States continuously for seven years. Aliens who served in the armed forces for ninety days were also eligible for naturalized citizenship.[147] To bolster further the system of readjustment, the government passed the Act of September 11, 1957, which granted relief from deportation if the person charged with illegal entry was the spouse, parent, or child of an American citizen or a permanent resident alien.[148] From 1957 to 1965, the annual reports of the INS indicated that there were at least 11,336 Chinese who entered the

United States under fraudulent claims of citizenship, and this finding implicated another 19,124 people and closed off 5,800 slots.[149] Although the Chinese Confession Program helped to halt Chinese illegal immigration, it was not until the passage of the 1965 Immigration Act that slot immigration became obsolete. The Confession Program, however, continued to be in effect until the early 1970s. It importantly highlighted how illegal immigration, since it was a crime invented by the state, could also be undone by the state.[150]

The Chinese extortion and slot rackets illustrate the broader struggle among Chinese Americans for the right to family unification. These events showed how Chinese American leaders made use of the U.S. Cold War agenda to advocate for the rights and privileges that were afforded to their European counterparts. Organizations such as the CCBA and the CACA persisted in petitioning for an immigration policy that placed Asian Americans on par with white Americans. As Henry Lem, grand president of the CACA, stated in his 1959 address before the twenty-fifth biennial national convention of the CACA,

> The price of liberty is eternal vigilance. We must, therefore, continue to work toward a clearer focus in the area of civil rights and for a more informed public opinion to bring about judicious legislation and democracy to human relations.[151]

The legacy of Chinese exclusion was the rise of a particular brand of activism that saw immigration reform as civil rights reform. In the next five years, tensions emerged within the CACA as the San Francisco contingent sought to bypass the leadership of the grand lodge and sponsor various immigration bills as a way to wield greater power and prestige for the members in San Francisco.[152] As the CACA worked through these divisions, its efforts, together with those of the CCBA as well as the JACL, helped to bring about the passage of the 1965 Immigration and Nationality Act. Following the passage of this act, immigration quotas were no longer based on race and nationality. The system of preferential categories instituted by this act also did not discriminate based on race and nationality.

The 1965 Immigration and Nationality Act marked the third landmark civil rights reform that was passed by the Johnson administration, which had already signed into law the 1964 Civil Rights Act and the 1965 Voting

Rights Act. The passage of this immigration measure carried out the recommendation of the President's Commission on Immigration and Naturalization, which argued for repealing the 1952 McCarran-Walter Act on the grounds that the nation "cannot defend civil rights in principle, and deny them in our immigration laws and practice."[153] Like desegregation policies, immigration reform allowed the federal government to justify its role as leader of the "free world" by showing its commitment to protecting civil rights.[154] Through their activism, Chinese American leaders also made use of the U.S. Cold War agenda to advocate for equal rights through immigration reform.

Conclusion

Cold War America and the
Appeal to See Past Race

On the day that President Lyndon B. Johnson was to sign the landmark 1964 Civil Rights Act into law, he addressed the nation to convey the historic significance of the occasion.[1] He reminded the nation of how its founding members pledged their lives and fortunes to fight for something bigger than political independence and the elimination of foreign rule. He contended that they battled for freedom, justice, and personal liberty. Their legacy, Johnson asserted, has continued to live on as people from far corners of the world still looked to these patriots for inspiration in their struggles for freedom and equality. Additionally, each generation of Americans must renew and expand on the nation's founding ideals. Johnson urged his fellow Americans to join soldiers in Vietnam and take up this responsibility. The purpose of outlawing discrimination based on race, color, religion, or national origin was to promote a "more abiding commitment to freedom, a more constant pursuit of justice, and a deeper respect for human dignity." It further sought to rid the country of its "last vestiges of injustice" and to show the world the superiority of American democracy.[2] As Johnson petitioned the nation to unite under this cause, he carried forward the demands of civil rights activists and the proposal of President John F. Kennedy. He also brought up to date the goals of President Truman. In a special 1948 message on civil rights to Congress, Truman had beseeched Congress to implement measures that would safeguard the rights of all in the nation so as to enhance the effectiveness of the United States as the leader of the "free world."[3]

Cold War civil rights worked to establish the credibility of U.S. democracy in a particular way. Beyond securing equal protection under the law to all people, they distinguished American democracy above all other forms of government. They explained why people in the United States lived fuller lives than those living in other parts of the world, especially in communist countries. More importantly, they spoke to the ability of American democracy to make free the unfree. This transformative capacity of American democracy put the nation on the path toward social progress and turned the promise of the good life into a viable reality. Cold War civil rights thus established the credibility of U.S. democracy by advancing the preeminence of the American way of life.

During the early Cold War years, as the notion of civil rights was understood primarily as the extension of equal rights to nonwhites, this signification importantly made race a defining construct that shaped the image of U.S. democracy. By examining the racial formation of Asian Americans, this book has sought to underscore the multiple and conflicting ways race defined the superiority of the American political system. Specifically, I have explored how the racialization of Asian Americans as the foreigners-within deepened the political significance of blurring the color line through desegregation policies and immigration reform. Besides affirming that U.S. democracy worked to safeguard the rights of all, the extension of equal rights to Asian Americans functioned to show the nation's goodwill toward all people in Asia. This was notable because it implied that the promise of a better life was not limited to those in the United States. By embracing the American way, other countries could also join the United States on the path to social advancement. In this view, the expansion of U.S. democracy did not impose its will on other countries as communism had, but led them to greater freedoms and liberties.

But as this study has shown, the federal government also limited the rights of Asian Americans in order to maintain the credibility of the American political system. As many Chinese and Korean Americans had subscribed to communist ideologies to create societies in China and in Korea that were free of colonial and feudal vestiges, their political dealings importantly undermined the belief that the American way was the only way to achieve freedom and equality for all. The federal government thereby suppressed the political dealings of Asian American progressives in its effort to assert the superiority of the American way of life. Additionally, the racial formation of Asian Americans as the foreigners-within worked to cast doubt on the loyalty of all Chinese and Korean Americans following the rise of the communist regime in China and the outbreak of the Korean War. This effect revealed the regulatory mechanisms of the state to police politics in the nation, which influenced the activism of Asian Americans in Cold War America. In view of these developments, this study has insisted that the examination of Cold War civil rights is not complete without an analysis of the measures that were passed or enforced to criminalize the activities of communists, as these acts also worked to establish the preeminence of the American way of life.

Citizens of Asian America has endeavored to show how Asian Americans as citizens of America and as representatives of Asia worked to promote the nation's Cold War agenda of internationalism and communist containment. In this concluding section, I hope to further analyze how race shaped the image of American democracy and promoted the nation's Cold War objectives. Specifically, I seek to call attention to an emerging racial paradigm that did not recognize Asian Americans as either citizens of America or as representatives of Asia. Rather, it saw Asian Americans, Latinos, blacks, and whites as members of the global family of man. By foregrounding the commonality of all mankind, this emerging paradigm advanced the importance of seeing past cultural, racial, and national differences for bringing about social harmony among all groups of people. During the early Cold War years, the federal government found images endorsing the belief in the shared humanity of mankind useful for advancing the superiority of the American way of life. It therefore endorsed the *Family of Man* photography exhibit that was created by Edward Steichen for the Museum of Modern Art in New York City.

The distinction of the *Family of Man* photography exhibit was that it featured photos of people from different parts of the world to demonstrate the existence of a universal set of life events that purportedly bound people together from across time and distance, in contrast to the social disparities that divided societies and disaggregated nations. The 1955 *Family of Man* exhibit at MOMA and a subsequent world tour helped to popularize the belief that equality and world peace were attainable once viewers learned to see past racial and cultural differences and embraced the humanity of all. As the federal government underwrote the cost of the world tour, this financial backing crucially attached the *Family of Man* exhibit to the task of promoting the U.S. Cold War agenda. It thus provided a look at how the state built the international appeal of U.S. democracy on its ability to see past social differences. This trait was significant because it imbued the nation with the capability of uniting the world under a common purpose of ensuring freedom and equality to all mankind.

Although the federal government relied largely on the enactment of civil rights reforms and the rising status of racialized minorities such as Asian American "firsts" to make known the benefits of the American way of life, the early Cold War years also saw the growing appeal of a multicultural vision that looked to bridge social and political divisions by transcending the recognition of difference. This concluding chapter argues through its examination of the *Family of Man* photography exhibit that the concept of shared humanity was a constructed belief, a social device that worked to shape our views of social differences instead of denoting a natural human condition. Currently, the idea that from the recognition of a common humanity comes a society free of prejudices holds much weight. The importance ascribed to this worldview calls for a look into the circumstances that made the appeal to see past racial and cultural differences desirable. This inquiry details how the vision of a multicultural society carried with it the terms and limits of U.S. democracy. It is guided by the understanding that racial equality, rather than being the inevitable outcome of U.S. democracy, results from an ongoing contestation over what democracy looks like.

Constructing the Oneness of Mankind

Hailed as the most popular photographic event of the 1950s, the *Family of Man* exhibit, curated by Edward Steichen and produced and shown first at the Museum of Modern Art in New York City, set attendance records for the museum during its run from January 24 to May 8, 1955. After the four-month show ended, the museum released a companion book of exhibition photographs that has sold over four million copies and become a coffee table staple.[4] The *Family of Man* exhibit remained active following its tenure at MOMA; with funding from the federal government, the exhibit toured the world for eight consecutive years. Between 1955 and 1962, various versions of the photography show appeared in thirty-eight countries and at ninety-one venues. These showings amassed a worldwide audience of over nine million people.[5] In 1989, the Luxembourg government restored the original MOMA photographs, which had been donated to the country of Steichen's birth by the U.S. government for a special exhibit at the Clervaux Castle commemorating Luxembourg's 150 years of nationhood.[6] Steichen had immigrated to the United States from Luxembourg as an infant and spent most of his childhood and young adult years in Milwaukee, Wisconsin. Before becoming the director of the department of photography at MOMA in 1947, Steichen distinguished himself as a war photographer for the U.S. army in World War I and for the U.S. navy in World War II. He also garnered acclaim for his work as a fashion photographer and with various advertising agencies.

Not surprisingly, Steichen's work on the *Family of Man* exhibit, which began in 1952, was punctuated by opposing ideals, given how there was nothing natural or transparent about the concept of enduring ideals that bound people together from across time and distance. The *Family of Man* exhibit made the oneness of mankind seem an inviting and wholly unguided approach to seeing the world. It showed not only how Steichen and his creative team tapped into the economy of mass culture to attract a wide audience, but also how they used the notion of mass to substantiate the existence of shared values. As the American studies scholar Eric J. Sandeen has detailed in his comprehensive study of the *Family of Man* exhibit, Steichen and his creative team built on the undertakings of *Harper's*, *Ladies Home Journal*, and most importantly, *Life* magazine, which had cultivated a readership around the use of photography during the war and postwar years. Whereas war photographers made visions of the world accessible to the average American, *Life* magazine had successfully built a business around being the interpreter of Western civilization and shaping visually America's place in it. But Sandeen asserts that unlike *Life*, which flooded its pages with consumer-friendly products that attested to the nation's postwar prosperity, Steichen accessed the economy of mass culture for the purpose of generating public interest in an egalitarian vision of the postwar world. Beyond this desire for a large audience, Steichen employed the concept of mass in order to authenticate his vision of shared humanity.

The endeavor to create an exhibit around the oneness of mankind reportedly began with a search for photographs that could piece together the commonality of man. This search, recounted by Wayne Miller, Steichen's chief assistant, led the team to comb through 3.5 million photographs from the archives of *Life* magazine.[7] As Steichen and his creative team relied on *Life* as their gateway into the genre of the mass appeal, their use of this aesthetic in the context of MOMA worked to blur the "high" and "low" art divide. This deployment further drew on a definition of mass to denote a unified majority to establish that the collection of photos featured in the *Family of Man* exhibit had sufficiently represented all of humanity. Miller's recounting of raking through 3.5 million photographs verified in this respect that the *Family of Man* exhibit was formulated on the basis of sound research. Even though the sheer amount of photos consulted for the show can also suggest the difficulties of pinpointing the commonalities of man, the quest for the desired outcome turned this large number into an indication that the exhibit contained only the most exemplary depictions of shared humanity.

Numerical expressions also played an important role in reinforcing the narrative arc of the *Family of Man* exhibit. As this show sought to put on display the oneness of mankind as a natural human condition, it notably submerged the particularities of a photographer's vision under the story about shared humanity. This undertaking not only led to the liberal cropping and enlarging of exhibition photographs, it also shaped how the photographers selected were foremost identified by their enumeration.[8] The oft-cited statistic of 503 pictures taken by 273 men and women from 68 countries to detail the contents of the show implied that the values portrayed in the exhibition were common to all. Likewise, highlighting the fact that the show's photographers consisted of amateurs and professionals suggested that regardless of who took the pictures and where the photos were shot, the images captured aspects of human existence that were truly timeless.[9] This approach effectively identified mass culture as not only an aesthetic, but also a mechanism that affirmed the existence of the universal.

The *Family of Man* exhibit also built on the structure and themes of a previous photographic series that appeared in the *Ladies Home Journal* in 1948 and 1949 entitled "People Are People the World Over," to frame and detail the experiences that were believed to be shared by all. In the

"People Are People" series, the *Journal* developed twelve two-page spreads that designated the family as the common denominator of all societies and featured aspects of family life such as eating, playing, washing, getting educated, sleeping, and worshipping to generate an image of sameness. These photos were placed around two globes to help viewers navigate where they were taking place. To buttress that the situations depicted were indeed universal, the *Journal* touted how the series had brought into view eighty-eight people from twelve families, three races, five religions, and eleven languages.[10] In so doing, the "People Are People" photographic series developed the use of numerical expressions to substantiate that its pictorials had captured the complete range of humanity. In this way it helped forge a framework that drew on a proliferation of shared experiences to create a common humanity.

In his analysis of the "People Are People" photographic series, Sandeen has cogently demonstrated the way the series ignored the biases that it used to interpret the oneness of mankind. For example, the emphasis on family life, rather than capturing a value that was shared equally by all cultures in all times, displayed the cultural leanings of 1950s America that promoted the heterosexual nuclear family as the basic building block of U.S. postwar society. As Sandeen contends, the patterns of family life featured in the "People Are People" series were not neutral representations of social activities; they worked to affirm the image of the United States as the beacon of progress, given how Americans were always shown to be interacting with the newest technologies, whereas people in non-Western countries were shown to be engaged only in practices handed down from centuries past.[11] Another standout point of Sandeen's review was that the *Ladies Home Journal* used racial and cultural differences to capture the oneness of mankind because it wanted to maintain a "nonpolitical" line in satiating the curiosity of readers and their tourist imaginations.[12] By casting particular worldviews as universal, the "People Are People" series endeavored to project an image of difference that did not call attention to the strictures of power. This multicultural projection, in turn, worked to verify the existence of a higher ideal through which to interpret the wide range of human experiences.

Although Steichen adopted this multicultural approach to create his vision of shared humanity, he did so as a way to resolve political issues, not as an attempt to avoid being political. To that end, Steichen aspired to direct the world's attention to the higher ideal of humanity so that people and nations could put aside their differences and work together to ensure peace and equal rights for all. He believed photography to be a powerful medium for bringing the oneness of mankind into focus and espoused a theory about photography and the knowledges that it produced to highlight the benefits of the medium. For Steichen, any photograph was a realistic depiction of actual events. As a result, the most important service that it could render history was "the recording of human relations, in explaining man to man."[13] Steichen considered photography distinctive in its ability to explicate human relations, given that it was able to transgress the boundaries of English-speaking countries and communicate to everyone throughout the world. He declared photography the only "universal language . . . requiring no translation."[14] Considering how Steichen extolled the benefits of photography in relation to his promotion of the *Family of Man* exhibit, his attention to the accessibility of photographs went beyond advancing photography as the universal language. He also sought to uphold the belief that there were aspects of human existence that required no explanation or contextualization. Steichen wanted to establish sameness as the indisputable basis for working out the social and political differences of the world.

The experiences that the *Family of Man* exhibit drew on to highlight the commonality of man were love, marriage, birth, joy, struggle, and death. As seen in the companion book of exhibition photographs, the *Family of Man* exhibit extracted various quotations from known and unknown sources and interspersed them with the photographs. Central to rendering universal a featured experience, the captions that accompanied each photograph made no mention of the photograph's date or specific historical context. They identified a photo wholly by the country depicted in the shot and the name of the photographer. Additionally, as observed in the segment on the anguish of children, the use of repetitive images, particularly the placement of six similar images of disheartened boys and girls from different parts of the world against a single backdrop of a thorny, barren bush, brought coherence to the range of struggles that youths were shown to have encountered.[15] This unity suggested the commonality of such incidents. A similar rank-and-file arrangement of nine headshots of demoralized-looking people of various ages, races, and nationalities further reinforced the idea that human suffering was a collective experience.[16]

Notably, critics like the French theorist Roland Barthes were quick to unsettle the use of the human condition, which Barthes deemed a "myth," as the lens through which all human actions were interpreted and understood. As Barthes noted in his 1957 review entitled "The Great Family of Man," the believability of the timelessness of human relations required that "Nature" be placed below "History."[17] While Barthes did not doubt that events such as birth and death were universal, he nevertheless considered it damaging to remove the particularities of time and place from the telling of life events, because it reduced the exercise of narrating life events into a practice of redundancy. For Barthes, the death of fourteen-year-old Emmett Till was noteworthy precisely because it brought into view the deep racial divide in Mississippi during the 1950s, where a black boy talking to a white woman was enough to incite a brutal murder. In this understanding, a death's history, not its essence, distinguished it and made it worth mentioning. The recognition of death's particularities could in this way help transform the immobile and ahistorical world of *The Family of Man* into a mobile and historically relevant one.[18] The resulting shift would unsettle not only the way the *Family of Man* exhibit bestowed on a single picture the ability to denote the experiences of all people, at all times, and in all places, but also the way it utilized images of the uncivilized black body to capture the whole of Africa.

As Barthes aptly showed, the myth of the human condition rendered invisible the particularities of lived experiences; nevertheless, he overlooked the very circumstances that drove the invention of this myth and made the timelessness of human actions worth propagating during the early Cold War years. As a result, what Barthes left unexamined was how the belief in the universal was conjured in order to help prevent the outbreak of another world war and the detonation of another atomic bomb. Moreover, rather than a dismissal of the problem of racism, the *Family of Man* exhibit had actually sought to mitigate the way race worked to divide people and splinter societies. While understanding this aspiration does not take away from the critiques that Barthes raised, it does deepen the recognition of shared humanity as a social device that was deployed to shape our views of human relations and to achieve a desired goal. Historicizing this construct is a productive endeavor because it directs attention away from the quest for a higher ideal, existing outside the realm of power relations, and toward a study of why the recognition of the equal worth of all people regardless of race, creed, or color was desirable in Cold War America.

Advancing the Superiority of U.S. Democracy

In an address to the Wisconsin Historical Society in 1957, Steichen discussed how he wanted to put on a show that not only featured the relationship of man to man and demonstrated how photography could reveal that bond, but also conveyed that people were all alike, regardless of race, color, or creed. He explained that the latter goal was a deeply personal one and that it stemmed from an incident that took place when he was just seven or eight years old growing up in Milwaukee. According to Steichen, this incident marked the true beginnings of the *Family of Man* exhibit.[19] Steichen recounted how one day when he was walking from school to his mother's millinery store, he saw a Jewish boy on the street and yelled, "You dirty kike!" He recalled how his mother, upon hearing him utter the slur, rushed out and dragged him to their upstairs apartment for a four-hour lecture. As Steichen related, his mother not only admonished him for failing to see that all people were alike, she also reminded him that this was America and that she had taken him here so that he could live in a world free of prejudices. He remembered her being "heartsick" because he had not understood this.[20] The *Family of Man* photography exhibit was Steichen's way of telling his mother that he had learned this lesson. It also became his way of sharing this lesson with the world so that the atrocity of the Holocaust would not occur again.

Notably, as Steichen's story illustrated, the prevention of another world war entailed not just promoting a message of equality but also promoting the view that the United States was the preeminent nation to bring about this ideal. Steichen's espousal of American exceptionalism led him to back the government's use of the exhibit to promote the superiority of U.S. democracy abroad. As the *Family of Man* exhibit embarked on a government-sponsored world tour, it importantly bolstered the efforts of other U.S. cultural ambassadors of the early Cold War years, such as the Olympic diver Sammy Lee and the author Jade Snow Wong, to testify to the benefits of the American way of life. But the *Family of Man* exhibit did not promote the advantages of U.S. democracy by putting on display its ability to respect and tolerate the cultural, racial, and national differences of the "East," as Lee and Wong had done. Rather, the exhibit extolled the nation's capacity to see past all social differences and embrace the commonality of mankind. This ability effectively enabled the United States to transcend national borders and to unite the world under its leadership so that an international body could come together to work for world peace and ensure equal rights to all.

A noteworthy segment of the *Family of Man* exhibit that demonstrated how the idea of shared humanity worked to advance a world free of prejudices was the installation of ten photographs that each contained the caption "We two form a multitude," taken from the poem *Metamorphoses* by the famed Roman poet Ovid.[21] As seen in the *Family of Man* companion book, each of the photos featured a heterosexual couple from a different part of the world.[22] Taken together, the photographs drew on this mode of partnership as the primary building block of a multicultural and multiracial world. From this reference point, the idea that it only took two to form a multitude worked to reinforce the exhibition's espousal of the universality of human experiences. Building on the assumed reproductive abilities of heterosexual couples, the installation propagated difference as a non-threatening replica of the same and established this type of reproduction as the natural course of life. This message further anchored the scattering of photographs throughout the exhibition that each showed two people engaged in various activities. Among these photos was a blown-up picture of a young black boy with his arm wrapped around a young white boy as they strolled down the street.[23] The display of racial harmony prominently advertised the fruits of a society that recognized the humanity of all. It served as a reminder of how the exhibit developed sameness in order to resolve the social and political tensions of the world. The "We two form a multitude" installation reinforced this intent as it culminated with the largest photo of the exhibit, which showed the United Nations and an excerpt from the preamble of its charter. Facing across from this oversized photo of the United Nations was an image of the atomic bomb.[24] The quotations extracted from the UN Charter's preamble thus conveyed what the recognition of the oneness of mankind could accomplish. Not only did this ideal work to unify all people under one political body to help protect "succeeding generations from the scourge of war," it also helped to "reaffirm faith in fundamental human rights, in the dignity and worth of the human person, in the equal rights of men and women and of nations large and small."[25]

Notwithstanding that the *Family of Man* exhibit showed the United States to be one of many nations that pledged to uphold the UN Charter, this was far from the underlying message of the traveling exhibit. Following its highly successful run at MOMA, the United States Information Agency (USIA), an agency devoted to the task of public diplomacy, approached the museum with the idea of funding a world tour for the exhibit. The USIA had chosen *The Family of Man* to be the nation's cultural ambassador because it considered the exhibit effective at showing the world how U.S. democracy was superior to communism. Specifically, the USIA believed that the exhibit effectively demonstrated that the United States attached great importance to the inexplicable bond between mankind, and that this attachment was in accord with the nation's democratic heritage. After securing the backing of Steichen and his creative team for a world tour, the USIA put its full weight behind promoting the *Family of Man* exhibit. It made magazine formats of exhibition photographs to provide a preview of the show to countries that it visited and distributed widely the companion book of exhibition photographs. The USIA also produced two short film clips that employed the show's theme to call for the formation of a noncommunist bloc. These clips were translated into multiple languages.[26]

Of the thirty-eight countries that the exhibit traveled to, the most important stop was the Soviet Union for the 1959 American National Exhibition in Moscow, where the famous Kitchen Debate erupted between the U.S. vice president Richard M. Nixon and the Soviet premier Nikita Khrushchev.[27] As *The Family of Man* was among the commodities selected by the U.S. government to display the benefits of the American way of life, the circulation of the message of shared humanity at this event functioned foremost to advance U.S. Cold War objectives. As a result, the message of shared humanity was not intended to serve as a call for the United States and the Soviet Union to put aside their differences and work together for world peace and the creation of a socially equitable world order. Instead, it supplied the United States with the moral authority to be the preeminent leader of the postwar world.

The USIA's use of the *Family of Man* exhibit to boost the image of the United States abroad paralleled the U.S. government's use of civil rights during the Cold War to demonstrate the superiority of the American way of life. By promising to mitigate the racial divide in U.S. society, civil rights reforms importantly turned the rising status of racialized minorities into a symbol of national progress. The appointment of Delbert Wong as the first Chinese American judge prompted for this reason the *Los Angeles*

Examiner to celebrate how the nation was ridding itself of "some ancient discriminations as unworthy of an enlightened society."[28] Interestingly, it also incited other Los Angeles–area newspapers, as chapter 3 has discussed, to come forward and declare that Wong was chosen based on his fitness for the position and not because of his race. As the *Hollywood Citizen News* maintained, the greatest testament to the credibility of American democracy, and hence the best way to combat communism, was to not allow the question of race to factor into how one is selected for a job.[29] In this view, the rising status of Asian Americans in U.S. society not only demonstrated that the nation was working to correct some historic mistakes, but also showed that the nation was advancing to a stage where it no longer saw racial, national, or cultural differences. In much the same way, the *Family of Man* photography exhibit advanced this idea as it sought to distinguish the preeminence of the American way of life through its capacity to see past all social differences and embrace the commonality of mankind. Notably, the effectiveness of this message rested not just in the way the concept of shared humanity was constructed as a natural human condition, but also in the way social progress was figured as the anticipated outcome of the American political system.

The Battle over Ethnic Studies

In the last two decades, the call to see past racial and cultural differences has become an influential approach for the creation of a socially equitable society. The 2008 election of Barack Hussein Obama as the nation's first black president importantly played out the belief that the United States was advancing to a place where race finally ceased to matter. After Obama assumed the presidency, many political pundits claimed that this historic feat marked the final passage across the racial divide, and showed that the nation had successfully moved past its preoccupation with the color of a person's skin. The election of the first black president thus ushered in a postracial age where claims to see past a person's color signified the greatest espousal of racial equality. But the emphasis on seeing past race allows us to ignore how the securing of equal access to society's resources had worked to mitigate the racial divide. The intent to do away with racial injustice by merely recognizing the individuality of the disenfranchised further turned acknowledgments of difference based on race into the reason social inequality persisted. It obscured the fact that social disparities were caused by the refusal to accept difference.

The contention that the election of President Obama marked the dawn of an era where race ceased to matter was not without its critics. If anything, it revealed an ongoing contestation over just how race was to shape the image of U.S. democracy. Given that Obama's candidacy also exposed how deeply divided Americans were over the prospect of having a black president whose father was foreign-born, many argued that the notion of the postracial signified an attempt to evade the problem of racism rather than the successful eradication of the racial divide. But the proliferation of reports that attested to the realities of racism in the wake of Obama's presidency did not necessarily dim the effect of the postracial logic. This was because the concept of postracial also denoted an approach to combating racial inequalities and not just the dawn of an age where race ceased to matter. As the Cold War discourse about shared humanity has shown, the appeal to see past race served as a compelling remedy, given that it was premised on an essentialist belief in the commonality of man and on the belief that the ability to see past race marked the next step in the nation's advancement toward social progress. The postracial logic has for this reason remained a relevant rationale.

The effect of this logic has been apparent in the recent struggle over ethnic studies in Arizona. As state officials sought to ban ethnic studies from the school districts and charter schools of Arizona following student and community protest against the state's proposed immigration policy, many considered this campaign to be a deliberate attempt to suppress criticisms of an immigration policy that unfairly targeted Latinos and fostered hostility toward them. State officials, however, contended that ethnic studies courses promoted racial strife by refusing to see people as individuals. The campaign against ethnic studies advanced in this way the belief that the best approach to racial harmony was to avoid drawing attention to racial and cultural differences. It attempted to shift the terms that defined the benefits of a multicultural education in the wake of the state's enactment of a controversial immigration policy. Not surprisingly, this endeavor went against the efforts of those who initiated the institutionalization of ethnic studies over forty years ago.

CONCLUSION

As the community activist Mike Murase has detailed in his article "Ethnic Studies and Higher Education for Asian Americans," the fight to increase the access of racialized and economically disadvantaged students to higher education came to a head on the campus of San Francisco State University in 1968. This struggle resulted in the longest student strike in the nation's history, organized under the auspices of the Third World Liberation Front, a coalition of black, Chicano, Native American, and Asian American student groups and community activists.[30] Notably, the San Francisco State strike related the fight against the policy of tracking (which drew on existing social disparities to justify steering working-class and racialized students away from four-year colleges) to the need for the introduction of college courses that covered the histories of the working class and of racialized groups without demeaning stereotypes about them.[31] The demand for courses that included the perspectives of racialized and economically disadvantaged groups sought in this way to contest the bias of the school's existing admissions policy and educational curriculum toward upper- and middle-class white Americans. The Third World Liberation Front thus called for an educational curriculum that met the diverse needs of San Francisco State's student population.

This initial fight for the institutionalization of ethnic studies, which spread to multiple campuses across California, resulted in state institutions making conciliatory gestures to the demands of student and community groups. For instance, Charles Young, chancellor of the University of California, Los Angeles, responded to student petitions by agreeing to create the American Cultures Project, which established separate research units for black, Chicano, Asian American, and Native American studies. While Young relied on the creation of these centers to show that UCLA was committed to recognizing the "uniqueness of each individual group," he also used this initiative to denounce student demonstrations as damaging to the university. He wanted to distinguish UCLA as a quality campus by its absence of student demonstrations. As these early research units were not authorized to teach or offer courses on ethnic studies but were only encouraged to make recommendations for reform, they were severely limited in their ability to alter the curriculum at UCLA.[32] The university used the mere presence of the research units to affirm its commitment to multicultural education, even if it did not adequately fund such programs or explore other means to help meet the needs of its diverse student population. Besides engaging student and community activists, the battle for ethnic studies thus revealed the goals of the state.

In Arizona, the passage of House Bill 2281 on May 13, 2010, to ban ethnic studies courses in Arizona's public and charter schools occurred just a few weeks after the state signed into law the nation's toughest anti–illegal immigration measure. The campaign to ban ethnic studies was in this way connected to the state's endeavor to secure greater access to jobs and other societal resources to its citizens than to its immigrants. Although the immigration measure was ostensibly enacted to stop the flow of undocumented immigrants to the state, it nevertheless contained provisions to limit the rights of aliens by making it a misdemeanor for aliens to be in Arizona without proper documentation.[33] Moreover, given the popular perception that all undocumented immigrants were Latinos and that the vast majority of Latinos in the United States were foreign-born, this immigration measure disproportionately affected Latinos over other groups in Arizona.

The ban on ethnic studies in Arizona grew out of efforts to manage dissent against the immigration measure. Specifically, it looked to suppress criticism that the bill was out of line with the nation's democratic principles. The incident that reportedly prompted Tom Horne, Arizona superintendent of public education, to launch a campaign against ethnic studies was a heated exchange that took place between the labor activist Dolores Huerta and Arizona deputy superintendent of public instruction Margaret Garcia Dugan. Reportedly, when Dugan tried to refute Huerta's claim that the proposed state immigration bill was racist, particularly Huerta's incendiary remark that "Republicans hate Latinos," students at Tucson High Magnet School walked out in protest. Following this 2006 incident, Horne launched an attack against the ethnic studies curriculum at Tucson Unified School District and its Mexican American studies department. Without ever visiting a class or conducting a formal review of the curriculum, he proclaimed that ethnic studies courses taught students to resent whites and fostered a destructive brand of ethnic chauvinism.[34] What the student walkouts had thereby signaled to Horne was the need to adopt a more aggressive approach to secure consent for the proposed immigration bill and more importantly, to squash any suggestion that the bill had unfairly sought to limit the access of Latinos to state resources.

Herein lies the effectiveness of the postracial logic of the campaign against ethnic studies. As Horne emphasized the importance of looking past racial, cultural, and national differences for creating a learning environment that was free of prejudice, this logic enabled him to frame the ban on ethnic studies as a necessary educational reform that would lead to the design of a more equitable curriculum in Arizona's public schools. Horne was known to have remarked on numerous occasions that he considered ethnic studies courses damaging to race relations, as they prevented students from treating each other as individuals while drawing undue attention to their racial and cultural differences. In this view, the best way to mitigate the racial divide entailed not the petitioning against an immigration measure that infringed on the civil liberties of racialized immigrants and citizens. Rather, it required the development of a curriculum that eliminated the study of race and racism. Horne's appeal to see past racial and cultural differences thus worked to suppress activities and ideas that went against the state's political agenda.

The use of a postracial logic to contain rather than promote differences of opinions crucially demonstrates the need to contextualize appeals to see past race. Such appeals must be analyzed as social devices that work to shape our views of difference and equality. In the campaign to ban ethnic studies in Arizona, the appeal to see past race was invoked to advance uniformity of thought and to suppress the activities of those who contested the state's endeavor to limit the access of Latinos to state resources. The campaign resulted in Arizona governor Jan Brewer signing House Bill 2281 to eliminate ethnic studies courses from the public schools of Arizona. Notably, the bill's first stipulation included the popular Cold War directive to prohibit the teaching of ideas that promoted the overthrow of the government. During the height of the Smith Act and McCarran Act persecutions, the federal government had interpreted this edict liberally in its attempt to criminalize a whole host of activities that were believed to go against the status quo, many of which were antiracist activities. But rather than rendering irrelevant antiracist articulations, this clamp down helped turn race into a meaningful category of analysis that worked to reveal the terms and limits of U.S. democracy. In the case of Arizona, the ban on ethnic studies has effectively unsettled the ability of the postracial logic to create a society that is free of prejudices. It has made us question whether we want to arrive at a world where race has ceased to matter, and has made us begin to accept that race, in fact, does matter.

NOTES

INTRODUCTION

1. President's Committee on Civil Rights, *To Secure These Rights* (New York: Simon and Schuster, 1947), 30–32.
2. Ibid., 32–33.
3. Several studies have examined why Truman agreed to sign Executive Order 9808, which created in 1946 the President's Committee on Civil Rights and requested the submission of a written report with recommendations on how the federal government could best act to protect the civil liberties of all. Some reasons include Truman's need for the black vote, the urgings of more liberal members of the Truman administration, the rising influence of the NAACP, the Cold War, and Truman's commitment to civil rights. While these studies often differed in their explanations for why Truman made civil rights a national priority, they nevertheless agreed that the signing of Executive Order 9808 marked a change in national policy, after which the federal government took an active role to ensure racial equality during the postwar era. See Barton J. Bernstein, "The Ambiguous Legacy: The Truman Administration and Civil Rights," in *Politics and Policies of the Truman Administration,* ed. Barton J. Bernstein (Chicago: Quadrangle, 1971), 269–314; Raymond H. Geselbracht, ed., *The Civil Rights Legacy of Harry Truman* (Kirksville: Truman State University Press, 2007); and Michael R. Gardner, *Harry Truman and Civil Rights* (Carbondale: Southern Illinois University Press, 2002).
4. President's Committee on Civil Rights, *To Secure These Rights,* 146–48.
5. The President's Committee on Civil Rights emphasized the importance of civil rights with President Truman's March 1947 address before a joint session of Congress in mind. In this address, known popularly as the Truman Doctrine, Truman declared that every nation must choose between two ways of life. The first is a life based on the will of the majority, distinguished by free institutions; the second is based on the will of a minority forcibly imposed on the majority. Truman proclaimed the United States the presumptive leader of the "free world." As a result, the United States had a political obligation "to support free peoples who are resisting attempted subjugation by armed minorities or by outside pressure" and to spread American democracy. These remarks came to define U.S. Cold War policy as one of communist containment and internationalism. See President Harry S. Truman, speaking for the Recommendation for Assistance to Greece and

Turkey, on March 12, 1947, to the joint session of the Senate and the House of Representatives, 80th Cong., 1st sess.

Drawing on the analysis of the historian John Lewis Gaddis, I use the phrase "Cold War internationalism" to highlight the ways the federal government framed U.S. postwar expansionist initiatives as internationalism. Moreover, building on Christina Klein's analysis of U.S. Cold War foreign policy, I use the phrase to underscore the way internationalism became inextricably linked to communist containment. See John Lewis Gaddis, *The United States and the Origins of the Cold War*, rev. ed. (New York: Columbia University Press, 2000); and Christina Klein, *Cold War Orientalism: Asia in the Middlebrow Imagination, 1945–1961* (Berkeley: University of California Press, 2003), 19–60.

6. As the cultural critic Lisa Lowe has argued, the task of imagining the nation as homogeneous in its makeup, which I take to mean solely European American, requires the formation of a separate racial imagination whereby Asians in the United States remain "fundamentally 'foreign'" and averse to the mores of American society. Thus, despite the repeal of the whites-only rule in naturalization and in spite of how many Asians were American-born, the task of imagining the nation as homogeneous continues to relegate Asians in the United States to the status of foreigners-within. See Lisa Lowe, *Immigrant Acts: On Asian American Cultural Politics* (Durham: Duke University Press, 1996), 4–6. Because the racialization of Asians as the foreigners-within works to mark Asians as mere extensions of their countries of ancestry, irrespective of being American-born or length of residence in the United States, I use the terms "Asians in the United States" and "Asian Americans" to denote both American citizens of Asian descent and Asian immigrants.

7. As Harry H. L. Kitano and Roger Daniels have argued, following the communist takeover of China in 1949 and the entrance of China into the Korean conflict against the United States a year later, Chinese in the United States feared that they would be incarcerated the way Japanese Americans were in World War II. What prevented this from happening, Kitano and Daniels contend, was that "the American view of China and Chinese became plural." The perception that there were now two Chinas, Mao Zedong's communist China and Chiang Kai-shek's Republic of China, worked to allow for distinctions to be made "between the 'good' and 'bad' Asians." See Harry H. L. Kitano and Roger Daniels, *Asian Americans: Emerging Minorities* (Upper Saddle River, NJ: Prentice Hall, 2001), 44.

8. See Ronald Takaki, *Strangers from a Different Shore: A History of Asian Americans* (New York: Penguin, 1989), 357–405; and Sucheng Chan, *Asian Americans: An Interpretive History* (New York: Twayne, 1991), 121–42.

9. Elena Tajima Creef, *Imaging Japanese America: The Visual Construction of Citizenship, Nation and the Body* (New York: New York University Press, 2004), 150–51.

10. Takaki, *Strangers from a Different Shore*, 392.

11. Mae M. Ngai, *Impossible Subjects: Illegal Aliens and the Making of Modern America* (Princeton: Princeton University Press, 2004), 175.

12. Neil Gotanda, "Towards Repeal of Asian Exclusion," in *Asian Americans and Congress: A Documentary History*, ed. Hyung-chan Kim (Westport, CT: Greenwood, 1996), 312.

13. Ibid., 311–14. For a solid discussion of Japan's endeavors to create a pan-Asian alliance during the Pacific War, see John W. Dower, *War without Mercy: Race and Power in the Pacific War* (New York: Pantheon, 1986).

14. Fred W. Riggs, *Pressures on Congress: A Study of the Repeal of Chinese Exclusion* (New York: King's Crown, 1950).

15. For an insightful analysis of the ways Germany and Japan publicized racist practices in the United States in their attempts to discredit the superiority of U.S. democracy, see Dower, *War without Mercy*, 3–14.

16. For a solid discussion of how the federal government drew on the construct of "military necessity" to legalize the internment of Japanese residents on the West Coast, see Takaki, *Strangers from a Different Shore*, 379–405.

17. Brenda Gayle Plummer, *Rising Wind: Black Americans and U.S. Foreign Affairs, 1935–1960* (Chapel Hill: University of North Carolina Press, 1996).

18. Mary L. Dudziak, *Cold War Civil Rights: Race and the Image of American Democracy* (Princeton: Princeton University Press, 2000). Dudziak importantly situates her work within a broader historiography that explores how U.S. foreign affairs shaped domestic civil rights reforms. These works include Plummer, *Rising Wind*; Gerald Horne, *Black and Red: W. E. B. Du Bois and the Afro American Response to the Cold War* (Albany: State University of New York Press, 1986); and Derrick A. Bell Jr., "*Brown v. Board of Education* and the Interest-Convergence Dilemma," *Harvard Law Review* 93 (January 1980): 518–33.

19. Dudziak, *Cold War Civil Rights*, 13.

20. Ibid., 14.

21. President's Committee on Civil Rights, *To Secure These Rights*, 16.

22. Ibid., 30–34.

23. Ibid., x.

24. See Commission on Race and Housing, *Where Shall We Live? Report of the Commission on Race and Housing* (Berkeley: University of California Press, 1958).

25. Claire Jean Kim, "The Racial Triangulation of Asian Americans," *Politics and Society* 27, no. 1 (March 1999): 105–38.

26. Leslie Bow, "Racial Interstitiality and the Anxieties of the 'Partly Colored,'" *Journal of Asian American Studies* 10, no. 1 (February 2007): 4–5.

27. See Lowe, *Immigrant Acts*, 4–8.

28. See Klein, *Cold War Orientalism*, 240.

29. President's Committee on Civil Rights, *To Secure These Rights*, 3.

30. Ibid., 10.

31. In her essay "Gender: A Useful Category of Historical Analysis," the feminist historian Joan Wallach Scott sought to develop through the category of gender a theory that would explicitly work to unsettle existing paradigms guiding the writing of histories—paradigms that have elided the study of women. My substitution of the term "race" for "gender" is not meant to suggest that these categories are interchangeable modes of inquiry. Rather, I want to signal that this book goes beyond examining Asian Americans as the subjects of historical inquiry; it analyzes Asian American racial formation as a mode of historical inquiry. See Joan Wallach Scott, "Gender: A Useful Category of Historical Analysis," in *Gender and the Politics of History*, rev. ed. (New York: Columbia University Press, 1999), 28–50.

32. Lowe, *Immigrant Acts*, 8.

33. Ibid., 4, 6.

34. Michal Belknap, *Cold War Political Justice: The Smith Act, the Communist Party, and American Civil Liberties* (Westport, CT: Greenwood, 1977).

35. Victor Navasky, *Naming Names* (New York: Viking Adult, 1980); Ellen Schrecker, *Many Are the Crimes: McCarthyism in America* (Princeton: Princeton University Press, 1998).

36. See Daniel Tichenor, *Dividing Lines: The Politics of Immigration Control in America* (Princeton: Princeton University Press, 2002); and Gabriel J. Chin, "The Civil Rights Revolution Comes to Immigration Law: A New Look at the Immigration and Nationality Act of 1965," *North Carolina Law Review* 75 (1996–1997): 273–345.

37. Charlotte Brooks, *Alien Neighbors, Foreign Friends: Asian Americans, Housing, and the Transformation of Urban California* (Chicago: University of Chicago Press, 2009).

38. See Scott Kurashige, *The Shifting Grounds of Race: Black and Japanese Americans in the Making of Multiethnic Los Angeles* (Princeton: Princeton University Press, 2008).

39. Brooks, *Alien Neighbors, Foreign Friends*, 2.

CHAPTER 1

1. Tommy Amer, interview by author, Los Angeles, CA, August 26, 2000, and September 30, 2002.

2. Ibid.

3. Cheryl I. Harris, "Whiteness as Property," in *Critical Race Theory*, ed. Kimberle Crenshaw, Neil Gotanda, Gary Peller, and Kendall Thomas (New York: New Press, 1995), 277–78, 282.

4. Leslie Bow, *Partly Colored: Asian Americans and Racial Anomaly in the Segregated South* (New York: New York University Press, 2010).

5. California Constitution (1876), art. 19, sec. 4. Article XIX, which is simply entitled "The Chinese," remained in effect until November 1952. See California State Senate, *The Constitution of the State of California* (1958), 140.

6. The Alien Land Laws, first enacted in 1913, remained in effect until 1946, after the U.S. Supreme Court ruled in the case of *Oyama v. State of California* that these laws were unconstitutional. See *Oyama v. State of California* (68 S. Ct. 269). While these laws affected all Asians, they were primarily directed against Japanese Americans.

7. See Loren Miller, "Housing and Racial Covenants," *Frontier Magazine*, February 1, 1950, 11–13. See also Loren Miller, "The Power of Restrictive Covenants," *Survey Graphic* 35 (January 1947): 46. According to Miller, during the three decades of judicial enforcement of restrictive covenants from 1919 to 1948, California courts had consistently refused to oust persons of Mexican descent, "no matter how large their degree of Indian blood," from homes that had barred other non-Caucasians, given that Mexicans were classified as Caucasians in the California census.

8. Loren Miller, "Race Restrictions on Ownership or Occupancy of Land," *Lawyers Guild Review* 7 (1947): 99. See also Miller, "The Power of Restrictive Covenants"; California Constitution (1876), art. 19, sec. 4.

9. *In re Lee Sing* (43 F. 359).

10. *Gandolfo v. Hartman* (49 F. 181). This case was brought before the San Diego circuit court after the defendant Hartman attempted to rent to two Chinese a portion of a lot that he purchased from a man named Steward. While the racial restrictive covenant was originally agreed upon between owners Gandolfo and Steward, it included a clause that stated, "And said party of the second part agrees for himself and *heirs* that he will never rent any of the property hereby conveyed to Chinaman or Chinamen," thus making Hartman liable for breaking this covenant (emphasis mine).

11. *Gandolfo v. Hartman*.

12. James Stenius Roberts, "Racial Restrictive Covenants," *Sociology and Social Research* 32 (November–December 1947): 617. See also Yi-Seng Kiang, "Judicial Enforcement of Restrictive Covenants in the United States," *Washington Law Review* 24 (February 1949): 9.

13. *Buchanan v. Warley* (38 S. Ct. 16).

14. Clement E. Vose, *Caucasians Only: The Supreme Court, the NAACP, and the Restrictive Covenant Cases* (Berkeley: University of California Press, 1959), 3.

15. Filipinos were exempted from the stipulations of the Immigration Act of 1924, which prohibited the immigration of aliens ineligible for citizenship to the United States. As the Philippines was a colony of the United States, Filipinos were afforded the status of "nationals" and not "aliens." The legal designation "nationals" allowed for the immigration of Filipinos to the United States even though they remained ineligible for naturalized citizenship. The restriction of Filipino immigration to the United States came about following the passage of the 1934 Tydings-McDuffie Act.

16. Miller, "Race Restrictions on Ownership or Occupancy of Land," 100. See also D. O. McGovney, "Racial Residential Segregation by State Court Enforcement of Restrictive Agreements, Covenants or Conditions in Deeds Is Unconstitutional," *California Law Review* 33 (1945): 8.

17. *Corrigan v. Buckley* (271 U.S. 323); *Corrigan v. Buckley* (299 F. 899).

18. Kiang, "Judicial Enforcement of Restrictive Covenants," 2.

19. Vose, *Caucasians Only*, 7–8. See also J. Max Bond, "The Negro in Los Angeles" (PhD diss., University of Southern California, 1936), 85.

20. *Amer v. Superior Court of the State of California*, October term, 1947, no. 429.

21. Commission on Race and Housing, *Where Shall We Live?* (Berkeley: University of California Press, 1958), 10–34.

22. Ralph Guzman, "The Hand of Esau," *Frontier* 7–8 (June 1956): 13.

23. Herman H. Long and Charles S. Johnson, *People vs. Property: Race Restrictive Covenants in Housing* (Nashville: Fisk University Press, 1947), 39–55.

24. This study builds on the notion of suburbanization as urbanization that the historian Greg Hise developed in his study of postwar suburban growth in Los Angeles. What Hise sought to dismantle by adopting the concept of suburbanization as urbanization was the hierarchical and oppositional relationship between the city and the suburbs that urbanists drew on to characterize the growth of postwar suburbs as both peripheral and parasitic to the city. By showing how the growth of postwar suburbs in Los Angeles was driven by factors that differed from those driving the building of cities, Hise exposes the center/periphery model to be an overdetermined framework not wholly useful for understanding the proliferation of postwar suburbs. See Greg Hise, *Magnetic Los Angeles: Planning the Twentieth-Century Metropolis* (Baltimore: Johns Hopkins University Press, 1997).

25. Kenneth T. Jackson, *Crabgrass Frontier: The Suburbanization of the United States* (New York: Oxford University Press, 1985), 234–38.

26. Ibid., 241.

27. Given that the suburbs served as a gateway to the broader social amenities available in a neighborhood, the material benefits of whiteness included better access to schools, hospitals, and other public and institutional services. Eshref

Shevky and Molly Lewin, *Your Neighborhood* (Los Angeles: Haynes Foundation, 1949), 1.

28. Mary L. Dudziak, *Cold War Civil Rights: Race and the Image of American Democracy* (Princeton: Princeton University Press, 2000), 79–92.

29. *Amer v. Superior Court of the State of California*, 1–2.

30. Keith Collins, *Black Los Angeles: The Maturing of the Ghetto, 1940–1950* (Saratoga: Century Twenty One Publishing, 1980), 18. The sociologist Rose Hum Lee also observed the increased migration of Chinese in the United States to urban areas, particularly Los Angeles, Minneapolis, Oakland, Portland, San Francisco, Seattle, Washington, DC, and New York. Lee detailed how the burgeoning defense industries in these cities spurred on the migration of the Chinese to these areas between 1930 and 1940. This trend continued during the post–World War II period. See Rose Hum Lee, "The Decline of Chinatowns in the United States," *American Journal of Sociology* 54 (March 1949): 428.

31. Collins, *Black Los Angeles*, 19, 20. For a good account of black migration to Los Angeles from 1920 to 1930, see Lawrence B. De Graaf, "The City of Black Los Angeles: Emergence of the Los Angeles Ghetto, 1890–1930," *Pacific Historical Review* 39 (August 1970): 323–52.

32. Thomas Allen McDannold, "Development of the Los Angeles Chinatown, 1850–1970" (MA thesis, California State University, Northridge, 1973), 21; Wen-Hui Chung Chen, "Changing Socio-Cultural Patterns of the Chinese Community in Los Angeles" (PhD diss., University of Southern California, 1952), 53; and U.S. Bureau of the Census, *Sixteenth Census of the United States 1940*, vol. 2, *Characteristics of the Population, Part 1: United States Summary and Alabama-District of Columbia* (Washington, DC: U.S. Government Printing Office, 1943), 664.

33. Charles B. Spaulding, "Housing Problems of Minority Groups in Los Angeles County," *Annals of the American Academy of Political and Social Science* 248 (November 1946): Governor's Advisory Commission on Housing Problems, *Report on Housing in California* (San Francisco, 1963), 9.

34. U.S. Bureau of the Census, *Sixteenth Census of the United States, 1940*, vol. 2, *Characteristics of the Population, Part 1: United States Summary and Alabama-District of Columbia* 664; U.S. Bureau of the Census, *A Report of the Seventeenth Decennial Census of the United States, 1950*, vol. 2, *Characteristics of the Population, Part 5: California (Washington, DC: U.S. Government Printing Office, 1952)*, 179.

35. U.S. Bureau of the Census, *Sixteenth Census of the United States, 1940*, vol. 2, *Characteristics of the Population, Part 1: United States Summary and Alabama-District of Columbia*, 630; U.S. Bureau of the Census, *A Report of the Seventeenth Decennial Census of the United States. 1950*, vol. 2, *Characteristics of the Population, Part 5: California*, 179.

36. Paul F. Coe, "The Nonwhite Population Surge into Our Cities," *Land Economics* 35 (August 1959): 196.

37. Collins, *Black Los Angeles*, 19.

38. Spaulding, "Housing Problems of Minority Groups in Los Angeles County," 222.

39. Robert C. Weaver, *The Negro Ghetto* (New York: Russell and Russell, 1967), 87–90.

40. Kyung Lee, "Settlement Patterns of Los Angeles Koreans" (MA thesis, University of California, Los Angeles, 1969), 52, 54.

41. See Scott Kurashige, *The Shifting Grounds of Race: Black and Japanese Americans in the Making of Multiethnic Los Angeles* (Princeton: Princeton University Press, 2008).

42. Robin Scott Fitzgerald, "The Mexican-American in the Los Angeles Area, 1920–1950" (PhD diss., University of Southern California, 1971), 65–68; George Sanchez, "'What's Good for Boyle Heights Is Good for the Jews': Creating Multiracialism on the Eastside during the 1950s," *American Quarterly* 56, no. 3 (September 2004): 637.

43. Chen, "Changing Socio-Cultural Patterns of the Chinese Community in Los Angeles," 73–90. See also Suellen Cheng and Munson Kwok, "The Golden Years of Los Angeles Chinatown: The Beginning," in *The Golden Years: 1938–1988* (Los Angeles: 1988), 39–41, 45, 47.

44. Roberts, "Racial Restrictive Covenants," 617.

45. "Statistics Concerning Negro Population and Restrictive Covenants," ca. 1946, Ben Margolis and John McTernan Papers, Southern California Library for Social Studies and Research, Los Angeles, California (hereafter cited as Southern California Library for Social Studies and Research).

46. Chen, "Changing Socio-Cultural Patterns of the Chinese Community in Los Angeles," 63–67.

47. Shevky and Lewin, *Your Neighborhood*, 10.

48. Spaulding, "Housing Problems of Minority Groups in Los Angeles County," 222.

49. *Pacific Citizen*, May 25, 1946.

50. Brief for California as *amicus curiae*, *McGhee v. Sipes*, 5.

51. *Los Angeles Daily News*, May 13, 1946.

52. Los Angeles Council for Civic Unity, "The Ku Klux Klan in California," *Uni-Facts*, June 1946. See also *California Eagle*, May 16, 1946.

53. Los Angeles Council for Civic Unity, "The Ku Klux Klan in California."

54. *California Eagle*, May 23, 1946. Earl Robinson penned "The House I Live In," a popular song protesting the practice of residential segregation.

55. Chen, "Changing Socio-Cultural Patterns of the Chinese Community in Los Angeles," 64–66. I believe that the "Dr. K" to whom Chen refers in her study is Yin Kim, given that there was only one Korean American doctor who lived on Gramercy Street, earned his dentistry degree from the University of Southern California, and was engaged in fighting residential segregation in both the state courts of California and the U.S. Supreme Court.

56. The All People's Christian Church and Community Center had acquired the property of the Japanese Christian Institute during the time of the Japanese evacuation. During this early Cold War period, it emerged as the key interracial institution that supported the fight against discriminatory practices against racial minorities in Los Angeles. See *Pacific Citizen*, June 8, 1946.

57. The Japanese American Citizens League also contributed financial and legal support for both the Amer and Kim cases. See *Pacific Citizen*, June 15, 1946, December 7, 1946.

58. Kurashige, *Shifting Grounds of Race*.

59. Shana Bernstein, *Bridges of Reform: Interracial Civil Rights Activism in Twentieth-Century Los Angeles* (Oxford: Oxford University Press, 2011).

60. Tommy Amer, interview by author, Los Angeles, CA, August 26, 2000, and September 30, 2002.

61. Chen, "Changing Socio Cultural Patterns of the Chinese Community in Los Angeles," 71–72.

62. Kiang, "Judicial Enforcement of Restrictive Covenants," 10.

63. Brief for California as *amicus curiae*, *McGhee v. Sipes*, 2–3.

64. *Pacific Citizen*, May 25, 1946.

65. Brief for California as *amicus curiae*, *McGhee v. Sipes*, 4.

66. For a good discussion of the Sugar Hill and Laws cases, see Kevin Allen Leonard, *The Battle for Los Angeles: Racial Ideology and World War II* (Albuquerque: University of New Mexico Press, 2006); and Josh Sides, *L.A. City Limits: African American Los Angeles from the Great Depression to the Present* (Berkeley: University of California Press, 2003). See also Roberts, "Racial Restrictive Covenants," 617.

67. Weaver, *The Negro Ghetto*.

68. Louis Wirth, *The Ghetto* (Chicago: University of Chicago Press, 1928).

69. Robert C. Weaver, *Hemmed In: ABC's of Race Restrictive Housing Covenants* (Chicago: American Council on Race Relations, 1945), 13.

70. Louis Wirth, "The Unfinished Business of American Democracy," *Annals of the American Academy of Political and Social Science* 244 (March 1946): 2.

71. Vose, *Caucasians Only*, 64–68, 160–63.

72. "Proceedings of the Conference on Housing and Racial Discrimination," February 24, 1945, Frank Wilkinson Papers, Southern California Library for Social

Studies and Research; "Proceedings of the Los Angeles Citizens Housing Council Conference on Housing," January 18, 1947, Los Angeles Subject Files: Los Angeles Citizens Housing Council, Southern California Library for Social Studies and Research.

73. Grace E. Snouis, "Judge Stanley Mosk Rules Race Covenants Illegal, 'Un-American,'" *Los Angeles Sentinel*, October 30, 1947.

74. President's Committee on Civil Rights, *To Secure These Rights* (New York: Simon and Schuster, 1947), 69–70.

75. Ibid., 3–9.

76. The U.S. Supreme Court in 1945 denied the petition for a writ of certiorari to the *Mays v. Burgess* case. Justices Murphy and Rutledge, however, favored a review. The disagreement among the justices was significant, for it showed the growing willingness of the Supreme Court to review the constitutionality of racial restrictive covenants. The "rule of four" had stipulated that the consent of four justices is needed to grant a writ of certiorari. In light of the willingness of some justices to rule on the issue of racial restrictive covenants, the NAACP convened at Howard University in February 1947 to discuss filing petitions for writs of certiorari. While no definitive conclusions were made at this conference, lawyers for the Shelley case made a unilateral decision to petition their case before the U.S. Supreme Court on April 21, 1947. This instigated the filing of the McGhee case along with the two cases from the District of Columbia. See Vose, *Caucasians Only*, 156–57.

77. Vose, *Caucasians Only*, 157–58, 212.

78. Ibid., 158.

79. The four cases involving African Americans were *Shelley v. Kraemer* (68 S. Ct. 836); *McGhee v. Sipes* (68 S. Ct. 836); *Hurd v. Hodge* (68 S. Ct. 847); and *Urciolo v. Hodge* (68 S. Ct. 847). While Raphael Urciolo was a white real estate agent, Hodge nevertheless sued him for selling restricted properties to blacks.

80. Richard R. W. Brooks, "Incorporating Race," *Columbia Law Review* 106 (2006): 2060; *Trustees of the Monroe Avenue Church of Christ v. Fred C. Perkins* (68 S. Ct. 1069).

81. *Tom D. Amer v. Superior Court of the State of California* (68 S. Ct. 1069); *Yin Kim v. Superior Court of the State of California* (68 S. Ct. 1069).

82. Transcript of Record for Yin Kim, U.S. Supreme Court, October term, 1947, no. 430, 1.

83. Transcript of Record for Tom D. Amer, U.S. Supreme Court, October term, 1947, no. 429, 1. *Tom D. Amer v. Superior Court of the State of California*, 1.

84. *Los Angeles Sentinel*, May 23, 1946; *Poly Optimist*, May 23, 1946.

85. *Los Angeles Times*, May 17, 1946, May 20, 1946.

86. Brief of the Japanese American Citizens League as *amicus curiae*, *Hurd v. Hodge*, 4–5. See also *Pacific Citizen*, May 8, 1948.

87. *Amer v. Superior Court of California*; *Yin Kim v. Superior Court of California*, October term, 1947, no. 430, 4–5.

88. Brief of the Japanese American Citizens League as *amicus curiae*, on Petitions for Writs of Certiorari to the Supreme Court of the State of California, *Amer v. Superior Court of California; Yin Kim v. Superior Court of California*, 2–3.

89. As the legal scholar Neil Gotanda has argued, before the passage of the 1952 McCarran-Walter Act, which lifted the racial qualification of whites only to naturalized citizenship, the bypassing of the whites-only rule was stipulated through a step-by-step, group-by-group, and ethnic-by-ethnic approach. Separate statutes were enacted to determine, for example, blacks and Chinese as exceptions to the whites-only rule to naturalization. See Neil Gotanda, "Towards Repeal of Asian Exclusion," in *Asian Americans and Congress*, ed. Hyung-chan Kim (Westport, CT: Greenwood, 1996), 324–26.

90. For an in-depth discussion of the various factors that led to the filing of the amicus curiae brief by the Truman Justice Department for the Shelley et al. cases, see Philip Elman, "The Solicitor General's Office, Justice Frankfurter, and Civil Rights Litigation, 1946–1960," interview by Norman Silber in *Harvard Law Review* 100 (1987): 817–52; Randall Kennedy, "A Reply to Philip Elman," *Harvard Law Review* 100 (1987): 1938–57. See also Dudziak, *Cold War Civil Rights*, 275–77.

91. As cited in Dudziak, *Cold War Civil Rights*, 91. See also Vose, *Caucasians Only*, 168–74.

92. Brief for the United States as *amicus curiae*, *Shelley v. Kraemer*, *McGhee v. Sipes*, *Hurd v. Hodge*, *Urciolo v. Hodge*, 19–25.

93. The American Association for the United Nations was a nationwide, nonprofit organization dedicated to promoting the U.S. government's adherence to the United Nations Charter. Brief for the American Association for the United Nations as *amicus curiae*, *Shelley v. Kraemer*, *McGhee v. Sipes*, *Hurd v. Hodge*, *Urciolo v. Hodge*, 2, 31. See also Arthur G. Altschul, "U.N. Cited to High Court to End Bias in Realty Covenants," *New York Times*, December 5, 1947.

94. Brief for the United States as *amicus curiae*, *Shelley v. Kraemer*, *McGhee v. Sipes*, *Hurd v. Hodge*, *Urciolo v. Hodge*, 3, 37–38.

95. See Brief for Petitioners, *McGhee v. Sipes*, 334 U.S. 1 (1948); and Brief for Petitioners, *Shelley v. Kraemer* 334 U.S. 1 (1948).

96. See Vose, *Caucasians Only*, 160–67.

97. See John Mark McQuiston, *Negro Residential Invasion in Los Angeles County* (Los Angeles: McQuiston Associates, 1969).

98. The final U.S. Supreme Court ruling on the issue of racial restrictive

covenants was issued on June 15, 1954, when the Court ruled in *Barrows v. Jackson* that a racial restrictive covenant may not be enforced by law in a suit for damages. *Barrows v. Jackson* was a Los Angeles–based case whereby three property owners sued Mrs. Loela Jackson for (1) not incorporating in the deed the restriction contained in the covenant; and (2) breaking the covenant by selling to Negroes, thereby making her liable for damages. This case was filed on behalf of the Los Angeles Realty Board with the support of the National Association of Real Estate Boards. Additionally, white property owners in Los Angeles and other cities put their full weight behind this case as a last-ditch effort to preserve the practice of residential segregation based on race that involved at least twenty such organizations in Los Angeles alone. See Vose, *Caucasians Only*, 234–46.

99. *California Eagle*, May 6, 1948.

100. Ibid.

CHAPTER 2

1. Eric Avila, *Popular Culture in the Age of White Flight: Fear and Fantasy in Suburban Los Angeles* (Berkeley: University of California Press, 2004), 4.

2. Ibid., 14–16.

3. Caroline Chung Simpson, *An Absent Presence: Japanese Americans in Postwar American Culture, 1945–1960* (Durham: Duke University Press, 2001), 176–85.

4. See Nayan Shah, *Contagious Divides: Epidemics and Race in San Francisco's Chinatown* (Berkeley: University of California Press, 2001); Jennifer Ting, "Bachelor Society: Deviant Heterosexuality and Asian American Historiography," in *Privileging Positions*, ed. Gary Y. Okihiro, Marilyn Alquizola, Dorothy Fujita Rony, and K. Scott Wong (Pullman: Washington State University Press, 1995), 271–79.

5. See Thomas C. Reeves, *Freedom and the Foundation: The Fund for the Republic in the Era of McCarthyism* (New York: Knopf, 1969); Robert M. Hutchins, *Freedom, Education, and the Fund: Essays and Addresses, 1946–1956* (New York: Meridian, 1956).

6. Hutchins, *Freedom, Education, and the Fund*, 214.

7. Reeves, *Freedom and the Foundation*, 92; Commission on Race and Housing, *Where Shall We Live? Report of the Commission on Race and Housing* (Berkeley: University of California Press, 1958), v.

8. Commission on Race and Housing, *Where Shall We Live?*, v.

9. Ibid., 3.

10. Ibid., 8.

11. Ibid., 6, 8.

12. Ibid., 8.

13. "When Nixon Took on Khrushchev," *U.S. News and World Report*, August 3, 1959; *New York Times*, July 25, 1959. See also Elaine Tyler May, *Homeward Bound: American Families in the Cold War Era* (New York: Basic, 1988), 16–20.

14. May, *Homeward Bound*, 20.

15. William H. Whyte Jr., *The Organization Man* (New York: Simon and Schuster, 1956), 310.

16. Commission on Race and Housing, *Where Shall We Live?*, 9.

17. Ibid.

18. Davis McEntire, *Residence and Race* (Berkeley: University of California Press, 1960), 114–15.

19. Ibid., 115.

20. Ibid., 115–16.

21. Commission on Race and Housing, *Where Shall We Live?*, 8–9.

22. For a solid discussion of this sociological tradition, see Henry Yu, *Thinking Orientals: Migration, Contact, and Exoticism in Modern America* (Oxford: Oxford University Press, 2001), 38–39.

23. McEntire, *Residence and Race*, 105–18.

24. Ibid., 112.

25. Ibid., 111.

26. Ibid., 111–12.

27. Commission on Race and Housing, *Where Shall We Live?*, 13.

28. McEntire, *Residence and Race*, 46–47.

29. Commission on Race and Housing, *Where Shall We Live?*, 13.

30. May, *Homeward Bound*, 5–9.

31. Ibid., 3.

32. Ibid., 13.

33. Robert G. Lee, *Orientals: Asian Americans in Popular Culture* (Philadelphia: Temple University Press, 1999), 160–61. See also May, *Homeward Bound*, 94–95.

34. David K. Johnson, *The Lavender Scare* (Chicago: University of Chicago Press, 2004); John D'Emilio, *Making Trouble* (New York: Routledge, 1992), 57–73.

35. Rose Hum Lee, "The Decline of Chinatowns in the United States," *American Journal of Sociology* 54 (March 1949): 432.

36. Ibid.

37. Henry Yu, "The 'Oriental Problem' in America, 1920–1960: Linking the Identities of Chinese American and Japanese American Intellectuals," in *Claiming America*, ed. K. Scott Wong and Sucheng Chan (Philadelphia: Temple University Press, 1998), 202–3.

38. Rose Hum Lee, "The Recent Chinese Families of the San Francisco-Oakland Area," *Marriage and Family Living* 18 (February 1956): 14.

39. Ibid., 14–15. See also Wen-Hui Chung Chen, "Changing Socio-Cultural Patterns of the Chinese Community in Los Angeles" (PhD diss., University of Southern California, 1952), 40–41; Xiaojian Zhao, *Remaking Chinese America: Immigration, Family, and Community, 1940–1965* (New Brunswick: Rutgers University Press, 2002), 80.

40. Betty Lee Sung, *Mountain of Gold: The Story of the Chinese in America* (New York: Macmillan, 1967), 9.

41. Ibid., 108–9.

42. Ibid., 111.

43. Ibid., 115.

44. Ibid.

45. Ibid., 118.

46. "America's Chinese," *Life*, January 8, 1951, 70–77.

47. Ibid., 74–77.

48. Jerry Hulse, "Chinatown Changing as Suburbs Call Residents," *Los Angeles Times*, October 26, 1959.

49. Ibid.

50. For accounts of the Sheng case, see Rose Hum Lee, *The Chinese in the United States of America* (Hong Kong: Hong Kong University Press, 1960), 315–19; Robert Lee, "Community Exclusion: A Case Study," *Phylon Quarterly* 15, no. 2 (1954): 202–5; and Charlotte Brooks, *Alien Neighbors, Foreign Friends: Asian Americans, Housing, and the Transformation of Urban California* (Chicago: University of Chicago Press, 2009), 201–9.

51. Carolyn Anspacher, "Democracy Put to Test in South City," *San Francisco Chronicle*, February 16, 1952.

52. Alan Hynding, *From Frontier to Suburb* (Belmont, CA: Star Publishing, 1982), 106–8.

53. Linda Kauffman, *South San Francisco: A History* (South San Francisco: South San Francisco Bicentennial Committee, 1976), 40–41; Alvin D. Hyman, *The Suburbs of San Francisco* (San Francisco: Chronicle, 1969), 70.

54. Bernard Taper, "Southwood Finds Out It Isn't an 'All-White' Community, After All," *San Francisco Chronicle*, February 23, 1952. Since the U.S. census did not survey the racial composition of cities in San Mateo County during this time, a systematic breakdown of South San Francisco's population by race cannot be obtained.

55. Christina Klein, *Cold War Orientalism: Asia in the Middlebrow Imagination, 1945–1961* (Berkeley: University of California Press, 2003), 5.

56. Bernard Taper, "South S.F. Area Votes to Exclude a Chinese Family," *San Francisco Chronicle*, February 17, 1952.

57. Ibid.

58. "Southwood to the World," *San Francisco Chronicle*, February 19, 1952.
59. Ibid.
60. Anspacher, "Democracy Put to Test in South City."
61. Bernard Taper, "Homes Are Offered to Excluded Chinese," *San Francisco Chronicle*, February 18, 1952.
62. Dai-Ming Lee, "Brotherhood Week in South San Francisco," *Chinese World*, February 19, 1952.
63. "Additional Problems Related to the Sing Sheng Case," *Chinese Pacific Weekly*, February 23, 1952; translation mine.
64. Lee, "Brotherhood Week in South San Francisco."
65. "Additional Problems Related to the Sing Sheng Case."
66. "Public Reaction to the Sheng Case," *San Francisco Chronicle*, February 24, 1952.
67. Taper, "South S.F. Area Votes to Exclude a Chinese Family."
68. "Southwood Meets to Discuss Sing Sheng Case," *Chinese World*, February 22, 1952.
69. "No Second Ballot for Sing Sheng," *Chinese World*, February 23, 1952; "Bitter Debate Marks Southwood Minority Group Meeting," *Chinese World*, February 25, 1952.
70. Dai-ming Lee, "None Are So Blind as They Who Will Not See," *Chinese World*, February 26, 1952.
71. "Negro's Purchase of Richmond Home Creates Incident," *Chinese World*, March 6, 1952.
72. Dai-ming Lee, "Racial Prejudice in a Democracy," *Chinese World*, March 7, 1952.
73. "A 'Southwood' Incident at Dayton," *Chinese World*, February 29, 1952.
74. "Spokane Affair Ala 'Sing Sheng,'" *Chinese World*, June 23, 1952; "Spokane Residents Aid Chinese Couple in Search of a Home," *Chinese World*, June 28, 1952.
75. "Down Payment on House Returned to Hawaiian Couple," *Chinese World*, March 17, 1952.
76. "Brotherhood Week Article Points Finger at Sing Sheng's Exclusion," *Chinese World*, February 28, 1952.
77. "Chinese Welcomed into Sonoma All-White Tract," *Chinese World*, March 14, 1952; "Cases of Sheng and Wing Focus U.S. Interest on Oriental Status," *Chinese World*, March 18, 1952.
78. "Cases of Sheng and Wing."
79. Roger Daniels, *Asian America: Chinese and Japanese in the United States since 1850* (Seattle: University of Washington Press, 1988), 300; Lee, *The Chinese in the United States of America*, 315–19.

CHAPTER 3

1. *Los Angeles Times*, March 15, 1943; *L.A. Daily News*, March 15, 1943.
2. "Sport: Rookie of the Year," *Time*, September 22, 1947.
3. "Albert Armendariz, Sr.," Interview by Maggie Rivas-Rodriguez. VOCES Oral History Project, University of Texas at Austin, http://www.lib.utexas.edu/voces/template-stories-indiv.html?work_urn=urn%3Autlol%3Awwlatin.006&work_title=Armendariz%2C+Sr.%2C+Albert (accessed August 1, 2011).
4. See Keith Osajima, "Asian Americans as the Model Minority: An Analysis of the Popular Press Image in the 1960s and 1980s," in *Contemporary Asian America: A Multidisciplinary Reader*, ed. Min Zhou and James V. Gatewood (New York: New York University Press, 2000), 449–58.
5. Manuel G. Gonzales, *Mexicanos: A History of Mexicans in the United States* (Bloomington: Indiana University Press, 2009), 167–68; Ronald Takaki, *Strangers from a Different Shore: A History of Asian Americans* (New York: Penguin, 1989), 406; and Sucheng Chan, *Asian Americans: An Interpretive History* (New York: Twayne, 1991), 139–40.
6. Rose Hum Lee, *The Chinese in the United States of America* (Hong Kong: Hong Kong University Press, 1960), 47–48; Brenda Gayle Plummer, *Rising Wind: Black Americans and U.S. Foreign Affairs, 1935–1960* (Chapel Hill: University of North Carolina Press, 1996), 217–18.
7. Plummer, *Rising Wind*, 217–18.
8. Christina Klein, *Cold War Orientalism: Asia in the Middlebrow Imagination, 1945–1961* (Berkeley: University of California Press, 2003).
9. Benjamin Welles, "Lee Takes High Dive as Harlan, Also of the United States, Is Second," *New York Times*, August 6, 1948; "Swim Marks Shattered at Wembley," *Los Angeles Times*, August 6, 1948.
10. "Russian Tricks Major Lee with Peace Dove but U.S. Diver Then Gives Soviet the Bird," *New York Times*, July 16, 1952.
11. Ibid.
12. Ibid.
13. "Major Lee Named for Sullivan," *New York Times*, December 31, 1953.
14. *New York Times*, August 20, 1955.
15. "Major Lee Named for Sullivan."
16. "Major Lee, in Korea, Happy over Award: 'It's Like Winning Olympic Title,'" *New York Times*, January 1, 1954.
17. Sammy Lee, interview by Margaret Costa, December 1999, Amateur Athletic Foundation of Los Angeles, Los Angeles, CA.
18. Ibid.

19. Ibid.

20. "Olympic Champion's Fight for Home Backed," *Los Angeles Times*, August 20, 1955; "2 Realty Dealers Bar Olympic Star," *New York Times*, August 20, 1955; "Nixon to Help Lee Buy a Coast Home," *New York Times*, August 21, 1955; "The Case of Sammy Lee," *New York Times*, August 24, 1955; "Sammy Lee Gets Home," *New York Times*, September 2, 1955; and "Korean-Ancestry Waived and Major Gets a House," *New York Times*, September 25, 1955.

21. Sammy Lee, interview by Costa.

22. Ibid.

23. Elaine Kim, *Asian American Literature: An Introduction to the Writings and Their Social Context* (Philadelphia: Temple University Press, 1982), 59.

24. Ibid., 60.

25. Amy Ling, *Between Worlds: Women Writers of Chinese Ancestry* (New York: Pergamon, 1990), 120.

26. Jade Snow Wong, *No Chinese Stranger* (New York: Harper and Row, 1975), 54.

27. Jade Snow Wong, *Fifth Chinese Daughter* (Seattle: University of Washington Press, 1989), vii, viii; Kim, *Asian American Literature*, 60.

28. Frank Chin, Jeffery Paul Chan, Lawson Fusao Inada, and Shawn Hsu Wong, eds., *Aiiieeeee! An Anthology of Asian American Writers* (New York: Mentor, 1991), 14–17.

29. Wong, *Fifth Chinese Daughter*, 108–9.

30. Wong, *No Chinese Stranger*, 55.

31. Ibid., 82.

32. Ibid., 73–92.

33. Ibid., 74.

34. Ibid., 92.

35. Ellen D. Wu, "'America's Chinese': Anti-Communism, Citizenship, and Cultural Diplomacy during the Cold War," *Pacific Historical Review* 77, no. 3 (2008): 410–11.

36. Wong, *No Chinese Stranger*, 92.

37. Ibid., 83

38. Ibid., 108–9.

39. Gail Hershatter, *Women in China's Long Twentieth Century* (Berkeley: University of California Press, 2007), 79.

40. Lee Ming-Hua, "What I Have Seen in My Motherland," *Women of China*, March–April 1957, 1–3.

41. "Our New Judge," *Los Angeles Examiner*, January 24, 1959.

42. "Judge Wong's Case," *Hollywood Citizen News*, February 3, 1959.

43. "Our New Judge."

44. Robert Alden, "Congress Gets 2 of Asian Descent," *New York Times*, July 30, 1959.

45. "442nd Hero Elected Hawaii's Congressman," *Pacific Citizen*, July 31, 1959.

46. For a solid account of how Saund was elected from Imperial Valley, California, as the nation's first congressman of Asian descent as well as a critical reading of Saund's 1961 autobiography, *Congressman from India*, see Sandhya Shukla, *India Abroad: Diasporic Cultures of Postwar America and England* (Princeton: Princeton University Press, 2003), 141–49.

47. Alden, "Congress Gets 2 of Asian Descent."

48. *Pacific Citizen*, September 25, 1953.

49. "Our New Judge."

50. *Hollywood Citizen News*, February 3, 1959.

51. Judge Delbert Wong, interview by author, December 19, 2000, Los Angeles, tape recording.

52. Ibid.

53. Ibid.

54. Ibid.

55. Ibid.

56. Ibid.

57. Ibid.

58. Ibid.

59. Dolores Wong, interview by author, March 5, 2001, Los Angeles, tape recording.

60. "Success Story of One Minority Group in the U.S.," *U.S. News and World Report*, December 26, 1966; "Asian Americans: A 'Model Minority,'" *Newsweek*, December 6, 1982; *New York Times*, January 9, 1966.

61. "Success Story of One Minority Group," 73.

62. Ibid., 76.

63. Don Freeman, *Angelenos: Then and Now* (Los Angeles: Los Angeles Unified School District, 1966), iii.

CHAPTER 4

1. Kingsley K. Lyu, "Korean Nationalist Activities in Hawaii and America, 1901–1945," in *Counterpoint*, ed. Emma Gee (Los Angeles: UCLA Asian American Studies Center, 1976), 106–33; Kingsley K. Lyu, "Korean Nationalist Activities in Hawaii and the Continental United States, 1900–1945," pt. 1, *Amerasia* 4, no. 1 (1977): 23–85; pt. 2, *Amerasia* 4, no. 2 (1977): 53–100.

2. Alice Yang Murray, "Ilse Women and the Early Korean American Community," in *Unequal Sisters*, 3rd ed., ed. Vicki L. Ruiz and Ellen Carol DuBois (New York: Routledge, 2000), 205–13; Lili M. Kim, "Redefining the Boundaries of Traditional Gender Roles," in *Asian/Pacific Islander American Women*, ed. Shirley Hune and Gail M. Nomura (New York: New York University Press, 2003), 106–19.

3. Bruce Cumings, *The Origins of the Korean War: Liberation and the Emergence of Separate Regimes, 1945–1947*, vol. 1 (Princeton: Princeton University Press, 1981), 444.

4. Michal R. Belknap, *Cold War Political Justice: The Smith Act, the Communist Party, and American Civil Liberties* (Westport, CT: Greenwood, 1977), 126.

5. American Civil Liberties Union, *The Smith Act and the Supreme Court* (New York: ACLU, 1952), 4–5.

6. Belknap, *Cold War Political Justice*, 81.

7. The twelve who were arrested by FBI officers on July 26, 1951, were William Schneiderman, Al Richmond, Philip M. Connelly, Rose Chernin Kusnitz, Dorothy Rosenblum Healey, Albert Jason Lima, Ernest Otto Fox, Henry Steinberg, Carl Rude Lambert, Oleta O'Connor Yates, Loretta Starvus Stack, and Bernadette Doyle. The three arrested on August 31, 1951, were Frank Spector, Frank Carlson, and Ben Dobbs. On April 24, 1952, Judge William Mathes ordered the case of the ailing defendant Bernadette Doyle to be severed from the fifteen. See "Chronology of California Smith Act Cases," ca. 1951, Smith Act Cases Collection, Southern California Library for Social Studies and Research; "The California 15 Biographies," ca. 1951, Smith Act Cases Collection, Southern California Library for Social Studies and Research; and California Emergency Defense Committee, *The Bill of Rights* (Los Angeles: California Emergency Defense Committee, 1952).

8. "Los Angeles 21," 1948, Civil Rights Congress, Los Angeles, Southern California Library for Social Studies and Research; "Memorandum to Members of the Bar on Civil Rights," ca. 1948, Civil Rights Congress, Los Angeles, Southern California Library for Social Studies and Research.

9. The three black witnesses were Timothy Evans Jr., Louis Rosser, and Paul Estrada. Estrada was actually of mixed-race background as his father was Mexican and his mother was black.

10. House Committee on Un-American Activities, *The American Negro in the Communist Party* (Washington, DC: U.S. Government Printing Office, 1954), 4.

11. Ibid., 1.

12. Ibid.

13. Ibid., 2.

14. The three clients whom Branton represented were Henry Steinberg, Carl Rude Lambert, and Ben Dobbs.

15. *People's World*, October 11, 1951. For accounts on why blacks had a special interest in the Smith Act trials, see Richard E. Westbrooks and Earl B. Dickerson, "The Smith Act and the Negro People: Excerpts," September 27, 1951, Smith Act Cases Collection, Southern California Library for Social Studies and Research; "Democracy Is Indivisible: A Statement by Negro Leaders to the President and Attorney General of the United States on the Trial of the 12 Communist Leaders," ca. 1951, Smith Act Cases Collection, Southern California Library for Social Studies and Research; and Lloyd L. Brown, *Stand Up for Freedom! The Negro People vs. the Smith Act* (New York: New Century, 1952).

16. "Excerpts of Branton Argument to Jury," ca. 1952, Smith Act Cases Collection, Southern California Library for Social Studies and Research.

17. Ibid.

18. Senate Committee on the Judiciary, *Hearings before the Subcommittee on Immigration and Naturalization: Communist Activities among Aliens and National Groups, Part III—Appendixes I-VIII*, 81st Cong., 1st sess., 1949, A1, A4.

19. Subversive Activities Control Act of 1950, H.R. 9490, Pub. Law 831, 81st Cong., 2nd sess., 2.

20. Abner Green, *The Deportation Drive vs. the Bill of Rights: The McCarran Act and the Foreign Born* (New York: New Century, 1951), 3–4. Among the most notable Smith Act deportees was Claudia Jones, an immigrant from the West Indies, who was part of the second-string arrests in New York.

21. U.S. Department of Justice, *Annual Report of the Immigration and Naturalization Service for the Fiscal Year Ended June 30, 1953* (Washington, DC: U.S. Government Printing Office, 1953), 65.

22. Brief for the Respondent in the case of *Frank Carlson, Miriam Christine Stevenson, David Hyun and Harry Carlisle, petitioners v. Herman R. Langdon, District Director of Immigration and Naturalization Service, U.S. Department of Justice*, U.S. Supreme Court, October term, 1951, no. 35, 3–4. The list compiled from the confidential files identified another eight past members in Los Angeles.

23. "Brief History of the Los Angeles Committee for Protection of Foreign Born (Sep. 1950–Aug. 1955)," August 26, 1955, Los Angeles Committee for Protection of Foreign Born Records, 1938–1973, Southern California Library for Social Studies and Research.

24. The most notable of these sweeps was the 1954 Operation Terror, in which federal agents rounded up an estimated forty thousand Mexicans in Los Angeles and turned the Elysian Park Recreation Center into a security facility to detain those arrested. The LACPFB published some of the most insightful materials on these roundups, which included a 1959 petition to the United Nations charging that the U.S. government's treatment of Mexican Americans had violated the

Universal Declaration of Human Rights adopted by the United Nations in 1948; see American Committee for Protection of Foreign Born, *Our Badge of Infamy: A Petition to the United Nations on the Treatment of the Mexican Immigrant* (New York: American Committee for Protection of Foreign Born, 1959); Patricia Morgan, *Shame of a Nation: Police-State Terror against Mexican-Americans in the U.S.A.* (Los Angeles: Los Angeles Committee for Protection of Foreign Born, 1954). The petition *Our Badge of Infamy* built on the appeal that William Patterson and the Civil Rights Congress made in 1951 to the United Nations entitled *We Charge Genocide*, protesting the unjust and inhumane treatment of blacks in the United States. The CRC argued that the U.S. government in refusing to take action against the lynching of blacks in the United States had violated Article II of the UN Genocide Convention. Some other important publications of the American Committee for Protection of Foreign Born and the LACPFB that contested the efforts of the U.S. government to repatriate Mexican Americans during the early Cold War years include Isabel Gonzalez, *Step-Children of a Nation: The Status of Mexican-Americans* (New York: American Committee for Protection of Foreign Born, 1947); "The Role of the United States Immigration and Naturalization Service in Relation to the Mexican People," Los Angeles Committee for Protection of Foreign Born Records, 1938–1973, box 1, folder 18, Southern California Library for Social Studies and Research. See also Ralph Guzman, *Roots without Rights: A Study of the Loss of United States Citizenship by Native-Born Americans of Mexican Ancestry* (Los Angeles: East Los Angeles Chapter of the American Civil Liberties Union, 1958); and Jeffrey M. Garcilazo, "McCarthyism, Mexican Americans, and the Los Angeles Committee for Protection of Foreign-Born, 1950–1954," *Western Historical Quarterly* 32, no. 3 (2001): 273–95.

25. The four individuals of Japanese and Okinawan descent who were facing deportation because of their political activities and had sought the assistance of the LACPFB were Paul Shinsei Kochi, Shuji Matsui, Edo Mita, and Kameo Yamashiro. The one case in which the LACPFB assisted a Filipino American was that of Eulogio de la Cruz, who was denaturalized due to his alleged membership in the Communist Party in 1954 and served with an order of deportation. The three individuals of Korean descent who were facing deportation because of their political activities and had sought the assistance of the LACPFB were David Hyun, John Juhn, and Diamond Kimm. See "List of Deportees," ca. 1956, Los Angeles Committee for Protection of Foreign Born Records, 1938–1973, Southern California Library for Social Studies and Research; "Grouped Deportees by Nationality," ca. 1956, Los Angeles Committee for Protection of Foreign Born Records, 1938–1973, Southern California Library for Social Studies and Research. For a detailed look at the 1954 denaturalization trial of Eulogio de la Cruz, see

Los Angeles Committee for Protection of Foreign Born Records, 1938–1973, series III, case files, 1949–1969, Southern California Library for Social Studies and Research.

26. Brief for the Respondent in the case of *Frank Carlson, Miriam Christine Stevenson, David Hyun and Harry Carlisle, petitioners v. Herman R. Langdon*, 3–4.

27. Transcript of Record in the case of *Frank Carlson, Miriam Christine Stevenson, David Hyun and Harry Carlisle, petitioners v. Herman R. Langdon, District Director of Immigration and Naturalization Service, U.S. Department of Justice*, U.S. Supreme Court, October term, 1951, no. 35, 117.

28. Peter Hyun, *In the New World: The Making of a Korean American* (Honolulu: University of Hawaii Press, 1991), 264.

29. *New York Times*, October 24, 1950.

30. See Political Prisoners' Welfare Committee—Los Angeles, *Information Bulletin* 1, no. 1 (1950). A copy of this bulletin can be found in the Los Angeles Committee for Protection of Foreign Born Records, 1938–1973, Southern California Library for Social Studies and Research.

31. Transcript of Record in the case of *Frank Carlson, Miriam Christine Stevenson, David Hyun and Harry Carlisle, petitioners v. Herman R. Langdon*, 136.

32. Transcript of Record in the case of *David Hyun, petitioner v. Herman R. Langdon, District Director of Immigration and Naturalization Service, U.S. Department of Justice*, U.S. Supreme Court, October term, 1955, no. 201, 21–22.

33. Transcript of Record in the case of *Frank Carlson, Miriam Christine Stevenson, David Hyun and Harry Carlisle, petitioners v. Herman R. Langdon*, 118–19.

34. See Frank Chin, Jeffery Paul Chan, Lawson Fusao Inada, and Shawn Wong, eds., *Aiiieeeee! An Anthology of Asian American Writers* (New York: Mentor, 1991), 1–7.

35. Friends and Neighbors of David Hyun, *Exile: The Story of David Hyun* (Los Angeles, ca. 1956).

36. Ibid., 5.

37. For a good discussion on the changes that took place in deportation policies from 1917 to 1940, see Mae M. Ngai, *Impossible Subjects: Illegal Aliens and the Making of Modern America* (Princeton: Princeton University Press, 2004), 56–90.

38. Friends and Neighbors of David Hyun, *I Am Appealing on Behalf of My Youngest Son . . .* (Los Angeles, ca. 1956).

39. Transcript of Record in the case of *Diamond Kimm v. George R. Rosenberg, District Director, Immigration and Naturalization Service*, U.S. Supreme Court, October term, 1959, no. 139, 14–16.

40. Ibid., 31–33.

41. House Committee on Un-American Activities, *Investigation of Communist*

Activities in the Los Angeles, Calif., Area—Part 1, 84th Cong., 1st sess. (Washington, DC: U.S. Government Printing Office, 1955), 1563.

42. House Committee on Un-American Activities, *Annual Report for the Year 1955* (Washington, DC: U.S. Government Printing Office, 1956), 27; *Los Angeles Times*, January 16, 1952.

43. Committee to Save the Life of John Juhn, *Save the Life of John Juhn* (Los Angeles, ca. 1955); "Press Release," September 2, 1955, Los Angeles Committee for Protection of Foreign Born Records, 1938–1973, Southern California Library for Social Studies and Research.

44. Transcript of Record in the case of *Diamond Kimm v. George R. Rosenberg*, 49.

45. Ibid., 51.

46. The relevant sources may all be found in the Diamond Kimm Papers, Southern California Library for Social Studies and Research: Letter to Embassy of Czechoslovakia from Kimm Kang (Diamond Kimm), October 8, 1960; "Biographical Sketch of Diamond Kimm—prepared for application for asylum to Czechoslovakia and Soviet Union," ca. 1960; "Biographical Sketch of Fania Goorwitch—prepared for application for asylum to Czechoslovakia and Soviet Union," ca. 1960; "Affidavit of Diamond Kimm," June 12, 1961; "Affidavit of Fania Goorwitch," June 12, 1960; and Letter to William Samuels from Diamond Kimm and Fania Goorwitch from Prague, Czechoslovakia, January 24, 1962.

47. "Affidavit of Diamond Kimm"; "Affidavit of Fania Goorwitch."

48. The letter in its entirety was reproduced in the 1955 HUAC proceedings. House Committee on Un-American Activities, *Investigation of Communist Activities in the Los Angeles, Calif., Area—Part 1*, 1561–65.

49. Peter Hyun, the elder brother of David Hyun, indicated in his autobiography, *In the New World*, that Wellington Chong may have fled to Czechoslovakia in order to dodge the draft to fight in the Korean War for the United States. Wellington was a premedical student at UCLA during the outbreak of the Korean War and completed his medical degree in Prague. Peter Hyun's autobiography also details the tragic ending of Wellington and Alice. Wellington committed suicide and Alice was executed by the Democratic People's Republic of Korea. See Hyun, *In the New World*, 227.

50. House Committee on Un-American Activities, *Investigation of Communist Activities in the Los Angeles, Calif., Area—Part 1*, 1561–65.

51. Ibid., 1562–63.

52. House Committee on Un-American Activities, *Investigation of Communist Activities in the Pacific Northwest Area—Part 7 (Seattle)*, 83rd Cong., 2nd sess. (Washington, DC: U.S. Government Printing Office, 1954), 6489–6509.

53. Ibid., 6506.

54. Ibid., 6490.

55. Ibid., 6490–91.

56. Ibid., 6509.

57. House Committee on Un-American Activities, *Investigation of Communist Activities in the Los Angeles, Calif., Area—Part 1*, 1545.

58. Ibid., 1550.

59. Cumings, *Origins of the Korean War*, vol. 1, 86.

CHAPTER 5

1. Gerald T. White, "The Chinese and Immigration Law," *Far Eastern Survey* 19, no. 7 (April 1950): 68–70.

2. Christina Klein, *Cold War Orientalism: Asia in the Middlebrow Imagination, 1945–1961* (Berkeley: University of California Press, 2003), 240. In her study of U.S. Cold War culture, Klein examines the 1957 novel by C. Y. Lee, *The Flower Drum Song*, to show how the U.S. Cold War imperative of internationalism fostered the promotion of a dual identity of Asians in the United States as both foreign and American over the assimilation of Asians into the homogeneity of postwar whiteness. Klein argues that the maintenance of this dual identity "had everything to do with the global imperatives," which drove the nation to promote pluralist views and not just assimilationist ones.

3. Shih-shan Henry Tsai, *China and the Overseas Chinese in the United States, 1868–1911* (Fayetteville: University of Arkansas Press, 1983), 104–23.

4. Ibid., 105–8.

5. Daniel J. Tichenor, *Dividing Lines: The Politics of Immigration Control in America* (Princeton: Princeton University Press, 2002), 178.

6. Ibid., 178, 208, 212.

7. Gabriel J. Chin, "The Civil Rights Revolution Comes to Immigration Law: A New Look at the Immigration and Nationality Act of 1965," *North Carolina Law Review* 75 (1996–1997): 273–345.

8. Mae M. Ngai, *Impossible Subjects: Illegal Aliens and the Making of Modern America* (Princeton: Princeton University Press, 2004), 228–29.

9. Sue Fawn Chung, "Fighting for Their American Rights: A History of the Chinese American Citizens Alliance," in *Claiming America*, ed. K. Scott Wong and Sucheng Chan (Philadelphia: Temple University Press, 1998), 95–126.

10. George L. Beronious, "Chino-Americans Dread Relocation," *Los Angeles Times*, December 16, 1950.

11. "Chinese in Los Angeles Are Troubled," *Chinese Press*, December 29, 1950.

12. "Trouble in Chinatowns of West Coast," *Nation*, January 13, 1951, 23.

13. Ibid.

14. "Abuse of Chinese Found," *New York Times*, December 18, 1950.

15. Editorial, *San Francisco Chronicle*, December 5, 1950; Beronious, "Chino-Americans Dread Relocation."

16. "Trouble in Chinatowns of West Coast."

17. "Chinese in Los Angeles Are Troubled."

18. Editorial, *Chinese Press*, February 9, 1951.

19. Editorial, *San Francisco Chronicle*, December 5, 1950.

20. "Chinese in California Show Fine Spirit of Loyalty," *Los Angeles Daily News*, March 12, 1951.

21. "Chinese-Americans," *Chinese World*, October 16, 1952.

22. Ibid.

23. Ibid.

24. Beronious, "Chino-Americans Dread Relocation"; John Sharkmik, "Mott Street Communiqué," *New York Times*, May 14, 1950; "Chinese Here Denounce Reds in Native Land," *Los Angeles Times*, December 9, 1950.

25. "Mao Repudiated by Chinese Here," *New York Times*, December 3, 1950.

26. "Chinese Here Denounce Reds in Native Land."

27. Him Mark Lai, "The Chinese Press in the United States and Canada since World War II: A Diversity of Voices," *Chinese America: History and Perspectives*, 1990, 107–55. See also Ronald Leslie Soble, "A History of the *Chinese World*, 1891–1961" (MA thesis, Stanford University, 1962).

28. This count is based on Him Mark Lai's listing of daily newspapers in the United States and Canada in 1943. See Lai, "Chinese Press in the United States," 108.

29. Him Mark Lai, "China and the Chinese American Community: The Political Dimension," *Chinese America: History and Perspectives*, 1999, 8.

30. Correspondence between Y. C. Hong and Ngai Ho regarding the October 9 incident, ca. 1949, Hong Business Files, Huntington Research Library and Botanical Gardens, San Marino, CA (hereafter cited as Huntington Library).

31. "Public statement on the Oct 9th Incident" and "Open Letter" written by Y. C. Hong, ca. 1949, Hong Business Files, Huntington Library. While Henry Lem was the elected president of the CACA in 1949, he was forced to resign due to illness, and Y. C. Hong stepped in as president.

32. Him Mark Lai, "A Voice of Reason: Life and Times of Gilbert Woo, Chinese American Journalist," *Chinese America: History and Perspectives*, 1992, 101.

33. Lai, "Chinese Press in the United States," 112–13; Lai, "Voice of Reason," 98–107.

34. Soble, "History of the *Chinese World*," 11. The circulation numbers for

Chinese periodicals in San Francisco in 1960 listed the *Chinese Times* as having a daily circulation of 9,515 and the *Chinese World*, a daily circulation of 9,230.

35. Ibid., 98–99.
36. Ibid., 18–26, 27–32.
37. George de Carvalho, "Red Ransom Racket on Chinese Here Revealed," *San Francisco Chronicle*, November 10, 1951.
38. "Reds Put Squeeze on Chinese in U.S.," *New York Times*, November 14, 1951.
39. "Rackets: Chinese Torture," *Newsweek*, November 26, 1951, 26.
40. "State Dept. Seeks Data on Red China Ransom Racket," *San Francisco Chronicle*, November 14, 1951.
41. George de Carvalho, "Treasury to Act against Red Extortion," *San Francisco Chronicle*, November 15, 1951.
42. "State Dept. Seeks Data"; "Chinese Extortion Studied," *San Francisco Chronicle*, November 21, 1951.
43. George de Carvalho, "No Action in Chinatown on Red Racket," *San Francisco Chronicle*, November 26, 1951; "China Plans U.N. Action on Red Extortion," *San Francisco Chronicle*, November 20, 1051.
44. "Chinese Extortion Studied." The two top officials were Matthew Marks, chief of the enforcement division of the Treasury's Foreign Assets Control Administration, and Neil Naiden, assistant to the assistant secretary of the Treasury.
45. De Carvalho, "No Action in Chinatown." Whereas the Chinese Consolidated Benevolent Association is the umbrella organization of Chinese associations across the United States, the Chinese Six Companies refers only to the Chinese Consolidated Benevolent Association in San Francisco. The Chinese Six Companies is notable because the vast majority of Chinese in the United States resided in California, particularly San Francisco, during the early Cold War years.
46. De Carvalho, "Treasury to Act against Red Extortion."
47. George de Carvalho, "Chinatown Acts against Red Racket," *San Francisco Chronicle*, November 11, 1951.
48. "Chinese Extortion Racket," *Life*, December 3, 1951, 57–58.
49. "No More Blackmail," *Time*, December 17, 1951, 20.
50. "We Want Her to Die Now," *Time*, December 10, 1951, 28–29.
51. Ibid., 29.
52. De Carvalho, "Treasury to Act against Red Extortion"; de Carvalho, "No Action in Chinatown." The *Chronicle* also noted that C. S. Mong, editor of the *Chinese Times*, also came forward to advise readers to stop making ransom payments.
53. Because the Manchus were a separate ethnic group from the Cantonese, and Chinese in the United States were mostly from the province of Canton in southern China, the founding editor of the *Chinese World*, Tong King Chong,

argued that the Chinese in San Francisco did not support the campaign of the Manchus from northern China to eradicate Christians from China. At the end of the upheaval in China, Tong discontinued the *Oriental and Occidental Press* but maintained that his efforts were critical to preventing attacks against the Chinese in San Francisco. See Soble, "History of the *Chinese World*," 25.

54. Dai-ming Lee, "No Illusions Concerning the Chinese Reds," *Chinese World*, November 6, 1951; "Red Ransom Demands," *Chinese World*, November 12, 1951.

55. Dai-ming Lee, "Grim Messages from Red China," *Chinese World*, November 10, 1951; "Red Ransom Demands."

56. Dai-ming Lee, "Measures to Counter the Red Ransom Racket," *Chinese World*, November 13, 1951; Dai-ming Lee, "Now Is the Time for Unity and Cooperation," *Chinese World*, November 14, 1951.

57. Dai-ming Lee, "An Open Letter to Yeh Chien-ying," *Chinese World*, November 17, 1951. For an in-depth discussion of communist China's policies regarding overseas Chinese, see Union Research Institute, *Programs of Communist China for Overseas Chinese* (Kowloon: Union Research Institute, 1956). According to this study, the Chinese government violated its official stance of extending "favorable treatment" to overseas Chinese; it extracted foreign exchange from overseas Chinese by three methods: (1) control of private overseas Chinese money orders; (2) investment companies; and (3) extortion of overseas Chinese. Union Research Institute, *Programs of Communist China for Overseas Chinese*, 57–70.

58. Dai-ming Lee, "State Department Action against the Red Racket," *Chinese World*, November 19, 1951.

59. Dai-ming Lee, "Help for the Victims of the Ransom Racket," *Chinese World*, December 12, 1951.

60. For the *Chinese World*'s coverage of the Jang and Hong case, see Dai-ming Lee, "A Chinese Mother Commits Suicide," *Chinese World*, December 3, 1951; and Dai-ming Lee, "Racket Victim Finds Solace in Suicide," *Chinese World*, December 11, 1951.

61. Lee, "State Department Action."

62. De Carvalho, "No Action in Chinatown."

63. "Six Companies Discuss Racket," *Chinese World*, November 29, 1951; "Chinese Red Ransom Racket Victims Map Counter Move in Chinatown Meet," *Chinese World*, November 27, 1951.

64. Dai-ming Lee, "Signatures Wanted on Protest Petitions," *Chinese World*, December 4, 1951; "Eleven Hundred Sign Protest against Red Ransom Extortion Racket," *Chinese World*, December 15, 1951; "Extortion Protests Are Sent to Peiping," *New York Times*, December 16, 1951; and Dai-ming Lee, "Mass Protest Message on Its Way," *Chinese World*, December 17, 1951.

65. "Chinatown Hits Racket," *Chinese World*, December 1, 1951. It should be

noted that in February 1951, before the widespread knowledge of the racket, the Chinese Consolidated Benevolent Association had issued a statement requesting that all members of the association abide by the U.S. government's regulations prohibiting remittances to communist China. See Union Research Institute, *Programs of Communist China for Overseas Chinese*, 74.

66. Union Research Institute, *Programs of Communist China for Overseas Chinese*, 74–77.

67. "Treasury Dept. Lauds Cooperation; Warns of Remittance Illegalities," *Chinese World*, December 10, 1951.

68. Dai-ming Lee, "The Chinese Reds Take Notice of Protests," *Chinese World*, December 7, 1951; Dai-ming Lee, "Actions Speak Louder Than Words," *Chinese World*, December 10, 1951.

69. "Remittances to Red China Drop," *Chinese World*, December 17, 1951; Dai-ming Lee, "Reds Ease Pressure on Racket Victims," *Chinese World*, December 24, 1951; and Dai-ming Lee, "Persecution Continues in Red China," *Chinese World*, January 18, 1952.

70. Dai-ming Lee, "Remittances to Red China," *Chinese World*, January 7, 1952 and March 8, 1952.

71. Dai-ming Lee, "Funds for Starving Relatives in China," *Chinese World*, March 12, 1952.

72. "Chinatown Petitions U.S.," *Chinese World*, March 14, 1952; Dai-ming Lee, "United Action Needed to Help Hungry People," *Chinese World*, March 14, 1952; "Treasury Dept. Confirms Continued Ban on Remittances to Red China," *Chinese World*, April 10, 1952; and Dai-ming Lee, "The Ban of Remittances to Red China," *Chinese World*, April 14, 1952.

73. "Red Ransom Continues," *Chinese World*, April 26, 1952.

74. "China Daily Indicted," *Chinese World*, April 30, 1952; "Hong Kong Bank Continues China Remittances," *Chinese World*, May 2, 1952.

75. For a detailed account of the harassment by FBI agents and KMT supporters of *China Daily News* subscribers, particularly the Chinese Hand Laundry Alliance during World War II and the early Cold War years, see Renqiu Yu, *To Save China, to Save Ourselves: The Chinese Hand Laundry Alliance* (Philadelphia: Temple University Press, 1995), 165–97; *Chinatown Files*, VHS, dir. Amy Chen (New York: Third World Newsreel, 2001); and Him Mark Lai, "To Bring Forth a New China, to Build a Better America: The Chinese Marxist Left in America to the 1960s," *Chinese America: History and Perspectives*, 1992, 3–82.

76. "China Daily Indicted."

77. *United States v. China Daily News*, 224 F.2d 670 (1955); Lai, "To Bring Forth

a New China," 49. Tom Sung died during the appeal of his conviction; as a result, his appeal was dismissed as moot. According to Lai, following the conviction of Moy and the three other laundry workers, the circulation of the *China Daily News* dropped sharply and its operating deficits could only be met by the financial contributions of loyal readers throughout the United States. In 1962, the paper changed to a semiweekly publication.

78. "Chiang Issues Plea to Chinese in the U.S.," *New York Times*, September 16, 1950; "China Plans U.N. Action on Red Extortion."

79. Dai-ming Lee, "The Kuomintang and a United Anti-Red Front," *Chinese World*, January 11, 1952.

80. Dai-ming Lee, "Chiang Kai-shek's New Year Message," *Chinese World*, January 4, 1952; Dai-ming Lee, "Double Talk Out of Taipeh," *Chinese World*, January 15, 1952; Dai-ming Lee, "Formosa Is Not Free China," *Chinese World*, February 18, 1952.

81. "Chinese Look for 'Third Force' to Save Motherland," *Chinese World*, March 20, 1952. For a solid survey of U.S. intelligence operations in Hong Kong following the communist takeover of China, see Johannes R. Lombardo, "A Mission of Espionage, Intelligence and Psychological Operations: The American Consulate in Hong Kong, 1949–1964," *Intelligence and National Security* 14, no. 4 (1999): 64–81. In charting the viability of Chinese American political activities through the rise and fall of Chinese periodicals in the United States, Him Mark Lai attributed the decline of the third political force to Dai-ming Lee's ill-considered move to establish a New York edition of the *Chinese World* in 1957. The paper apparently never recovered from the financial loss. Just two years after it started, the New York edition of the *Chinese World* was shut down and the San Francisco edition was negatively impacted. According to Lai, after Lee passed away in 1961, the paper lost its viability and closed down in 1969. See Lai, "Chinese Press in the United States," 115.

82. For a detailed account of the role of Chinese in the United States in the overthrow of the Manchus and the establishment of the Republic of China in 1911, see Tsai, *China and the Overseas Chinese in the United States*, 124–42. It should be noted that the bulk of academic literature on "overseas Chinese" concentrates on the activities of Chinese in Southeast Asia and their influence on Chinese politics. For a detailed account of the special role that Chinese in Southeast Asia played in the Chinese Revolution of 1911, see Qinghuang Yan, *The Overseas Chinese and the 1911 Revolution, with Special Reference to Singapore and Malaya* (Kuala Lumpur: Oxford University Press, 1976).

83. Lee, "Help for the Victims of the Ransom Racket."

84. Cheryl Shanks, *Immigration and the Politics of American Sovereignty, 1890–1990* (Ann Arbor: University of Michigan Press, 2001), 96–186. For a more general

discussion of the nation's move toward internationalism during the early Cold War years, see John Lewis Gaddis, *The United States and the Origins of the Cold War, 1941–1947* (New York: Columbia University Press, 2000).

85. While the 1952 McCarran-Walter Act granted naturalization rights to Asians and lifted the exclusion of Asians to the United States, it maintained the Chinese quota and established a single Asian quota to limit the number of Chinese and Asians to the United States based on ancestry or race rather than place of origin. A person of Chinese ancestry living in England seeking to immigrate to the United States would be, for example, counted against the Chinese quota over the national quota allotted to England. The 1952 act, moreover, kept intact the national origins quota system that calculated quotas based on the 1920 census to regulate the immigration of people from countries outside the Asia-Pacific Triangle. Besides generating debates over the importance of immigration quotas based on race and national origins, the passage of the 1952 McCarran-Walter Act also divided Congress over the enactment of additional provisions to exclude people based on their political beliefs and activities. See Shanks, *Immigration and the Politics of American Sovereignty*, 134–39.

86. Ibid., 107–12.

87. Ibid., 168–74.

88. Following the communist takeover of China in 1949, there emerged two groups of Chinese refugees: those who fled communist China for fear of political persecution; and Chinese students who became "stranded" in the United States after the takeover. While the passage of the Displaced Persons Act of 1948 granted 3,465 Chinese students, visitors, and seamen who were stranded in the United States permanent status, the quotas allotted for the admission of refugees were granted almost exclusively to European countries. Following the protests of Chinese American leaders, the U.S. government, under a special act of Congress, passed the Refugee Relief Act of 1953, which allowed the entry of 2,777 Chinese refugees from communist China and a total of 2,000 visas to Chinese whose passports had been endorsed by the Chinese Nationalist government. In addition, in response to the protests of Chinese American leaders, President Kennedy permitted the entrance of Chinese refugees from Hong Kong as parolees by signing the Presidential Directive of May 25, 1962. See Victor G. Nee and Brett de Bary Nee, *Longtime Californ': A Documentary Study of an American Chinatown* (Stanford: Stanford University Press, 1972), 410. See also Correspondences exchanged among Y. C. Hong, Kenneth Y. Fung, and Peter F. Snyder, Hong Business Files, 1949, Huntington Library; and Letter from Harry Wai Gee, president of the CCBA, to Senators Thomas Kuchel, Claire Engle, and Francis Walter, March 29, 1960, Hong Business Files, Huntington Library. For a solid account

of the plight of stranded Chinese in the United States, see Rose Hum Lee, "The Stranded Chinese in the United States," *Phylon Quarterly* 19, no. 2 (1957): 180–94.

89. For a survey of the CACA and its many activities, see Chung, "Fighting for Their American Rights," 95–126.

90. See United Parlor, Native Sons of the Golden State, and Chinese American Citizens Alliance, *A Plea for Relief* (San Francisco: United Publishing, 1925). On May 25, 1925, the U.S. Supreme Court upheld that the stipulation to deny the admission of aliens ineligible for citizenship applied to the alien Chinese wife of an American citizen. See *Chang Chan, Wong Hung Kay, Yee Sin Jung et al. v. Nagle*, 268 U.S. 346 (1925). Following the Supreme Court's decision, the only recourse left was to appeal to Congress for relief.

91. United Parlor et al., *A Plea for Relief*, 2–4.

92. "Change Is Proposed in Immigration Act," *United States Daily*, February 7, 1928.

93. "Collection of Bibliographic Information on Y. C. Hong," Hong Business Files, Huntington Library.

94. As Congress designated that 25 percent of the 105 annual Chinese quota was to be allotted for countries outside China, this reduced the number allotted for Chinese immigration to the United States from China to 75. Following the passage of the 1943 Magnuson Act, alien Chinese wives emigrating from China were counted against this annual Chinese quota of seventy-five.

95. House Subcommittee No. 1 of the Committee on Immigration and Naturalization, *Study of Problems Relating to Immigration and Deportation and Other Matters*, H.R. Rep. 52, 79th Cong., 1st sess., 1946, 331–33.

96. An Act to Place Chinese Wives of American Citizens on a Non-Quota Basis, H.R. 4844, 79th Cong., 2nd sess. (August 9, 1946).

97. Letter from Henry Lem to Hon. Patrick McCarran, March 14, 1949, Hong Business Files, Huntington Library.

98. Y. C. Hong, "A Brief History of the Chinese American Citizens Alliance," in *23rd Biennial Convention Booklet of the Chinese American Citizens Alliance* (Fresno: Chinese American Citizens Alliance, 1955), 11–13.

99. Common Council for American Unity, "On Immigration, Naturalization and Related Problems," *Interpreter Releases* 103, no. 41 (September 14, 1951): 264.

100. JACL letter to Hon. Chet Holifield, March 12, 1952, Hong Business Files, Huntington Library.

101. The relevant sources are all from the Hong Business Files, Huntington Library: JACL letter to Y. C. Hong, April 16, 1950; letter from Y. C. Hong to Honorable Pat McCarran, May 13, 1952; letter from Y. C. Hong, Randolf M. Sakada, General

Hilario C. Moncado, and Chin Ha Choy to Honorable Pat McCarran, May 20, 1952; and CACA letter to Honorable Philip Perlman, October 15, 1952.

102. House Committee on the Judiciary, *Hearings before the President's Commission on Immigration and Naturalization*, 82nd Cong., 2nd sess., 1952, 1145–48. Following these hearings and in response to President Truman's directive, the President's Commission on Immigration and Naturalization assembled a final report, entitled *Whom We Shall Welcome?*, to provide a comprehensive outline of how the 1952 act could be amended to more effectively regulate immigration and naturalization. See President's Commission on Immigration and Naturalization, *Whom Shall We Welcome?* (Washington, DC: U.S. Government Printing Office, 1953).

103. House Committee on the Judiciary, *Hearings before the President's Commission on Immigration and Naturalization*, 1146–47.

104. Ibid., 1147–48.

105. Everett F. Drumright, "Report on the Problem of Passport Fraud at Hong Kong," Foreign Service Dispatch 931, December 9, 1955, 4–26, file 122.4732/12-955.

106. Ibid., 31–32.

107. Ibid., 27–29.

108. Ibid., 34.

109. Ibid., 48–61.

110. Ibid., 33–34.

111. Ibid., 1.

112. Ibid., 80–84.

113. Everett F. Drumright, "Proposals to Better Cope with Problem of Fraud at Hong Kong," Foreign Service Dispatch 942, December 13, 1955, 1–6, file 122.4732/12-1355.

114. "U.S. Probe of Illegal Entries Spreads to H.K.," *Chinese World*, March 3, 1956.

115. "Chinese Business Hit by Grand Jury Probes in New York, S.F.," *Chinese World*, March 17, 1956.

116. Dai-ming Lee, "A Chinaman's Chance," *Chinese World*, February 18, 1956.

117. Ibid.; "Subpoenaing of Family Data Is Protested in San Francisco," *New York Times*, March 17, 1956.

118. There are many discrepancies over the total number of subpoenas issued on February 29, 1956. Mai Ngai lists thirty-four, while Him Mark Lai claims the number of subpoenas to be between twenty-four and twenty-six. See Ngai, *Impossible Subjects*, 213; Him Mark Lai, *Becoming Chinese American* (New York: AltaMira, 2004), 28. The *Chinese World* in various news features reported the number to be twenty-four, twenty-six, and thirty. See *Chinese World*, March 7, 1956, and March 17, 1956. The *Chinese World* also noted that the U.S. Attorney's office planned to issue more subpoenas and demand that a total of thirty-three Chinese organizations

turn over their membership rolls, personnel files, and photographs. See *Chinese World*, March 3, 1956. Major newspapers such as the *New York Times* relied on ambiguous terms like "numerous" or "more than two dozen" to denote the number of cases subpoenaed. See *New York Times*, March 17, 1956. I have chosen to list the number of cases subpoenaed as "at least twenty-four" because, as clearly stated in the full text of Judge Oliver J. Carter's memorandum delivered on March 20, 1956, the motions that were reviewed before the court were the motions submitted on behalf of twenty-four Chinese family and district associations to quash the subpoenas that were issued to them on February 29, 1956. See "Text of Judge Carter's Memorandum Opinion Ordering Subpoenas Quashed," *Chinese World*, March 22, 1956. There may certainly have been more subpoenas issued on that date and thereafter, but based on Judge Carter's memorandum, there were at least twenty-four issued. I do believe that the total number of subpoenas issued on February 29, 1956, was most likely twenty-six, with two of the family associations not filing an official motion to quash, either because they did not object to the seizure of records or because they were unwilling to submit even partial records within that initial twenty-four-hour period. Part of the purpose of the motions to quash was to keep the records of the twenty-four that did submit impounded at the federal court and inadmissible for review by the federal grand jury.

119. "Text of Judge Carter's Memorandum Opinion." The *Chinese World* reprinted the complete text of the memorandum.

120. "Subpoenaing of Family Data Is Protested." See also *Chinese World*, March 17, 1956.

121. "60 New York Chinese Groups Protest 'Blanket' Probe of SF Organizations," *Chinese World*, March 13, 1956.

122. "U.S. Inquiry Hurts Chinatown Probe," *New York Times*, March 17, 1956; "Chinese Business Hit by Grand Jury Probes."

123. Art Hoppe, "Ghost of an Old Fear in Chinatown," *San Francisco Chronicle*, March 18, 1956.

124. "Danger!!," *Sun Reporter*, March 17, 1956; See also *Chinese World*, March 20, 1956.

125. "Yorty Raps 'Blunderbuss' Probe of Chinese Family Associations," *Chinese World*, March 6, 1956.

126. Dai-ming Lee, "Sweeping Investigation Creates Resentment," *Chinese World*, March 14, 1956.

127. Dai-ming Lee, "Federal Grand Jury Probes Chinatown Associations," *Chinese World*, March 3, 1956.

128. "Judge Carter Blocks 'Inquisition' of Chinese Family Associations," *Chinese World*, March 21, 1956; "Text of Judge Carter's Memorandum Opinion."

129. "Judge Carter Stays Execution of Subpoena Order," *Chinese World*, March 26, 1956.

130. "Government Wins New Delay in Subpoena Case," *Chinese World*, April 3, 1956; "New U.S. Grand Jury to Continue Probe of Illegal Entry Racket," *Chinese World*, April 6, 1956.

131. Lai, *Becoming Chinese American*, 29.

132. "Six Companies Pledge Support to U.S.," *Chinese World*, March 22, 1956; Dai-ming Lee, "Time for Unity in Chinatown," *Chinese World*, March 23, 1956.

133. "Taipeh Denounces 'Highhanded' U.S. Probe of Chinese Associations," *Chinese World*, March 9, 1956.

134. "Taipeh Press Blasts 'Harsh' U.S. Methods in Immigration Probe," *Chinese World*, March 12, 1956.

135. "HK Standard Challenges U.S. State Dept. on Bogus Passport Racket," *Chinese World*, March 27, 1956.

136. "HK China Mail Accuses U.S. State Dept. of Bogus Allegations," *Chinese World*, March 29, 1956.

137. Dai-ming Lee, "The Sins of the Fathers and Grandfathers," *Chinese World*, April 19, 1956; Dai-ming Lee, "Drumright's Amazing Charges," *Chinese World*, April 20, 1956.

138. Dai-ming Lee, "Fifty Years after the Fire and Quake," *Chinese World*, April 18, 1956.

139. Dai-ming Lee, "Drumright Stoops to 'Third Degree' Methods," *Chinese World*, April 21, 1956; Dai-ming Lee, "Drumright Finds a Handy Weapon," *Chinese World*, April 23, 1956; Dai-ming Lee, "Citizenship Hinges on Clinical Tests," *Chinese World*, April 24, 1956; Dai-ming Lee, "Drumright's Version of a 'Five-Anti's' Campaign," *Chinese World*, April 27, 1956; Dai-ming Lee, "U.S. Consulate at H.K. Adopts Unique Standards," *Chinese World*, April 26, 1956; Dai-ming Lee, "A Few Questions for Mr. Drumright," *Chinese World*, May 2, 1956; and Dai-ming Lee, "Red Propaganda Mill Feeds on Anti-Chinese Policies," *Chinese World*, May 15, 1956.

140. Dai-ming Lee, "The Chinese Conference in Washington," *Chinese World*, March 7, 1957.

141. Dai-ming Lee, "Responsibilities of Conference Delegates," *Chinese World*, March 4, 1957.

142. "Chinese Communities in America Begin 3-Day Washington Confab," *Chinese World*, March 6, 1957; "Chinese Conference in Washington Hears White House Representative," *Chinese World*, March 7, 1957.

143. *Chinese World*, March 9, 1957; Dai-ming Lee, "Chinese in America Conclude Conference," *Chinese World*, March 11, 1957.

144. "Statement Submitted by CACA at the Public Hearing Conducted by the Senate Subcommittee on Immigration and Naturalization," November 30, 1955, Hong Family Collection, Huntington Library.

145. Letter to Henry Lem from Y. C. Hong, October 4, 1957, Hong Business Files, Huntington Library.

146. "Oriental-American's Clean Record," in *24th Biennial National Convention Booklet of the Chinese American Citizens Alliance* (Los Angeles: Chinese American Citizens Alliance, 1957), 21.

147. Ngai, *Impossible Subjects*, 218.

148. Nee and Nee, *Longtime Californ'*, 410.

149. Ngai, *Impossible Subjects*, 221.

150. *Yik Shuen Eng v. Immigration and Naturalization Service*, 464 F.2d 1265 (2d Cir. 1972).

151. "Message from the Grand President," in *25th Biennial National Convention Booklet of the Chinese American Citizens Alliance* (Oakland: Chinese American Citizens Alliance, 1959), 3.

152. In 1957, elected members of the CACA Grand Lodge were highly agitated and angry at the San Francisco Lodge for initiating direct correspondence with government officials, press, and other organizations declaring the support of the CACA San Francisco Lodge of a proposed bill to replace the 1952 McCarran-Walter Act. Members of the CACA Grand Lodge considered the defiance of its authority to be an "arrogant" response that needed to be stopped and required disciplinary actions. The San Francisco Lodge, members of the Grand Lodge charged, was clearly using the immigration issue to garner national attention and influence. See Letter from Ngai Ho Hong to Y. C. Hong, April 12, 1957, Hong Business Files, Huntington Library.

153. President's Committee on Immigration and Naturalization, *Whom Shall We Welcome?*, xv.

154. Shanks, *Immigration and the Politics of American Sovereignty*, 169.

CONCLUSION

1. Lyndon B. Johnson, "Radio and Television Remarks upon Signing the Civil Rights Bill," July 2, 1964 (446), in *Public Papers of the Presidents of the United States: Lyndon B. Johnson, 1963–64, vol. 2* (Washington, DC: U.S. Government Printing Office, 1965), 842–44.

2. Ibid., 843.

3. Harry S. Truman, "Special Message to the Congress on Civil Rights," February 2, 1948 (20), in *Public Papers of the Presidents of the United States: Harry S.*

Truman, January 1 to December 31, 1948 (Washington, DC: U.S. Government Printing Office, 1964), 121–26.

4. Eric J. Sandeen, *Picturing an Exhibition: The Family of Man and 1950s America* (Albuquerque: University of New Mexico Press, 1995), 40.

5. Ibid., 95, 96.

6. Ibid., 10.

7. Ibid., 41. It should be noted that the number of photographs from the archives of *Life* magazine that Miller remembered to have searched through was substantially larger than the number that Steichen gave. According to Steichen, he and his creative team examined over two million photographs from all sources, which included individuals, collections, and files. See Edward Steichen, *The Family of Man* (New York: Museum of Modern Art, 1955), 5.

8. Sandeen, *Picturing an Exhibition*, 53.

9. Steichen, *The Family of Man*, 5.

10. Ibid., 23–24.

11. Ibid., 23–25.

12. Ibid., 23.

13. Edward Steichen, "Photography: Witness and Recorder of Humanity," *Wisconsin Historical Magazine* 41, no. 3 (Spring 1958): 159.

14. Ibid., 160.

15. Steichen, *The Family of Man*, 49.

16. Ibid., 178.

17. Roland Barthes, "The Great Family of Man," in *Mythologies* (New York: Hill and Wang, 1957), 101. See also Sandeen, *Picturing an Exhibition*, 54–55.

18. Barthes, "The Great Family of Man," 101–2.

19. Steichen, "Photography: Witness and Recorder of Humanity," 161.

20. Ibid.

21. Ibid., 167.

22. Steichen, *The Family of Man*, 182–83.

23. Ibid., 136.

24. Steichen, "Photography: Witness and Recorder of Humanity," 167.

25. Steichen, *The Family of Man*, 184–85.

26. Sandeen, *Picturing an Exhibition*, 96–97.

27. For a thorough discussion of the *Family of Man* exhibit in Moscow, see Sandeen, *Picturing an Exhibition*, 125–53.

28. "Our New Judge," *Los Angeles Examiner*, January 24, 1959.

29. *Hollywood Citizen News*, February 3, 1959.

30. Mike Murase, "Ethnic Studies and Higher Education for Asian Americans,"

in *Counterpoint: Perspectives on Asian America*, ed. Emma Gee (Los Angeles: UCLA Asian American Studies Center, 1976), 205–23.

31. Ibid., 220.

32. Ibid., 209.

33. The day before the Arizona Senate Bill 1070 was to take effect, a federal judge handed down an injunction making controversial portions of this strict immigration bill unenforceable. Among the provisions struck down by the judge was the requirement that all aliens in Arizona have proper documentation on them at all times.

34. Tamar Lewin, "Citing Individualism, Arizona Tries to Rein in Ethnic Studies in School," *New York Times*, May 13, 2010.

BIBLIOGRAPHY

MANUSCRIPT COLLECTIONS

Citizens Committee to Preserve American Freedoms. Southern California Library for Social Studies and Research.
Civil Rights Congress, Los Angeles. Southern California Library for Social Studies and Research.
First Unitarian Church of Los Angeles Records. Southern California Library for Social Studies and Research.
Leo Gallagher Papers. Southern California Library for Social Studies and Research.
You Chung Hong Business Files. Huntington Library.
You Chung Hong Family Collection. Huntington Library.
Diamond Kimm Papers. Southern California Library for Social Studies and Research.
Los Angeles Committee for Protection of Foreign Born Records. Southern California Library for Social Studies and Research.
Los Angeles Subject Files. Southern California Library for Social Studies and Research.
Ben Margolis and John McTernan Papers. Southern California Library for Social Studies and Research.
Smith Act Cases Collection. Southern California Library for Social Studies and Research.
Twentieth Century Organizational Files. Southern California Library for Social Studies and Research.
Frank Wilkinson Papers. Southern California Library for Social Studies and Research.

GOVERNMENT DOCUMENTS

An Act to Place Chinese Wives of American Citizens on a Non-Quota Basis. H.R. 4844, 79th Cong., 2nd sess., 1946.
California Constitution (1876).
California State Senate. *The Constitution of the State of California*. 1958.
Drumright, Everett F. "Report on the Problem of Passport Fraud at Hong Kong." Foreign Service Dispatch 931, December 9, 1955, 4–26, file 122.4732/12-955.
———. "Proposals to Better Cope with Problem of Fraud at Hong Kong." Foreign Service Dispatch 942, December 13, 1955, 1–6, file 122.4732/12-1355.

Governor's Advisory Commission on Housing Problems. *Report on Housing in California*. San Francisco, 1963.
House Committee on the Judiciary. *Hearings before the President's Commission on Immigration and Naturalization*. 82nd Cong., 2nd sess., 1952.
House Committee on Un-American Activities. *The American Negro in the Communist Party*. Washington, DC: U.S. Government Printing Office, 1954.
———. *Annual Report for the Year 1955*. Washington, DC: U.S. Government Printing Office, 1956.
———. *Investigation of Communist Activities in the Los Angeles, Calif., Area—Part 1*. 84th Cong., 1st sess. Washington, DC: U.S. Government Printing Office, 1955.
———. *Investigation of Communist Activities in the Pacific Northwest Area—Part 7 (Seattle)*. 83rd Cong., 2nd sess. Washington, DC: U.S. Government Printing Office, 1954.
House Subcommittee No. 1 of the Committee on Immigration and Naturalization. *Study of Problems Relating to Immigration and Deportation and Other Matters*. H.R. Rep. 52, 79th Cong., 1st sess., 1946.
President's Commission on Immigration and Naturalization. *Whom Shall We Welcome?* Washington, DC: U.S. Government Printing Office, 1953.
President's Committee on Civil Rights. *To Secure These Rights*. New York: Simon and Schuster, 1947.
Public Papers of the Presidents of the United States: Harry S. Truman, January 1 to December 31, 1948. Washington, DC: U.S. Government Printing Office, 1964.
Public Papers of the Presidents of the United States: Lyndon B. Johnson, 1963–64. Washington, DC: U.S. Government Printing Office, 1965.
Senate Committee on the Judiciary. *Hearings before the Subcommittee on Immigration and Naturalization: Communist Activities among Aliens and National Groups, Part III—Appendixes I-VIII*. 81st Cong., 1st sess., 1949.
Subversive Activities Control Act of 1950. H.R. 9490, Pub. Law 831, 81st Cong., 2nd sess.
Truman, Harry S. "Recommendation for Assistance to Greece and Turkey." 80th Cong., 1st sess., March 12, 1947.
U.S. Bureau of the Census. *A Report of the Seventeenth Decennial Census of the United States 1950. Vol. 2, Characteristics of the Population. Part 5: California*. Washington, DC: U.S. Government Printing Office, 1952.
———. *Sixteenth Census of the United States 1940. Vol. 2, Characteristics of the Population. Part 1: United States Summary and Alabama-District of Columbia*. Washington, DC: U.S. Government Printing Office, 1943.
U.S. Department of Justice. *Annual Report of the Immigration and Naturalization Service for the Fiscal Year Ended June 30, 1953*. Washington, DC: U.S. Government Printing Office, 1953.

BIBLIOGRAPHY

LEGAL CASES AND BRIEFS

Amer v. Superior Court of the State of California. October term, 1947, no. 429.
Tom D. Amer v. Superior Court of the State of California, 68 S. Ct. 1069 (1948).
Brief for California as *amicus curiae, McGhee v. Sipes.*
Brief for the Respondent, *Frank Carlson, Miriam Christine Stevenson, David Hyun and Harry Carlisle v. Herman R. Langdon.* U.S. Supreme Court. October term, 1951, no. 35.
Brief for the United States as *amicus curiae, Shelley v. Kraemer, McGhee v. Sipes, Hurd v. Hodge, Urciolo v. Hodge.*
Brief of the Japanese American Citizens League as *amicus curiae, Amer v. Superior Court of California; Yin Kim v. Superior Court of California.*
Brief of the Japanese American Citizens League as *amicus curiae, Hurd v. Hodge.*
Buchanan v. Warley, 38 S. Ct. 16 (1917).
Corrigan v. Buckley, 299 F. 899 (1926).
Gandolfo v. Hartman, 49 F. 181 (1892).
Hurd v. Hodge, 68 S. Ct. 847 (1948).
In re Lee Sing, 43 F. 359 (Circuit Court, N. D. California, 1890).
McGhee v. Sipes, 68 S. Ct. 836 (1948).
Oyama v. State of California, 68 S. Ct. 269 (1948).
Shelley v. Kraemer, 68 S. Ct. 836 (1948).
Transcript of Record for *David Hyun v. Herman R. Langdon.* U.S. Supreme Court. October term, 1955, no. 201.
Transcript of Record for *Diamond Kimm v. George R. Rosenberg.* U.S. Supreme Court. October term, 1959, no. 139.
Transcript of Record for *Frank Carlson, Miriam Christine Stevenson, David Hyun and Harry Carlisle v. Herman R. Langdon.* U.S. Supreme Court. October term, 1951, no. 35.
Transcript of Record for Tom D. Amer. U.S. Supreme Court. October term, 1947, no. 429.
Transcript of Record for Yin Kim. U.S. Supreme Court. October term, 1947, no. 430.
Trustees of the Monroe Avenue Church of Christ v. Fred C. Perkins, 68 S. Ct. 1069 (1948).
United States v. China Daily News, 224 F.2d 670 (1955).
Urciolo v. Hodge, 68 S. Ct. 847 (1948).
Yin Kim v. Superior Court of the State of California, 68 S. Ct. 1069 (1948).

NEWSPAPERS AND PERIODICALS

California Eagle.
Chinese Pacific Weekly.
Chinese Press.
Chinese World.
Hollywood Citizen News.
Korean Independence.
Life Magazine.
Los Angeles Daily News.
Los Angeles Examiner.
Los Angeles Sentinel.
Los Angeles Times.
Nation.
Newsweek.
New York Times.
Pacific Citizen.
Pan American Chinese Weekly.
People's World.
Rafu Shimpo.
San Francisco Chronicle.
Time Magazine.
U.S. News and World Report.
Women of China.

ORAL HISTORY INTERVIEWS

Amer, Tommy. Interview by author, 26 August 2000, Los Angeles. Tape recording.

———. Interview by author, 30 September 2002, Los Angeles. Tape recording.

Armendariz, Albert. Interview by Maggie Rivas-Rodriguez. VOCES Oral History Project, University of Texas at Austin. http://www.lib.utexas.edu/voces/template-stories-indiv.html?work_urn=urn%3Autlol%3Awwlatin.006&work_title=Armendariz%2C+Sr.%2C+Albert. Accessed August 1, 2011.

Lee, Sammy. Interview by Margaret Costa, December 1999. Amateur Athletic Foundation of Los Angeles, Los Angeles.

Wong, Delbert. Interview by author, December 19, 2000, Los Angeles. Tape recording.

Wong, Dolores. Interview by author, March 5, 2001, Los Angeles. Tape recording.

BOOKS

Almaguer, Tomas. *Racial Fault Lines: The Historical Origins of White Supremacy in California.* Berkeley: University of California Press, 1994.

American Civil Liberties Union. *The Smith Act and the Supreme Court.* New York: ACLU, 1952.

American Committee for Protection of Foreign Born. *Our Badge of Infamy: A Petition to the United Nations on the Treatment of the Mexican Immigrant.* New York: American Committee for Protection of Foreign Born, 1959.

Anderson, Kay J. *Vancouver's Chinatown: Racial Discourse in Canada, 1875–1980.* Montreal: McGill-Queens University Press, 1991.

Avila, Eric. *Popular Culture in the Age of White Flight: Fear and Fantasy in Suburban Los Angeles.* Berkeley: University of California Press, 2004.

Barthes, Roland. *Mythologies.* New York: Hill and Wang, 1957.

Belknap, Michal. *Cold War Political Justice: The Smith Act, the Communist Party, and American Civil Liberties.* Westport, CT: Greenwood, 1977.

Bernstein, Barton J. "The Ambiguous Legacy: The Truman Administration and Civil Rights." In *Politics and Policies of the Truman Administration*, ed. Barton J. Bernstein, 269–314. Chicago: Quadrangle, 1970.

Bernstein, Shana. *Bridges of Reform: Interracial Civil Rights Activism in Twentieth-Century Los Angeles.* Oxford: Oxford University Press, 2011.

Bow, Leslie. *Betrayal and Other Acts of Subversion: Feminism, Sexual Politics, Asian American Women's Literature.* Princeton: Princeton University Press, 2001.

———. *Partly Colored: Asian Americans and Racial Anomaly in the Segregated South.* New York: New York University Press, 2010.

Brooks, Charlotte. *Alien Neighbors, Foreign Friends: Asian Americans, Housing, and the Transformation of Urban California.* Chicago: University of Chicago Press, 2009.

Brown, Lloyd L. *Stand Up for Freedom! The Negro People vs. the Smith Act.* New York: New Century, 1952.

Case, Fred, and James H. Kirk. *The Housing Status of Minority Families.* Los Angeles: UCLA Real Estate Research Program in cooperation with the Los Angeles Urban League, 1958.

Chan, Sucheng. *Asian Americans: An Interpretive History.* Boston: Twayne, 1991.

———. *Entry Denied.* Philadelphia: Temple University Press, 1991.

Cheng, Suellen, and Munson Kwok. "The Golden Years of Los Angeles Chinatown: The Beginning." In *The Golden Years, 1938–1988.* Los Angeles, 1988.

Chin, Frank, Jeffery Paul Chan, Lawson Fusao Inada, and Shawn Hsu Wong, eds. *Aiiieeeee! An Anthology of Asian-American Writers.* New York: Mentor, 1991.

Civil Rights Congress. *We Charge Genocide: The Historic Petition to the United Nations for Relief from a Crime of the United States Government against the Negro People.* New York: International, 1970.

Collins, Keith. *Black Los Angeles: The Maturing of the Ghetto, 1940–1950.* Saratoga: Century Twenty One, 1980.

Commission on Race and Housing. *Where Shall We Live? Report of the Commission on Race and Housing.* Berkeley: University of California Press, 1958.

Committee to Save the Life of John Juhn. *Save the Life of John Juhn.* Los Angeles, ca. 1955.

Creef, Elena Tajima. *Imaging Japanese America: The Visual Construction of Citizenship, Nation, and the Body.* New York: New York University Press, 2004.

Cumings, Bruce. *The Origins of the Korean War: Liberation and the Emergence of Separate Regimes, 1945–1947.* Vol. 1. Princeton: Princeton University Press, 1981.

Daniels, Roger. *Asian America: Chinese and Japanese in the United States since 1850.* Seattle: University of Washington Press, 1988.

Dear, Michael J., ed. *From Chicago to L.A.: Making Sense of Urban Theory.* Thousand Oaks, CA: Sage, 2001.

D'Emilio, John. *Making Trouble.* New York: Routledge, 1992.

Dower, John W. *War without Mercy: Race and Power in the Pacific War.* New York: Pantheon, 1986.

Draney, R. Whitney. *Americans: Then and Now.* Los Angeles: Los Angeles Unified School District, 1966.

———. *Californians: Then and Now.* Los Angeles: Los Angeles Unified School District, 1966.

Dudziak, Mary L. *Cold War Civil Rights: Race and the Image of American Democracy.* Princeton: Princeton University Press, 2000.

Fogelson, Robert M. *The Fragmented Metropolis: Los Angeles, 1850–1930.* Cambridge: Harvard University Press, 1967.

Foucault, Michel. *Power/Knowledge: Selected Interviews and Other Writings, 1972–1977.* Ed. Colin Gordon. New York: Pantheon, 1980.

Freeman, Don. *Angelenos: Then and Now.* Los Angeles: Los Angeles Unified School District, 1966.

Friends and Neighbors of David Hyun. *Exile: The Story of David Hyun.* Los Angeles, ca. 1956.

———. *I Am Appealing on Behalf of My Youngest Son...* Los Angeles, ca. 1956.

Gaddis, John Lewis. *The United States and the Origins of the Cold War.* Rev. ed. New York: Columbia University Press, 2000.

Gardner, Michael R. *Harry Truman and Civil Rights.* Carbondale: Southern Illinois University Press, 2002.

Geselbracht, Raymond H., ed. *The Civil Rights Legacy of Harry Truman*. Kirksville: Truman State University Press, 2007.

Gonzales, Manuel G. *Mexicanos: A History of Mexicans in the United States*. Bloomington: Indiana University Press, 2009.

Gonzalez, Isabel. *Step-Children of a Nation: The Status of Mexican-Americans*. New York: American Committee for Protection of Foreign Born, 1947.

Green, Abner. *The Deportation Drive vs. the Bill of Rights: The McCarran Act and the Foreign Born*. New York: New Century, 1951.

Guzman, Ralph. *Roots without Rights: A Study of the Loss of United States Citizenship by Native-Born Americans of Mexican Ancestry*. Los Angeles: East Los Angeles Chapter of the American Civil Liberties Union, 1958.

Harris, Cheryl. "Whiteness as Property." In *Critical Race Theory*, ed. Kimberle Crenshaw, Neil Gotanda, Gary Peller, and Kendall Thomas, 276–91. New York: New Press, 1995.

Hershatter, Gail. *Women in China's Long Twentieth Century*. Berkeley: University of California Press, 2007.

Hirata, Lucie Cheng. "Chinese Immigrant Women in Nineteenth-Century California." In *Women of America: A History*, ed. Carol Ruth Berkin and Mary Beth Norton, 223–44. Boston: Houghton Mifflin, 1979.

Hise, Greg. *Magnetic Los Angeles: Planning the Twentieth-Century Metropolis*. Baltimore: Johns Hopkins University Press, 1997.

Hong, Y. C. "A Brief History of the Chinese American Citizens Alliance." In *23rd Biennial Convention Booklet of the Chinese American Citizens Alliance*, 11–13. Fresno: Chinese American Citizens Alliance, 1955.

Horne, Gerald. *Black and Red: W. E. B. Du Bois and the Afro American Response to the Cold War*. Albany: State University of New York Press, 1986.

———. *Communist Front? The Civil Rights Congress, 1946–1956*. Plainsboro, NJ: Associated University Presses, 1988.

Hutchins, Robert M. *Freedom, Education, and the Fund: Essays and Addresses, 1946–1956*. New York: Meridian, 1956.

Hyman, Alvin D. *The Suburbs of San Francisco*. San Francisco: Chronicle, 1969.

Hynding, Alan. *From Frontier to Suburb*. Belmont, CA: Star, 1982.

Hyun, Peter. *In the New World: The Making of a Korean American*. Honolulu: University of Hawaii Press, 1991.

Jackson, Kenneth T. *Crabgrass Frontier: The Suburbanization of the United States*. New York: Oxford University Press, 1985.

Johnson, David K. *The Lavender Scare*. Chicago: University of Chicago Press, 2004.

Kang, Laura Hyun Yi. *Compositional Subjects*. Durham: Duke University Press, 2002.

Kauffman, Linda. *South San Francisco: A History*. South San Francisco: South San Francisco Bicentennial Committee, 1976.

Kim, Elaine. *Asian American Literature: An Introduction to the Writings and Their Social Context*. Philadelphia: Temple University Press, 1982.

Kim, Hyun-chan, ed. *Asian Americans and Congress: A Documentary History*. Westport, CT: Greenwood, 1996.

Kim, Lili M. "Redefining the Boundaries of Traditional Gender Roles." In *Asian/Pacific Islander American Women*, ed. Shirley Hune and Gail M. Nomura, 106–19. New York: New York University Press, 2003.

Kitano, Harry H. L., and Roger Daniels. *Asian Americans: Emerging Minorities*. Upper Saddle River, NJ: Prentice Hall, 2001.

Klein, Christina. *Cold War Orientalism: Asia in the Middlebrow Imagination, 1945–1961*. Berkeley: University of California Press, 2003.

Krenn, Michael L., ed. *Race and U.S. Foreign Policy during the Cold War*. New York: Garland, 1998.

Kurashige, Scott. *The Shifting Grounds of Race: Black and Japanese Americans in the Making of Multiethnic Los Angeles*. Princeton: Princeton University Press, 2007.

Kwan. "Pioneer Judges: Judge Delbert E. Wong." In *1993 Chinatown Souvenir Book*, 21. Los Angeles: Chinese Chamber of Commerce, 1993.

Laclau, Ernesto. *Emancipations*. London: Verso, 1996.

Lai, Him Mark. *Becoming Chinese American*. New York: AltaMira, 2004.

Lee, Marjorie, ed. *Duty and Honor: A Tribute to Chinese American World War II Veterans of Southern California*. Los Angeles: Chinese Historical Society of Southern California, 1998.

Lee, Robert G. *Orientals: Asian Americans in Popular Culture*. Philadelphia: Temple University Press, 1999.

Lee, Rose Hum. *The Chinese in the United States of America*. Hong Kong: Hong Kong University Press, 1960.

Lefebvre, Henri. *The Production of Space*. Trans. Donald Nicholson-Smith. Cambridge, MA: Blackwell, 1991.

Leonard, Kevin Allen. *The Battle for Los Angeles: Racial Ideology and World War II*. Albuquerque: University of New Mexico Press, 2006.

Ling, Amy. *Between Worlds: Women Writers of Chinese Ancestry*. New York: Pergamon, 1990.

Lipsitz, George. *Rainbow at Midnight: Labor and Culture in the 1940s*. Urbana: University of Illinois Press, 1994.

Long, Herman H., and Charles S. Johnson. *People vs. Property: Race Restrictive Covenants in Housing*. Nashville: Fisk University Press, 1947.

Lowe, Lisa. *Immigrant Acts: On Asian American Cultural Politics*. Durham: Duke University Press, 1996.
Lyu, Kingsley K. "Korean Nationalist Activities in Hawaii and America, 1901–1945." In *Counterpoint: Perspectives on Asian America*, ed. Emma Gee, 106–33. Los Angeles: UCLA Asian American Studies Center, 1976.
Manalansan, Martin F., IV, ed. *Cultural Compass: Ethnographic Explorations of Asian America*. Philadelphia: Temple University Press, 2000.
Mark, Diane Mei Lin, and Ginger Chih. *A Place Called Chinese America*. Iowa: Kendall/Hunt, 1993.
May, Elaine Tyler. *Homeward Bound: American Families in the Cold War Era*. New York: Basic, 1988.
McEntire, Davis. *Residence and Race*. Berkeley: University of California Press, 1960.
McQuiston, John Mark. *Negro Residential Invasion in Los Angeles County*. Los Angeles: McQuiston Associates, 1969.
Morgan, Patricia. *Shame of a Nation: Police-State Terror against Mexican-Americans in the U.S.A.* Los Angeles: Los Angeles Committee for Protection of Foreign Born, 1954.
Murase, Mike. "Ethnic Studies and Higher Education for Asian Americans." In *Counterpoint: Perspectives on Asian America*, ed. Emma Gee, 205–23. Los Angeles: UCLA Asian American Studies Center, 1976.
Myrdal, Gunnar. *An American Dilemma: The Negro Problem and Modern Democracy*. Vol. 1. New York: Harper, 1944.
Navasky, Victor. *Naming Names*. New York: Viking Adult, 1980.
Nee, Victor G., and Brett de Bary Nee. *Longtime Californ': A Documentary Study of an American Chinatown*. Stanford: Stanford University Press, 1972.
Ngai, Mae M. *Impossible Subjects: Illegal Aliens and the Making of Modern America*. Princeton: Princeton University Press, 2004.
Osajima, Keith. "Asian Americans as the Model Minority: An Analysis of Popular Press in the 1960s and 1980s." In *Contemporary Asian America: A Multidisciplinary Reader*, ed. Min Zhou and James V. Gatewood. New York: New York University Press, 2000.
Palumbo-Liu, David. *Asian/American: Historical Crossings of a Racial Frontier*. Stanford: Stanford University Press, 1999.
Peffer, George Anthony. *If They Don't Bring Their Women Here*. Urbana: University of Illinois Press, 1999.
Pitt, Leonard. *The Decline of the Californios: A Social History of the Spanish-Speaking Californians, 1846–1890*. Berkeley: University of California Press, 1970.
Plummer, Brenda Gayle. *Rising Wind: Black Americans and U.S. Foreign Affairs, 1935–1960*. Chapel Hill: University of North Carolina Press, 1996.

Portelli, Alessandro. *The Battle of Valle Giula: Oral History and the Art of Dialogue.* Wisconsin: University of Wisconsin Press, 1997.

———. *The Death of Luigi Trastulli and Other Stories: Form and Meaning in Oral History.* Albany: State University of New York Press, 1991.

Reeves, Thomas C. *Freedom and the Foundation: The Fund for the Republic in the Era of McCarthyism.* New York: Knopf, 1969.

Riggs, Fred W. *Pressures on Congress: A Study of the Repeal of Chinese Exclusion.* New York: King's Crown, 1950.

Riley, Denise. *"Am I That Name?"* Minneapolis: University of Minnesota Press, 1988.

Sandeen, Eric J. *Picturing an Exhibition: The Family of Man and 1950s America.* Albuquerque: University of New Mexico Press, 1995.

Saund, D. S. *Congressman from India.* Hialeah: Dutton, 1960.

Schrecker, Ellen. *Many Are the Crimes: McCarthyism in America.* Princeton: Princeton University Press, 1998.

Scott, Joan W. "Experience." In *Feminists Theorize the Political*, ed. Judith Butler and Joan W. Scott, 22–40. New York: Routledge, 1992.

———. *Gender and the Politics of History.* Rev. ed. New York: Columbia University Press, 1999.

Shah, Nayan. *Contagious Divides: Epidemics and Race in San Francisco's Chinatown.* Berkeley: University of California Press, 2001.

Shanks, Cheryl. *Immigration and the Politics of American Sovereignty, 1890–1990.* Ann Arbor: University of Michigan Press, 2001.

Shevky, Eshref, and Molly Lewin. *Your Neighborhood.* Los Angeles: Haynes Foundation, 1949.

Shukla, Sandhya. *India Abroad: Diasporic Cultures of Postwar America and England.* Princeton: Princeton University Press, 2003.

Sides, Josh. *L.A. City Limits: African American Los Angeles from the Great Depression to the Present.* Berkeley: University of California Press, 2003.

Simpson, Caroline Chung. *An Absent Presence: Japanese Americans in Postwar American Culture, 1945–1960.* Durham: Duke University Press, 2001.

Soja, Edward, and Allen J. Scott, eds. *The City: Los Angeles and Urban Theory at the End of the Twentieth Century.* Berkeley: University of California Press, 1996.

Steichen, Edward. *The Family of Man.* New York: Museum of Modern Art, 1955.

Sung, Betty Lee. *Mountain of Gold: The Story of the Chinese in America.* New York: Macmillan, 1967.

Takaki, Ronald. *Strangers from a Different Shore.* New York: Penguin, 1989.

Tichenor, Daniel. *Dividing Lines: The Politics of Immigration Control in America.* Princeton: Princeton University Press, 2002.

Ting, Jennifer. "Bachelor Society: Deviant Heterosexuality and Asian American Historiography." In *Privileging Positions*, ed. Gary Y. Okihiro, Marilyn Alquizola, Dorothy Fujita Rony, and K. Scott Wong, 271–79. Pullman: Washington State University Press, 1995.

Tsai, Shih-shan Henry. *China and the Overseas Chinese in the United States, 1868–1911*. Fayetteville: University of Arkansas Press, 1983.

Union Research Institute. *Programs of Communist China for Overseas Chinese*. Hong Kong: Union Research Institute, 1956.

United Parlor, Native Sons of the Golden State, and Chinese American Citizens Alliance. *A Plea for Relief*. San Francisco: United Publishing, 1925.

Vose, Clement. *Caucasians Only: The Supreme Court, the NAACP, and the Restrictive Covenant Cases*. Berkeley: University of California, 1959.

Wallerstein, Immanuel. "The Unintended Consequences of Cold War Area Studies." In *The Cold War and the University*, ed. Andre Schiffrin, 195–231. New York: New Press, 1997.

Weaver, Robert C. *Hemmed In: ABC's of Race Restrictive Housing Covenants*. Chicago: American Council on Race Relations, 1945.

———. *The Negro Ghetto*. New York: Russell and Russell, 1967.

Wei, Min She. *Chinese Working People in America*. San Francisco: United Front Press, 1979.

Whyte, William. *The Organization Man*. New York: Simon and Schuster, 1956.

Wirth, Louis. *The Ghetto*. Chicago: University of Chicago Press, 1928.

Wong, Jade Snow. *Fifth Chinese Daughter*. Seattle: University of Washington Press, 1989.

———. *No Chinese Stranger*. New York: Harper and Row, 1975.

Wong, K. Scott. *Americans First: Chinese Americans and the Second World War*. Cambridge: Harvard University Press, 2005.

Wong, K. Scott, and Sucheng Chan, eds. *Claiming America: Constructing Chinese American Identities during the Exclusion Era*. Philadelphia: Temple University Press, 1998.

Wong, Marshall. "Delbert E. Wong, Pioneer Chinese American Judge." In *Bridging the Centuries: History of Chinese Americans in Southern California*, 108–11. Los Angeles: Chinese Historical Society of Southern California, 2001.

Yan, Qinghuang. *The Overseas Chinese and the 1911 Revolution, with Special Reference to Singapore and Malaya*. Kuala Lumpur: Oxford University Press, 1976.

Yang Murray, Alice. "Ilse Women and the Early Korean American Community." In *Unequal Sisters*, 3rd ed., ed. Vicki L. Ruiz and Ellen Carol DuBois, 205–13. New York: Routledge, 2000.

Yu, Henry. *Thinking Orientals: Migration, Contact, and Exoticism in Modern America*. Oxford: Oxford University Press, 2001.

Yu, Renqiu. *To Save China, to Save Ourselves: The Chinese Hand Laundry Alliance*. Philadelphia: Temple University Press, 1995.

Zhao, Xiaojian. *Remaking Chinese America: Immigration, Family, and Community, 1940–1965*. New Brunswick: Rutgers University Press, 2002.

ARTICLES

Allen, Barbara. "Story in Oral History: Clues to Historical Consciousness." *Journal of American History* 79 (September 1992): 606–11.

Bell, Derrick A., Jr. "*Brown v. Board of Education* and the Interest-Convergence Dilemma." *Harvard Law Review* 93 (January 1980): 518–33.

Bow, Leslie. "Racial Interstitiality and the Anxieties of the 'Partly Colored.'" *Journal of Asian American Studies* 10, no. 1 (February 2007): 1–30.

Brooks, Richard R. W. "Incorporating Race." *Columbia Law Review* 106 (2006): 2023–94.

Bu, Liping. "Educational Exchange and Cultural Diplomacy in the Cold War." *Journal of American Studies* 33 (1999): 393–415.

Chin, Gabriel J. "The Civil Rights Revolution Comes to Immigration Law: A New Look at the Immigration and Nationality Act of 1965." *North Carolina Law Review* 75 (1996–1997): 273–345.

Coe, Paul L. "The Nonwhite Population Surge into Our Cities." *Land Economics* 35 (August 1959): 195–210.

Common Council for American Unity. "On Immigration, Naturalization and Related Problems." *Interpreter Releases* 103, no. 41 (September 14, 1951): 264.

De Graaf, Lawrence B. "The City of Black Los Angeles: Emergence of the Los Angeles Ghetto, 1890–1930." *Pacific Historical Review* 39 (August 1970): 323–52.

Elman, Philip. "The Solicitor General's Office, Justice Frankfurter, and Civil Rights Litigation, 1946–1960." Interview by Norman Silber. *Harvard Law Review* 100 (1987): 817–52.

Garcilazo, Jeffrey M. "McCarthyism, Mexican Americans, and the Los Angeles Committee for Protection of Foreign-Born, 1950–1954." *Western Historical Quarterly* 32, no. 3 (2001): 273–95.

Guzman, Ralph. "The Hand of Esau." *Frontier* 7–8 (June 1956): 13, 16.

Kennedy, Randall. "A Reply to Philip Elman." *Harvard Law Review* 100 (1987): 1938–57.

Kiang, Yi-Seng. "Judicial Enforcement of Restrictive Covenants in the United States." *Washington Law Review* 24 (February 1949): 1–20.

Kim, Claire. "The Racial Triangulation of Asian Americans." *Politics and Society* 27, no. 1 (March 1999): 105–38.

Lai, Him Mark. "China and the Chinese American Community: The Political Dimension." *Chinese America: History and Perspectives*, 1999, 1–32.

———. "The Chinese Press in the United States and Canada since World War II: A Diversity of Voices." *Chinese America: History and Perspectives*, 1990, 107–55.

———. "To Bring Forth a New China, To Build a Better America: The Chinese Marxist Left in America to the 1960s." *Chinese America: History and Perspectives*, 1992, 3–82.

———. "A Voice of Reason: Life and Times of Gilbert Woo, Chinese American Journalist." *Chinese America: History and Perspective*, 1992, 83–123.

Lee, Robert. "Community Exclusion: A Case Study." *Phylon Quarterly* 15, no. 2 (1954): 202–5.

Lee, Rose Hum. "The Decline of Chinatowns in the United States." *American Journal of Sociology* 54 (March 1949): 422–32.

———. "The Recent Chinese Families of the San Francisco-Oakland Area." *Marriage and Family Living* 18 (February 1956): 14–29.

———. "The Stranded Chinese in the United States." *Phylon Quarterly* 19, no. 2 (1957): 180–94.

Lombardo, Johannes R. "A Mission of Espionage, Intelligence and Psychological Operations: The American Consulate in Hong Kong, 1949–1964." *Intelligence and National Security* 14, no. 4 (1999): 64–81.

Lyu, Kingsley K. "Korean Nationalist Activities in Hawaii and the Continental United States, 1900–1945." Pt. 1, *Amerasia* 4, no. 1 (1977): 23–85; pt. 2, *Amerasia* 4, no. 2 (1977): 53–100.

McGovney, D. O. "Racial Residential Segregation by State Court Enforcement of Restrictive Agreements, Covenants or Conditions in Deeds Is Unconstitutional." *California Law Review* 33 (1945): 5–39.

Miller, Loren. "Housing and Racial Covenants." *Frontier Magazine*, February 1, 1950, 11–13.

———. "The Power of Restrictive Covenants." *Survey Graphic* 35 (January 1947): 46.

———. "Race Restrictions on Ownership or Occupancy of Land." *Lawyers Guild Review* 7 (1947): 99–111.

Ngai, Mae M. "Legacies of Exclusion: Illegal Chinese Immigration during the Cold War Years." *Journal of American Ethnic History* 18 (fall 1998): 3–37.

Roberts, James Stenius. "Racial Restrictive Covenants." *Sociology and Social Research* 32 (November–December 1947): 616–24.

Sanchez, George. "'What's Good for Boyle Heights Is Good for the Jews': Creating Multiracialism on the Eastside during the 1950s." *American Quarterly* 56, no. 3 (September 2004): 663–61.
Spaulding, Charles B. "Housing Problems of Minority Groups in Los Angeles County." *Annals of the American Academy of Political and Social Science 248 (November 1946):*, June 1946, 220–25.
Steichen, Edward. "Photography: Witness and Recorder of Humanity." *Wisconsin Historical Magazine* 41, no. 3 (Spring 1958): 159–67.
White, Gerald T. "The Chinese and Immigration Law." *Far Eastern Survey* 19, no. 7 (April 1950): 68–70.
Wirth, Louis. "The Unfinished Business of American Democracy." *Annals of the American Academy of Political and Social Science* 244 (March 1946): 1–9.
Wu, Ellen D. "'America's Chinese': Anti-Communism, Citizenship, and Cultural Diplomacy during the Cold War." *Pacific Historical Review* 77, no. 3 (2008): 391–422.

DISSERTATIONS, THESES, AND UNPUBLISHED PAPERS

Bingham, Edwin R. "The Saga of the Los Angeles Chinese." MA thesis, Occidental College, 1942.
Bond, J. Max. "The Negro in Los Angeles." PhD diss., University of Southern California, 1936.
Chen, Wen-Hui Chung. "Changing Socio-Cultural Patterns of the Chinese Community in Los Angeles." PhD diss., University of Southern California, 1952.
———. "A Study of Chinese Family Life in Los Angeles as Compared with the Traditional Family Life in China." MA thesis, University of Southern California, 1940.
Fitzgerald, Robin Scott. "The Mexican-American in the Los Angeles Area, 1920–1950." PhD diss., University of Southern California, 1971.
Kwan, Kian Moon. "Assimilation of the Chinese in the United States: An Exploratory Study in California." PhD diss., University of California, Berkeley, 1958.
Lee, Kyung. "Settlement Patterns of Los Angeles Koreans." MA thesis, University of California, Los Angeles, 1969.
Lyu, Kingsley K. "Korean Nationalist Activities in Hawaii and American, 1901–1945." Paper submitted in partial fulfillment of the requirements for the research in History 300, University of Hawaii, 1950.
McDannold, Thomas Allen. "Development of the Los Angeles Chinatown, 1850–1970." MA thesis, California State University, Northridge, 1973.
Soble, Ronald Leslie. "A History of the *Chinese World*, 1891–1961." MA thesis, Stanford University, 1962.

INDEX

Acheson, Dean, 2
ACLU, 41
activism: and housing segregation, 24; interracial, 16, 23–24, 57; U.S. suppression of, 19, 117
Aiso, John, 106, 115
Alien Land Law (1913), 1
Alien Land Laws (CA), 1, 25, 213n6; *Oyama v. State of California*, 213n7
Alien Registration Act (1940), 124, 125
All People's Christian Church and Community Center, 41, 217n56
Amer, Tommy, 21–22, 30, 31, 35, 37 fig. 1.2, 38 fig. 1.3; court case of, 43–44, 46, 47–48, 55; restrictive covenant of, 28; Supreme Court case, 21–24, 217n57. *See also* restrictive covenants
American Association for the United Nations, 52, 219n93
American Committee for Protection of Foreign Born, 119, 126
Americanization, 117; of Chinese Americans, 70, 72; and suburbanization, 58–59, 62
American Homes Development Company, 82
American National Exhibition (Moscow), 62, 202
American Youth for Democracy, 41
anticommunism, 124; activists, surveillance of, 117; and 1950 McCarran Act, 125
Anti-Communist League of the Six Companies, 168–69

antiracism, as communist ploy, 120, 121, 124
Armendariz, Albert Sr., 86, 87
Asian American firsts: diversity, as appearance of, 113; double bind of, 108–9; stories of, 89–90, 93–94, 106, 114. *See also* Asian Americans; culture of the first
Asian Americans: and Asians, 10; assimilability of, 84; assimilation of, 4–5, 17–18, 58, 79–80; and blacks, 15, 55, 65, 153; black-white schema, position in, 8–10, 42–43, 75; and Cold War, 3; firsts, 89–90, 93–94, 106, 108–9; 113–14; as foreigners-within, 3, 6, 8, 10, 48, 64–65, 192, 193, 210n6; as model minority, 88; as nonwhite exceptions, 65–66; as nonwhites, 84; politics, suppression of, 192–93; racial ambiguity of, 31; as racial anomaly, 25; racial formation of, 3, 5, 10, 13, 14, 18, 20, 192; racialization of, 8, 12, 13, 15, 64, 153; as storytellers of democracy, 93–95; and U.S. foreign policy, 88. *See also* Chinese Americans; Korean Americans
assimilation, 44; of Asian Americans, 4–5, 17–18, 58, 79–80; of blacks, 63; and education, 65–66; and family, 69, 78; as ideological construct, 12, 87; and integration, 79; and segregation, 17–18; in Sheng case, 59, 74, 78–79; and social mobility, 62; and suburbanization, 59;

261

assimilation (cont'd): and *Where Shall We Live?*, 64; and Jade Snow Wong, 99, 102
Avila, Eric, 57

Barrows v. Jackson, 220n98
Barthes, Roland, 198–99
Bass, Charlotta, 54–55
Belknap, Michal, 14–15, 120
Bernstein, Shana, 42
blacks, U.S.: as "almost Americans," 62–63; as archetype of race, 8–10, 23, 48–49, 51, 54; assimilation of, 63; and Cold War, 8; and communism, 121, 122–23
black-white divide, 23–24, 25; Asian American positioning in, 8–10, 42–43, 75; legal reinforcement of, 51; white v. non-white, 52–53
Bow, Leslie, 9–10, 25
Branton, Leo, 122–23, 228n14
Brewer, Jan, 207
Brooks, Charlotte, 16–17
Brown, Edmund G. "Pat," 88, 105, 111
Brown v. Board of Education, 7

California Constitution, 26, 213n5
Carlisle, Harry, 127
Carlson, Frank, 127
Carter, Oliver J., 183
Chen, Wen-Hui Chung, 42
Chernin, Rose, 126
Chiang Kai-shek, 151, 156, 172
Chin, Frank, 97
Chin, Gabriel, 16, 153
China (People's Republic of China): America, 1905 boycott of, 150; communist revolution in, 3, 4, 210n7; gender in, 102–5; involvement in Korean War, 153–54, 161; and favorable treatment of overseas Chinese, 166; refugees from, 238n88; remittances to, 161; and United Nations, 157, 162. *See also* Taiwan
China Daily News, 237n77
China Daily News, Inc., 170–71
China Mail, 184–85
Chinatowns, 58; decline of, 66, 68, 69–70, 155; in *Fifth Chinese Daughter*, 97, 101–2; in *Life*, 72
Chinese American Citizens Alliance (CACA), 151, 157, 186–87, 188, 243n152; and family unification, 174–76; government surveillance of, 158; 1957 convention, 187; unlawful search and seizure of, 159
Chinese American Democratic Youth League, 158
Chinese Americans: Americanization of, 70, 72; assimilability of, 59, 67; assimilation of, 66, 71, 155; and communism, 192; and communist revolution, 17; demographics, 70, 71; family, reformation of, 66–67; as foreign, 150; as foreigners-within, 150; government surveillance of, 4, 19, 158; immigration reform, 149; internment, fear of, 153–55, 210n7; and KMT, 159, 236n75; in Los Angeles, 34; national allegiance of, 154–55, 155–56, 157; political persecution of, 15; suburbanization of, 58–59, 73; urban migration of, 215n30; whites, compared to, 65; and World War II, 11
Chinese Communist Party (CCP), 158, 160, 171. *See also* communism
Chinese Confession Program, 187–88

Chinese Consolidated Benevolent Association (CCBA), 42, 151, 234n45; and government surveillance, 158; and 1965 Immigration Act, 188; ransom racket, response to, 169, 236n65; and slot racket, 181–82; Washington conference, 185–86

Chinese Daily News, 158–59; FBI harassment of, 236n75

Chinese Democratic Constitutionalist Party, 160, 172

Chinese exclusion acts, 6, 10, 32, 150–51; repeal of, 6–7, 173, 174–75, 178, 238n85. *See also* immigration; immigration laws; immigration reform

Chinese extortion racket. *See* Chinese ransom racket

Chinese Hand Laundry Alliance, 158, 171

Chinese Nationalist government, 78, 86, 150–51, 157–59, 171–72

Chinese Pacific Weekly, 80, 81

Chinese Press, 154, 155

Chinese ransom racket, 151–52, 157–58, 160–73; Chinese press, influence of, 161, 232n28; *Chinese World* coverage of, 166–68, 171–72; Hong incident, 164; and immigration reform, 167; Jang case, 165; mainstream press coverage, 160–65, 167–68; Mar case, 164; victims, registration of, 162–63, 165. *See also* Chinese Consolidated Benevolent Association

Chinese Six Companies, 159, 163, 234n45

Chinese slot racket, 177–78, 178–85; Lee on, 181, 183; and immigration reform, 184, 185–86. *See also* Chinese Consolidated Benevolent Association; immigration laws

Chinese Times, 234n52; circulation of, 234n34

Chinese women: American perceptions of, 59–60; and assimilation, 72, 73; postwar population growth, 69; war brides, 72

Chinese Workers Mutual Aid Association, 158, 159

Chinese World, 80, 82–83, 105, 158; and Chinese Democratic Constitutionalist Party, 160; circulation of, 234n34; and immigration reform, 170; KMT, opposition to, 159–60; on national allegiance, 156; ransom racket, coverage of, 161–62, 166–68, 171–72; slot racket coverage, 184. *See also* Lee, Dai-Ming

Chinese Youth League, 158

Chin Hong Ming, 171

Chin You Gon, 170–71

Chong, Wellington, 142, 143, 231n49

Chung, Sue Fawn, 153

citizenship: and Amer and Kim cases, 49–50; derivative, 180; and heterosexuality, 71; and naturalization, 1, 51, 125, 176, 219n89

civil rights: and Asian American racial formation, 20; and Cold War, 192; and foreign policy, 7, 59, 211n18; Fourteenth Amendment, 26–27, 28, 48, 52–54; and immigration reform, 153; and Japanese internment, 1; protests, 114; and Truman administration, 60, 191–92; and World War II, 46

Civil Rights Act (1964), 191

Civil Rights Congress, 126, 229n24

Cold War: in Asia, 56, 74; and communism, 2–3; and internationalism,

Cold War (con'td): 150, 151, 172, 173, 193, 210n5, 238n84; model minority stories, 88; and multiculturalism, 194; and pluralism, 58; and racial equality, 58; suppression of dissent during, 117–18; and U.S. race relations, 2–3, 31; and U.S. segregation, 14; and working women, 105. *See also* communism; internationalism, Cold War

Commission on Race and Housing, 9–10, 60–61. See also *Residence and Race*; *Where Shall We Live?*

Committee for Free Asia, 81, 168

communism: and Asian Americans, perceptions of, 11; and blacks, 121, 122–23; and Chinese Americans, 17, 105, 192; and Cold War, 2–3; criminalization of, 193; cultural specificity of, 146–47; and equality, 13–14; as foreign, 120; and gender equality, 88–89; and homosexuality, 67–68; and Korean Americans, 117, 192; and racism, 143–43; and U.S. policy. *See also* Cold War; democracy, Cold War

Communist Party USA (CPUSA), 120–21, 123–23, 142, 158; black membership in, 121–22; criminalization of, 121

communist containment, 2–3, 60–61, 150, 193, 209n5, 210n5. *See also* internationalism, Cold War

Council for Civic Unity (Los Angeles), 35

Creef, Elena Tajima, 5

culture of the first, 86, 90. *See also* Asian American firsts

Cumings, Bruce, 119, 146

de la Cruz, Eulogio, 229n25

democracy, Cold War, 5–14, 31, 46, 79, 88–92, 146, 192. *See also* democracy, U.S.

democracy, U.S., 31, 45–46, 54–55, 95, 131, 191–93; legitimacy of, 80–81, 84, 95, 97, 109, 111, 114, 115 121–24, 141, 153; communism, as superior to, 46, 51–52, 58–59, 75–77, 81, 87, 94, 95, 131, 134, 147, 165, 191, 200, 202. *See also* democracy, Cold War

Democratic People's Republic of Korea (North Korea), 141–43; and Kimm case, 145–46. *See also* Korea; Republic of Korea

desegregation: as progress, 46, 53; and social progress, 46; Soviet propaganda, as counter to, 22; and U.S. democracy, 47; of U.S. armed forces, 3. *See also* segregation, housing

Dickerson, Lloyd L., 48

Displaced Persons Act (1948), 173, 238n88

dissent, U.S. suppression of, 15, 117–18, 139

Drumright, Everett F., 179–80, 184–86, 187

Dudziak, Mary, 7–8, 211n18

Dugan, Margaret Garcia, 206

Dulles, John Foster, 182

education: minority achievement, 65–66; multiculturalism in, 204–6

ethnic studies, 203, 204–6; Arizona ban on, 206

family: and assimilation, 69, 78; and nation, 67–68; unification of, 174–76; in *Where Shall We Live?*, 66–67

Family of Man (photography exhibit), 193–96, 197–202; Barthes on,

198–99; and democratic superiority, 200; heteronormativity in, 201; shared humanity in, 194, 195–96, 198
Far Eastern Survey, 149
Fiancées Act (1946), 69, 175
Fifth Chinese Daughter (Wong), 96–99; Chinatown in, 97, 101–2. *See also* Wong, Jade Snow
Filipino Americans, 175, 177, 214n15, 229n25; and immigration laws, 2, 11; and restrictive covenants, 52
Fong, Hiram, 106
Ford Foundation, 60
Foreign Assets Control Regulation (1950), 162
Fourteenth Amendment, Equal Protection Clause, 26, 48, 53, 54
Fund for the Republic, 60
Fung, Kenneth Y., 174, 175

Gaddis, John Lewis, 210n5
Gary, Wilbur D., 83
gender: as category of analysis, 12, 212n31; post-war domestic ideal, 67–68; in Sheng case, 78
Genung, Dan B., 41
ghettos, as symbols of segregation, 54
G.I. Bill of Rights, 89
Gold Mountain Companies (*Kum Shan Jongs*), 179
Goorwitch, Fania, 136 fig. 4.4, 141–42
Gotanda, Neil, 6, 219n89
Greater East Asia Co-Prosperity Sphere, 6
Great Migration, the (blacks), 27

Harris, Cheryl, 24
Hershatter, Gail, 102
Hickerson, H. G., 22, 35

Hillcrest Country Club, 112–13
Hise, Greg, 214n24
Hollywood Citizen News, 105, 109, 203
homosexuality: as communist menace, 67–68; lavender scare, 68
Hong, Chin, 164
Hong, Y. C., 159, 174, 177, 178, 186–87
Hong Kong Standard, 77, 184–85
Horne, Tom, 206–7
House Un-American Activities Committee (HUAC), 122–23; *American Negro in the Communist Party, The*, 122–23
Huerta, Dolores, 206
human condition, myth of, 199. *See also Family of Man*
Hurd v. Hodge, 47–48, 218n79
Hutchins, Robert Maynard, 60
Hyun, Alice, 142, 231n49
Hyun, David, 19, 117–19, 124, 126, 127–34, 135 fig. 4.1, 136 fig. 4.3, 147, 229n25; American Dream, narrative of, 131; assimilation of, 119; deportation proceedings, 128–30, 134; *Exile: The Story of David Hyun*, 130; *I am Appealing on Behalf of My Youngest Son . . .* , 133–34; and Korean War, 129–130; labor organizing, 132; and model minority construct, 130, 131
Hyun, Peter, 231n49
Hyun, Rev. Soon, 131, 133–34

immigration, illegal, Chinese, 177–78
Immigration Act (1918), 124
Immigration Act of 1924, 27, 69, 174, 214n15
Immigration and Nationality Act (1965), 15–16, 150, 152; as civil rights reform, 20, 153, 188–89

Immigration and Naturalization Service (INS), 125–26, 128, 131, 132
immigration laws: Act of August, 9, 1946, 175; Act of September 11, 1957, 187; and Cold War internationalism, 173; quotas, 173, 177, 238n85, 239n94. *See also* immigration reform; *and individual immigration acts*
immigration reform, 109–20, 149; and CCBA conference, 186; and Chinese ransom racket, 167; and Chinese slot racket, 184, 185–86; and civil rights, 153, 174; and *Chinese World*, 170; family unification, 150, 151, 152, 164, 167, 174–75, 188, 239n90; under Kennedy, 152–53; Dai-Ming Lee on, 184; under Truman, 152–53. *See also* immigration laws; *and individual immigration acts*
Inouye, Daniel K., 106
internationalism, Cold War, 2–4, 11, 16, 150–51, 173; 238n84; and Asian American identity, 232n2; and communist containment, 2–3, 60, 150, 193, 209n5; Dai-Ming Lee on, 172; and immigration laws, 173; Marxist, 146. *See also* Cold War
interracial activism, 16, 23, 57; in Los Angeles, 42, 55
Ishikawa, Samuel, 177

Jackson, Loela, 220n98
Jang, Joe Lum, 165
Japanese American Citizens League (JACL), 49–51, 106, 176, 187, 188–89, 217n57
Japanese Americans: naturalization of, 9; whites, compared to, 65 and World War II, 11. *See also* Asian Americans; Japanese internment

Japanese internment, 5–6, 106, 125, 211n16; and Amer and Kim cases, 50; and civil rights, 1
Jim Crow laws, 25, 115
Johnson, Lyndon B., 153, 191
Jones, Claudia, 228n20
Judd Bill, 175
Juhn, John, 138, 229n25

Kang Youwei, 160
Kennedy, John F., 88, 191; and immigration reform, 152
Kenny, Robert W., 35, 40
Kim, Claire Jean, 9
Kim, Lili, 118
Kim, Yin, 37 fig. 1.2, 39 fig. 1.4, 40–44, 217n55; court case of, 22–24, 43–44, 46, 47–48, 55, 217n57
Kimm, Diamond, 19, 117–19, 124, 135 fig. 4.2, 136 fig. 4.4, 137–47, 229n25; and assimilation, 119; deportation hearings, 137–38; HUAC hearing of, 141–42; *Korean Independence*, 138–39, 140, 145; as "North Korean," 145; Rhee, opposition to, 141
Kitano, Harry H. L., 210n7
Klein, Christina, 11, 89–90, 150, 232n2
Knowland, William F., 162, 163, 168
Kochi, Paul Shinsei, 229n25
Korea: division of, 118; Japanese annexation of, 118; 1919 March 1 uprising, 93, 118, 134. *See also* Democratic People's Republic of Korea; Republic of Korea
Korean Americans: and communism, 192; government surveillance of, 4; and Korean War, 17; in Los Angeles, 33; political suppression of, 15, 19; and World War II, 118. *See also* Asian Americans

Korean Communist Party, 142
Korean Independence, 138–39, 140, 145
Korean War, 75, 87; and anticommunism, 124; and Asian American social status, 79; China involvement in, 161; and communism, fear of, 117, 192; and desegregation, 3–4; and perceptions of Asian Americans, 4. *See also* Cold War
Kroeger, Frances, 31
Kroeger, Gus, 31
Krushchev, Nikita, 202
Ku Klux Klan, 35, 49
Kuomintang (KMT), 158–60, 168–72, 184; and Chinese American communism, 159, 236n75
Kurashige, Scott, 16, 41–42
Kwock, C. H., 166

labor; activism, 117, 132–33, 139, 206; immigrant, 10, 72; migration, 215n30; unions, 89; women, 67, 105
Ladies Home Journal, 195, 196–97. *See also* "People are People the World Over"
Lai, Him Mark, 158, 237n81, 240n118
Latinos, 206. *See also* Mexican Americans
Laws case, 43
Lee, C. Y., 232n2
Lee, Dai-Ming, 80–81, 82–83; on Chinese remittances, 169–70; on immigration reform, 184; and internationalism, 172; on "overseas Chinese," 171–72; slot racket, coverage of, 181, 183, 185; ransom racket, coverage of, 166–68, 171–72; third force, advocacy of, 171. See also *Chinese World*
Lee, Jennie, 85–86

Lee, Kenneth K., 163
Lee, Robert G., 66–67
Lee, Rose Hum, 68, 69, 215n30; on assimilation, 68–69
Lee, Sammy, 18, 88, 90–95, 96, 107 fig. 3.1, 114, 115, 200; and Korean War, 90; as model minority, 94; press coverage of, 90–92; residence, denial, 94; Russian athletes incident, 90–91; Sullivan award, 91–93
Lee Ming-Hua, 104
Lem, Henry, 186–87, 188
Levittown, NY, 30
Life, 72, 164, 195–96, 244n7
Ling, Amy, 96
Little Tokyo (Los Angeles), 34
Los Angeles, CA: black migration to, 32–33, 215n31; Chinese Americans in, 34; community activism in, 40; community organizations in, 41, 42; interracial activism in, 42, 55; Korean Americans in 33–34; Mexican Americans in, 33–34; neighborhoods of, 33, 36 fig. 1.1; racial demographics of, 32–34; restrictive covenants in, 31–32, 33, 34–35
Los Angeles Committee for Protection of Foreign Born (LACPFB), 119, 126; deportees, defense of, 126, 129, 229n25; and Terminal Island Four case, 127–28; and Hyun case, 126, 129; and Kimm case, 139; and Operation Terror, 228n24
Los Angeles Daily News, 155–56
Los Angeles Times, 49, 72–73, 94, 153–54; on Chinese American allegiance, 157
Los Angeles Unified School District, 114–15
Lowe, Lisa, 13, 210n6

Magnuson Act (1943), 6–7, 68, 69, 174–75, 239n94
Manchus, 166, 234n53, 237n82
Mao Zedong, 151, 153, 168, 172
Mar, Don, 164
Marks, Matthew, 234n44
Matsui, Shuji, 229n25
May, Elaine Tyler, 67
Mays v. Burgess, 218n76
McCarran, Patrick, 124–25, 175
McCarran Act (1950), 117, 120, 124, 126–27, 207
McCarran-Walter Act (1952), 176, 219n89, 238n85; advocacy for, 176–77; and derivative citizenship, 180; and isolationism, 173; repeal of, 189, 243n152
McGhee v. Sipes, 47–48, 218n79
Mexican Americans, 206, 228n24; in Los Angeles, 33–34; racial classification of, 25, 213n7; mass deportation drives of, 126, 228n24
Miller, Loren, 25–26, 41, 45, 54
Miller, Wayne, 196
Mita, Edo, 229n25
Mong, C. S., 234n52
Mosk, Stanley, 45–46
Moy, Eugene, 170–71, 237n77
multiculturalism, 194, 197–98; in education, 204–6
Murase, Mike, 205
Murray, Alice Yang, 118

NAACP, 53, 60, 209n3, 218n76
Naiden, Neil, 234n44
Nation, The, 154–55
National Association of Real Estate Boards, 29, 220n98
nationalism: Chinese, 101, 150–51, 160; Korean, 118–19, 133, 146; U.S., 147
Nationality Act (1940), 124
naturalization: of Japanese Americans, 9; revocation of, 125
Navasky, Victor, 15
neighborhood associations, 28, 29
New Chinatown (L.A.), 73
Newsweek, 161
New York Times, 84, 90–91, 94, 106, 127; on Chinese American allegiance, 157; ransom racket, coverage of, 161
Ngai, Mae, 6, 153, 240n118
Nixon, Richard, 62, 182, 202
North Korea. *See* Democratic People's Republic of Korea

Obama, Barack Hussein, 203–4
Operation Terror, 228n24
Oriental and Occidental Press, 166, 235n54
overseas Chinese, 20, 151, 158, 161, 166, 169, 171–72, 180, 183, 237n82, 235n57

Pacific Citizen, 105, 106, 108
Park, Sang Rhee, 138
Pearson, Drew, 127
"People are People the World Over," 195, 196–98; multiculturalism in, 197–98
People's Republic of China. *See* China
Perkins, Fred, 48
Perkins v. Trustees of Monroe Avenue Church of Christ, 47–48
Pfeiffer, Sachiko, 58
Plummer, Brenda Gayle, 7, 12, 89
postracism, 203, 207

Pravda, 92
President's Commission on Immigration and Naturalization, 178, 240n102
President's Committee on Civil Rights, 1–2, 8–9, 11–12, 209n3, 209n5, 46; African Americans, focus on, 9; and desegregation, 46; *To Secure These Rights*, 1, 8–9, 11, 61; and U.S. foreign relations, 52
press, Chinese, 151, 157–60, 161–62
progress: and communist China, 102, 103, 105; and "firsts," 18–19, 85, 89, 94; notions of, 11–14, 16, 17, 105, 197; and politics, 20, 106; social, 12, 23, 44, 53, 72, 113, 115, 192, 202–4
propaganda, 29; Chinese Nationalist, 161; communist, 77, 91, 102, 109, 183; Japanese, 6; Soviet, 7; 10, 22, 46, 51–52, 76; U.S., 70, 85; and World War II, 2, 6

race: in Arizona, 204; black-white schema of, 8–10, 23–24, 25; discourse of, 11, 12; in HUAC trials, 144–45; as ideological construct, 11, 12; and phenotype, 9; and "progress," 11–12, 16; and property values, 29–30; and Soviet propaganda, 51–52; and urban migration, 32–33; and U.S. democracy, 5; and World War II, 89. *See also* Asian Americans, and Asians; racial formation; racism
racial formation: of Asian Americans, 3, 5, 10, 13, 14, 18, 20, 192. *See also* Asian Americans; race
racism: and communism, 143–44; antiracism, 120, 121, 124; in Germany, 7; as "personal" issue, 87; as postracial logic, 203–4, 206–7; in U.S., 2, 211n15. *See also* Asian Americans; race
Randall, Harriet, 31
Refugee Relief Act (1953), 238n88
re Lee Sing, 26–27
Republic of China. *See* Taiwan
Republic of Korea (South Korea), 4, 91–92. *See also* Korea; Democratic People's Republic of Korea
Residence and Race (CRH), 61, 63–64; black families in, 63–64; whites as normative in, 65
restrictive covenants, 21–22; *Buchanan v. Warley*, 27; *Corrigan v. Buckley*, 28; DOJ amicus brief, 52, 219n90; and Fourteenth Amendment, 26–27, 28, 52; *Gandolfo v. Hartman*, 26, 28, 213n10; in Los Angeles, 31–32, 33, 34–35; restrictions, types of, 28–29; in Sheng case, 82; in South San Francisco, 74; succession, 34, 40–41, 42; Supreme Court cases, 24, 43, 45, 54, 218n79. *See also* Amer, Tommy; Kim, Yin
Rhee, Syngman, 92, 93, 133, 134, 138
Robinson, Earl, 216n54
Robinson, Jackie, 86–87
Roosevelt, Franklin Delano, 6
Rosie the Riveter, 85, 86
Rusk, Dean, 162

Saito, Sakuo, 43
Sandeen, Eric J., 195, 197
San Francisco Chronicle, 75–76, 77–78, 154, 155; ransom racket, coverage of, 160–64; slot racket, coverage of, 182; Sheng case, coverage of, 76–77

Saund, Dalip Singh, 106, 226n46
Scott, Joan Wallach, 12, 212n31
segregation, housing, 16, 17; and activism, 24; anti-Chinese laws, 25–26; and assimilation, 17–18; Bingham Ordinance (1890), 26; and Cold War, 14; and ghettoization, 23, 32; and integration, 42–43; Supreme Court rulings, 24; and urban development, 53; and U.S. blacks, 17. *See also* desegregation
Senate Bill 1070 (AZ), 245n33
shared humanity,194, 195–96, 198, 204. See also *Family of Man*; "People are People the World Over"
Shelley v. Kraemer, 47, 54, 218n79
Sheng, Sing, 18, 59, 74–84, 79 fig. 2.1; as assimilated, 59, 74, 78–79; veteran status of, 78. *See also* Sheng case
Sheng case, 222n50, 222n54; in Chinese media, 80–84; as democracy v. communism, 75–76; gender in, 78; mainstream press coverage, 81. *See also* Sheng, Sing
Shrecker, Ellen, 15
Simpson, Caroline Chung, 58
Smith Act, 14, 120, 125, 170, 207. *See also* Smith Act trials
Smith Act trials, 120–22, 123, 130, 228n15, 228n20; California fourteen, 121–22, 123–24, 227n7, 227n9. *See also* Smith Act
South Korea. *See* Republic of Korea
South San Francisco, CA, 74–75, 222n54
Steichen, Edward, 193, 194, 195, 197–98, 200; on American exceptionalism, 200
Stevenson, Miriam Christine, 127

suburbanization, 57, 214n24; and Americanization, 58–59, 62; and assimilation, 59; of Chinese Americans, 58–59, 73; and whiteness, 57, 61, 215n27
suburbs, as white space, 62
Sugar Hill case, 43
Sung, Betty Lee, 70–72
Sung, Tom, 170–71, 237n77
Sunoo, Harold W., 143–44
Sun Yat-sen, 160
Swift v. Rogers, 43

Taiwan (Republic of China), 4; Chinese American support of, 157. *See also* China
Takaki, Ronald, 6
Terminal Island Four, 127–28, 129
Third World Liberation Front, 205
Tichenor, Daniel, 16, 152–53
Till, Emmett, 199
Time, 86–87, 164
tokenism, 89, 113
Tom D. Amer v. Superior Court of the State of California, 47–48. *See also* Amer, Tommy
Tong King Chong, 160, 235n54
To Secure These Rights, 1, 8–9, 11, 61. *See also* President's Committee on Civil Rights
Trading with the Enemy Act (1917), 164–65, 170
Treasury Department, U.S., 162–64, 168–70, 234n44; remittances, banning of 169; Trading with the Enemy Act, 164–65, 170
Truman, Harry S, 2–3, 209n3, 142; on civil rights, 191–92; Executive Order 9809; and immigration reform, 152

Truman Doctrine, 209n5
Tsai, Shih-shan Henry, 150–51
Tydings-McDuffie Act (1934), 214n15

unions, racial barriers, 89
United Nations, 7, 162–63, 169, 201, 229n24; communist China, seating of, 157
United States Information Agency (USIA), 202
Urciolo v. Hodge, 47–48, 219n79
U.S. News and World Report, 114

Voice of America, 70, 77
Voorhis Act, 121
Vose, Clement, 45, 47, 53

War Brides Act (1945), 69, 175
Warren, Earl, 81, 108
Weaver, Robert, 44–45, 53
Where Shall We Live? (CRH), 9–10, 61–63, 66–67; and Americanization, 61–62; assimilation as remedy in, 64; family in, 66–67
White, Gerald T., 149
white flight, 57
whiteness: and inclusion, 76; "nonwhite," as term, 30; privilege of, 29, 57; as property, 24–25, 26, 30, 43; and suburbanization of, 57, 61, 215n27; value of, 30–31
Whyte, William, 62

Wing, Freddie, 82–83
Wirin, A. L., 41
Wirth, Louis, 44, 45, 53
Women of China, 102–4
Wong, Albert, 170–71
Wong, Delbert, 18–19, 88, 105–14, 108 fig. 3.3, 115, 202–3; "only," discourse of, 109–13; as token minority, 113; press coverage of, 102–9; World War II, service of, 109–10
Wong, Dolores, 113, 14, 108 fig. 3.3
Wong, Jade Snow, 18, 88, 95–102, 107 fig. 3.2, 200; Asian speaking tour, 96–97; assimilationist ideology of, 99, 102; Chinese communism, as counter to, 105; and cultural purity, notions of, 100–101; *No Chinese Stranger*, 99; as native informant, 97; overseas reception of, 99–100. See also *Fifth Chinese Daughter*
Wong Yang Sung v. McGrath, 128–29
World War II, 11, 118; propaganda in, 2, 6; and race, 89. See also Japanese internment
Wu, Ellen D., 100

Yamashiro, Kameo, 229n25
Yeh Chien-ying, 168
Yin Kim v. Superior Court of the State of California, 47–48. See also Kim, Yin
Yorty, Samuel, 182–83
Young, Charles, 205

ABOUT THE AUTHOR

Cindy I-Fen Cheng is Associate Professor of History and Asian American Studies at the University of Wisconsin–Madison, where she teaches Asian American history and culture and U.S. Cold War culture.

www.ingramcontent.com/pod-product-compliance
Lightning Source LLC
Chambersburg PA
CBHW020359080526
44584CB00014B/1091